T0317435

Serving a Wired World

BERKELEY SERIES IN BRITISH STUDIES

Edited by James Vernon

Serving a Wired World

LONDON'S TELECOMMUNICATIONS
WORKERS AND THE MAKING OF
AN INFORMATION CAPITAL

Katie Hindmarch-Watson

UNIVERSITY OF CALIFORNIA PRESS

University of California Press
Oakland, California

Library of Congress Cataloging-in-Publication Data

Names: Hindmarch-Watson, Katie, 1979– author.
Title: Serving a wired world : London's telecommunications workers and the
    making of an information capital / Katie Hindmarch-Watson.
Other titles: Berkeley series in British studies ; 17.
Description: Oakland, California : University of California Press, [2020] |
    Series: Berkeley series in British studies ; 17 | Includes bibliographical
    references and index.
Identifiers: LCCN 2020011739 (print) | LCCN 2020011740 (ebook) |
    ISBN 9780520344730 (cloth) | ISBN 9780520975668 (ebook)
Subjects: LCSH: Telecommunication—Employees. | Telegraphers—
    England—London—Social conditions—19th century. | Telephone
    operators—England—London—Social conditions—19th century. |
    Telegraphers—England—London—Social conditions—20th century.
    | Telephone operators—England—London—Social conditions—20th
    century. | Gender identity in the workplace—England—London—
    19th century. | Gender identity in the workplace—England—London—
    20th century. | Employee rights—England—London—19th century. |
    Employee rights—England—London—20th century.
Classification: LCC HD8039.T242 G75 2020 (print) | LCC HD8039.T242
    (ebook) | DDC 331.7/6138410942109034—dc23
LC record available at https://lccn.loc.gov/2020011739
LC ebook record available at https://lccn.loc.gov/2020011740

Manufactured in the United States of America

29   28   27   26   25   24   23   22   21   20
10   9   8   7   6   5   4   3   2   1

CONTENTS

FIGURES

ACKNOWLEDGMENTS

Serving a Wired World is the result of many different collaborations, and I have a world of people to thank for seeing this book through to completion. Many thanks to James Vernon, Niels Hooper, Robin Manley, Erika Büky, Kate Hoffman, and the University of California Press for their enthusiasm, support, and excellent advice. I also thank Chris Otter and the anonymous readers who provided very astute and detailed critiques. This book is much improved as a result of their input. Any missteps are of course very much my own. Thanks to the Social Sciences and Research Council of Canada, who funded much of the research in this monograph's first iteration as a dissertation. Thanks to Colorado State University and Johns Hopkins University for their generous support of junior faculty, and to McGill University, Dalhousie University, University College London, the University of Manchester, and London's Science Museum for providing forums to present and discuss this material with diverse and engaged scholars.

Many thanks to Barry Attoe and the wonderful staff at the Postal Museum (formerly the British Postal Museum and Archive) and the BT Archives in London, where I did the bulk of archival research for this book, for their expertise, kind support, and tolerance of my obsession with telegraph boys. Many thanks are also due to the staff at the National Archives, the London Metropolitan Archives, the Modern Records Center at the University of Warwick, the Women's Library at its shifting locations over recent decades, and the Archives and Local Studies Centre at the Manchester Central Library. Thanks also to the Haringey archivists at Blair Castle for their help with a unique trove of documents.

I owe a huge debt of gratitude to the Johns Hopkins history department, and in particular to Geminar, our gender- and sexuality–focused workshop.

Many, many thanks to those past and present who have worked through innumerable versions of these chapters, who have made Baltimore a hell of a lot of fun, and whose intelligence, curiosity, and kindness continue to make my life (academic and otherwise) such a positive one: Adam Bisno, Katie Hemphill, Sara Damiano, Claire Cage, Jessica Valdez, Dave Schley, Olivia Weisser, Claire Gherini, Jason Hoppe, Katie Jorgensen-Grey, Rob and Steph Gamble, Jonathan Guienapp, Joe Clark, Emily Mokros, Justin Roberts, Sandra Eder, Susan Lamb, Jamie Gianoutsis, Christopher Consolino, Rachel Hsu, Liz Ember, Mo Speller, Katie Boyce-Jacino, Jessica Keene, Jess Levy, Amira Davis, Meredith Gaffield, Joanna Behrman, Jennie Williams, Aya Nuriddin, Jilene Chua, Thera Naiman, Lauren Feldman, Emily Clark, Brooke Lansing, Yuri Amano, Anna Weerasinghe, Catherine Hinchliff, and Magdalene Klassen. Thanks are equally due to my colleagues, many of whom have mentored me at various stages of my career: Toby Ditz, Mary Ryan, Bill Leslie, Jessie Rosenthal, Gaby Spiegel, Michael Kwass, Yumi Kim, Tamer El-Leithy, Jessica Johnson, Tobie Meyer-Fong, Megan Zeller, and Rachel LaBozetta. Casey Lurtz and Liz Thornberry provided excellent critiques of later drafts; John Marshall's support has been invaluable over the last few years; Todd Shepard and Mary Fissell devoted much of their time and expertise to discussing the book's arguments with me and helped me wrestle with its more unruly sections. I am grateful to both of them for their support and enthusiasm. Special thanks are also due to Ren Pepitone, Laurel Flinn, Gabriel Klehr, Alice Wiemers, Katie Reinhardt, Chris Stolarski, Julia Cummiskey, Ian Beamish, David Woodworth, and Morgan Shahan. Will Brown deserves his own shout-out for being all-round MVP in this process. Jessica Clark and Amanda Herbert have been enmeshed in this project since its inception, and their contribution is impossible to overstate.

I am lucky to have received support and feedback from many other superb historians. Many thanks to my colleagues in Colorado: Sarah Payne, Anne Little, Adrian Howkins, and Ruth Alexander. Thanks also to Brian Lewis, Matt Houlbrook, Chris Bishoff, Julia Laitte, Paul Deslandes, Chris Waters, Frank Mort, Seth Koven, Deborah Cohen, Anna Clark, Kate Imy, David Minto, Jonathan Coleman, Ben Mechen, Jacob Ward, Mar Hicks, Matt Cook, Peter Bailey, Charles Upchurch, Amy Froide, Erica Rappaport, Joy Dixon, Nadja Durbach, Laura Kriegel, Lesley Hall, Sean Brady, Ellen Ross, Helen Glew, Simeon Koole, Mark Crowley, Liz Bruton, Mo Moulton, Amy Tooth Murphy, and Justin Bengry.

Three women in particular require special acknowledgment: Shirley Tillotson, who many years ago introduced me to gender history and set me on this path (I only found out much later that she had done pioneering work on telegraphists); Laura Doan, who provided excellent mentorship and continues to challenge our field to question its assumptions; and Judith Walkowitz, who has been the guiding force behind this work and very kindly took time to comment on the manuscript. As always, her insights and commitment were invaluable.

Many thanks to Amy Clausen and Nadine Carew. Many thanks also to Charlotte D'Ooge, for all kinds of reasons, and to Fran D'Ooge and Craig D'Ooge for all their support. Thanks also to Kate Drabinsky. I am lucky to have a large UK family to return to every year: Gemma and Amanda Bradley-Rigbye, Emma Bowers, Sean Beaver, Glen Stonebridge, PJ and Glenn Chubb, the Woodburns, and the Dartingtons. Perhaps the best outcome of this project has been new bonds of close friendship with my extended family. My cousin Tim Dartington has welcomed me into his home in North London for well over a decade, and his empathy, curiosity, wit, and love have added immeasurably to my life.

Many thanks to my family in Canada, Ireland, and the United States. My parents, Peter and Pat, have been fantastic backers throughout this long process, as have Chris, Tim, Jess, and Suze. This book is dedicated to Natalie Elder. She has been a constant force of support and humor, and she suffers no bullshit arguments. Thank you for all your wisdom, patience, and love.

Some parts of this manuscript have been published in other forms. Sections of chapter 6 appeared as "Male Prostitution and the London GPO: Telegraph Boy 'Immorality' from Nationalization to the Cleveland Street Scandal," *Journal of British Studies* 51 (2012): 594–617. Reprinted with permission from the Cambridge University Press. Parts of chapter 7 appeared in "Sex, Services, and Surveillance: The Cleveland Street Scandal Revisited," *History Compass* 14 (2016): 283–91. Reprinted with permission from Wiley. Components of chapters 2, 3, and 4 appear in "Embodying Telegraphy in Late-Victorian London," *Information and Culture: A Journal of History* 55 (2020): 10–29. Reprinted with permission from the University of Texas Press. I am grateful to all publishers for allowing me to republish this material.

Introduction

WHEN OSCAR WILDE PUBLISHED *The Picture of Dorian Gray* in 1890, one reviewer memorably described its parable of duplicity and degeneration as suitable "for none but outlawed noblemen and perverted telegraph-boys."[1] Eight years later, another writer linked telecommunications workers with troubling indiscretions, improper correspondences, and damaging revelations: Henry James's novel *In the Cage* depicts a young woman telegraphist with "odd caprices of curiosity." Sequestered in a telegraph receiving office, she is irresistibly drawn to her customers' electric correspondence. She actively intercedes in the exchange of telegrams between an adulterous couple, in doing so violating the sanctity of public consumers' private utterances and affairs.[2] By the early twentieth century, a fictive "wicked telephone girl" appeared in London's periodical press. Overly attentive to subscribers' conversations and fueled with vindictive jealousy after a failed love affair, she deliberately misdirected connections in order to cause her male customers similar agonies. Another journalist described the young women at telephone switchboards as "playing at the Fates... cutting or joining the lines of electric speech between man and man in a great city."[3] Public commentators expressed ambivalence in the stories they told about the telegraphists, telegraph messengers, and telephone operators at the intersections between themselves and the wires. They were concerned about the kinds of trust required of these information conduits.

The telecommunications workers who made information flow smoothly often seemed to be invisible, without agency, both passive and impassive conveyors of communication. British telecommunications administrators described the work as the kind that could be performed by "an ambi-dextrous monkey."[4] Yet electric communication depended on men and women to serve as mediators. This reality generated a nexus of concerns about privacy, information, and social inequality. When telecommunications workers themselves affirmed their presence, they exposed the dangers inherent in daily labor with the public's private missives. From aspiring telegraphists who laid bare the intellectual engagement that electric transcriptions required to telegraph boys who revealed their customers' secrets, telecommunications workers pushed back against their roles as transparent information conduits. Their corporeality was both their most valuable asset and their undoing.

Serving a Wired World follows London's telecommunication workers from the telegraph system's nationalization in 1870 to the middle of World War I. Over this period, Britons found themselves surrounded by new and expanding communications networks that became essential to modern business, statecraft, and social life. Metropolitan telegraph lines and stations grew rapidly in urban centers. Telegraph poles bordered country rail lines and rural byways. The scale and complexity of London's telecommunications infrastructure asserted the capital's position as the hub of imperial power.

While contemporaries frequently thought of electric information systems on a global scale, organized according to the centralizing logic of empire, they also viewed them on a more intimate level. The new occupations of telegraphist, telegraph messenger, and telephone operator generated overlapping concerns about the human conduits of electric information and their access to the confidential dialogues of others.

The workers who transcribed Morse-coded messages, dispatched telegrams, and operated switchboards disrupted the fantasies of elite users and overseers who envisioned telecommunications as the automatic conveyance of their thoughts, utterances, and desires. The system's users responded to the presence of people along the wires by ignoring, marginalizing, and demeaning the labor of information mediation. Telecommunications workers found their own social and economic aspirations continually obstructed by a consuming public and an administrative order troubled by the work of information mediation.

Technological development has always depended on human labor. When scientists and engineers supervised the laying of telegraph wires under London, over much of the kingdom, and across oceans to connect the Empire, they constructed a system that relied on an ever-expanding workforce. The telegraph and telephone came to depend on the cheap labor of young, aspiring men and women. Their bodies—down to specific body parts—were foundational to the design of public utilities. Under the auspices of the General Post Office, or GPO, British telecommunications developed as a state service whose workers made the largely intangible electric technology manifest and understandable.[5]

These new public servants were subject to a Victorian value system that put distinct emphases on communication networks. Telecommunications workers were entrusted with conveying the information of liberal subjects and in accordance with liberal demands. The practice of conveying and receiving information was central to the era's political innovations and to the conduct of economic and social life.[6] By controlling one's thoughts, personal interactions, consumption, and pleasures as an uninhibited actor, one developed the proper styles of presentation, cognition, and fortitude essential for an orderly public sphere.[7] The ideological division between the world of remunerative work and civic responsibility versus the private world of self-cultivation was necessary for the encouragement and practice of liberal notions of freedom. As the literary critic Lauren Goodland puts it, this meant an active commitment to "projects of liberating individuals from illegitimate authority while simultaneously ensuring their moral and spiritual growth."[8] The sanctity of information dovetailed with Victorian obsessions with privacy, resulting in a widely shared view that the written, typed, transcribed, and spoken word should be circulated as if it were wholly unimpeded and unmediated.[9]

Rigid distinctions between public and private spheres were impossible to maintain in practice, especially in a political environment where public order depended on personal character. The individual of liberal fantasy, who could easily navigate between the two realms as interest or duty demanded, was elite, gendered male, prone to lapses in character, and in constant need of all kinds of services to maintain his persona. Telecommunications workers bore much of the brunt of ensuring that liberal subjects were properly informed and that their information was suitably and securely conveyed.

The kinds of labor that went into producing the mobility, privileges, and knowledgeability of certain liberal subjects often remained as the Victorians wanted it: invisible. Service industries—professional, financial, bodily, and informational—constituted a broad sector of the British economy, and they have proved remarkably durable and prolific. Service providers engaged in necessary but often immaterial exchanges. Exploring the dynamics of these exchanges offers new insights into the kinds of agency that could develop among those who produced intellectual, cultural, and emotional capital for others.[10]

Telecommunications workers were crucial to liberal aspirations for ever more efficient streams of movement. Like sewage workers, park gardeners, shop assistants, barmaids, and the butchers in London's newly covered meat markets, the telecommunications workers of the late nineteenth and early twentieth centuries were essential to the unobtrusive flows of modern life. When they resisted work discipline and challenged the flow of information, they rendered liberalism's practices of discretion visible and revealed the coercive, stratified, and unruly aspects of this regime. This left workers with a unique but tenuous set of resources with which to assert their own worth.

Telecommunications workers did not just embody information systems: they used their perception, knowledgeability, and emotions—and their hands, eyes, and ears (and occasionally other body parts)—to contest and reshape the meaning of their work and their economic position. I describe these dynamics as "bodied labor:" the active negotiations between workers and the powers they are subject to. In contrast to "embodied" labor, which tends to denote the imposition of a labor regime's inherent values onto or into workers, bodied labor foregrounds human engagement. Even as they became both the tools and the targets of a growing surveillance state, telecommunications workers found the means to alter some of the trajectories intended for them by officialdom. Bodied labor describes the ruptures, pushback, and many ironic consequences that ensue when sociotechnical projects and human bodies collide. In the case of telecommunications workers, thinking in terms of bodied labor reveals that discretion was at the heart of the struggle among administrators, users, and workers to define the value of information service work. The forces unleashed by this struggle helped create a modern and distinctly British communications order.

A bodied-labor history of telecommunications requires the incorporation of many contingencies. London's social geography, both as the hub of Empire and as a city seemingly experiencing both unparalleled growth and unspeakable degeneration, shaped the structure of telecommunications systems and their labor force. Affluent urban consumers relied on these systems to maintain their own prestige and security. The social realities of telecommunications workers, their goals and associational politics, and the particular gender dynamics and sexual undercurrents of their work were shaped by the industry's requirements for discretion. Their creative responses were often self-defeating. Still, the work cultures of the telecommunications industry reflected a dynamism that has perhaps been missed in other histories attentive to biopolitics. Telegraphists, telephone operators, and telegraph boys informed how information technologies suffused and helped reshape British liberalism between the 1870s and the First World War.

Imperial grandiosity characterized popular depictions of telegraphy in the nineteenth century. In an article on London's new Central Telegraph Office in 1876, the journalist John Munro observed that "telegraph lines are the nerves of the world. . . . [W]e see them radiating in all directions, from the capital to the remotest hamlets, much in the same way as the nerves issue from the brain; and if we include the habitable world in our scan, we shall find them straggling by devious routes to the utmost parts of the Earth."[11] Historians of telecommunications have often followed suit, asserting the centrality of wired, high-speed information networks to global trade, finance, governance, cultural exchange, and war.[12] Britain's nineteenth-century telegraph network has been studied as a technology of imperial dominance, instrumental to the expansion and maintenance of colonial rule, but also as a target of imperial resistance and appropriation.[13] The telegraph, as Munro reminds us, was indicative of culturally embedded regulatory powers, expressed in metaphors of bodily circulation and flow.[14]

The metaphors and evocations of an all-encompassing, centralized system of electric intercourse obscure a more complex reality.[15] It would have been obvious to contemporaries, for example, that access to telegraphy and telephony was not universal but depended on wealth, education, occupation, and geography.[16] Londoners' access to new technologies was markedly different from that of rural, suburban, and urban Britons.

While Manchester, Liverpool, Newcastle, Penzance, and Dublin were the sites of certain innovations in information work, London's role in the forging of an imperial telecommunications network and labor force was unique.[17] The city dominated both the production and the dissemination of electric communications, from wire manufacturing to the international network hubs established by the GPO telegraph service.[18] Administrators envisaged a global telegraph system wired through London exchanges. The expansion of telephony was more complex: competition between private companies evolved into a heavily regulated monopoly, fully nationalized in 1911. Telephone use was likewise concentrated in and centered on the capital. Late Victorian and Edwardian London was the first iteration of the city's "unparalleled global connectivity," a status that London's financial districts would reclaim by the start of the twenty-first century.[19]

Service industries, including telecommunications, are multifarious, underhistoricized, and resilient economic drivers.[20] As C. H. Lee argued in the early 1980s, the concentration of services in the southeast of England in the nineteenth and early twentieth centuries demonstrated that they were not "derivative developments generated by industrial growth" but had dynamics of their own and were tied to wealth concentrations and economic processes distinct from industrial production and its attendant class forms.[21] Economic power, intellectual capital, cultural acumen, aesthetic value, and political influence accumulated in areas where services were concentrated. Despite the seismic shifts in British economic and social life elsewhere, London remained the center of power. Its telecommunications system was both an expression of this power and constitutive of it.

In the organization of both the telegraph and the telephone networks, problems affecting London often resulted in national solutions. This was true of labor as well as technology: administrative attempts to control the capital's troublesome employees resulted in nationwide disciplinary campaigns. At the same time, network design and gendered divisions of work varied significantly between London, provincial towns, and rural communities. Female postmistresses were not uncommon in small towns, for example, and female telegraph messengers appeared in rural landscapes here and there throughout the late nineteenth and early twentieth centuries. In British cities, by contrast, administrative anxieties about the dangers of urban street culture and city life—especially after dark—resulted in parameters designed to protect women and boys from commuting and working at certain times and places.[22]

London's influence on the shaping of British electric networks was further manifest in the parallel narratives of success and decline that characterized the city in the latter half of the nineteenth century.[23] Celebrations of its massive infrastructural developments—including those for the new underground railway system and the Thames embankments—existed alongside countless evocations of the perils of its dilapidated neighborhoods, the blind alleys of a morally and physically toxic city.[24] *Serving a Wired World* embraces a multifaceted approach in teasing out London's transformations and their effects on the rest of Britain's telecommunications up to the first years of the Great War.

SERVICE LABOR AND PROFESSIONAL MEDIATIONS

While this study mainly resists a teleological analysis of London's communications networks, I believe there are some underexamined legacies of the work of telecommunications in the late Victorian period. In narratives of modernizing labor, telegraphists and telephone operators have usually been slotted uneasily between industrial automatons and lower-middle-class clerks. Such ambiguity is in fact the defining feature of much information-service work, because aspects of it were (and are) both necessary and dangerous to social ordering.[25]

Information services are one component of a much larger service economy that encompasses occupations ranging from bank executives to street cleaners and all conventional ranks of wealth and social affiliation. This catch-all category, based on economists' traditional definition of *services* as any employment that does not result in tradable physical products, was a highly significant sector of the British economy. By the 1860s, 31 percent of the British workforce was involved in transport, distribution, banking and commerce, professions, government and defense, and "miscellaneous" services, and this figure grew to more than 41 percent in the 1910s.[26]

Understanding service industries, their stratifications, and the social and spatial contours of service-driven economies requires sharper distinctions and perhaps entirely new categories.[27] For example, both doctors and household servants fall under the category of service workers. Both often provide highly intimate services to their clients or employers, yet doctors usually occupy the middle to upper echelons of society. What separated doctors' work from that of personal servants in the nineteenth century was the directional flow of social capital.

Most personal service work produced intangible aesthetic, intellectual, physiological, or emotional value for the consumer but left the provider in a more tenuous position. Sometimes the very knowledge required to provide services—insights into traffic patterns or food preparation and delivery, awareness of physical ailments and emotional states, knowledge of how to enhance features or remove blemishes, the ability to provide pleasurable entertainment while hiding evidence of excess, or the power to channel private discourse through public networks—threatened to be detrimental to the consumer's processes of respectable self-fashioning if it were publicly rendered.[28]

In a social order based on "character," defined by self-control, discretion was a virtue of service provision. The more intimate the encounters between service providers and consumers, the more unsettling and volatile the relationship became. One response to the potential threat posed by the intimate knowledge held by service workers was to marginalize the work and render the workers socially invisible. Doctors escaped this tactic by wielding highly specialized and uniquely valuable knowledge (ultimately, the power of life and death), and—by the nineteenth century—enacting this knowledge through formalized displays of expertise. In other words, doctors (and other elite service providers) performed professionalism. This is a crucial distinguishing variable in assessing the status, monetary value, and social leverage of service work and one that has been recognized as a powerful value marker with many complex histories.[29]

Claims to professionalism and its attendant respectability shaped many of telegraphists' and telephone operators' interactions and disputes with officials, the public, and one another. For these workers, the fusion of technical prowess with multiple forms of literacy, along with the requirement of discretion, meant that they performed intellectual, not mechanical, labor. They saw themselves as respectable professionals who should be paid as such and entitled to privileges in the new information bureaucracy. Administrators and many public observers thought differently: they emphasized the unobtrusive, passive, repetitive nature of the work. The classes who ran and used the telegraph and the telephone networks, used to inferior social beings performing all kinds of personal services for them (often in close proximity to their bodies and utterances), tried to ensure that the work of information mediation remained marginal. This book explores how workers, administrators, and consumers all celebrated the new information technologies even as they imparted very different meanings to the daily performance of telecommunications work.

AFFECTIVE MEDIATIONS

Telecommunications workers were mediators who negotiated thresholds of privacy and transparency between the burgeoning telegraph and telephone systems and very specific sectors of the public. Telegraphists transcribed private communications into electrically transmittable code, continually managing machines, symbols, language, and people; the boys who delivered the resulting telegrams manifested the new technology on city streets and brought it to consumers' doorsteps; telephone operators' disembodied voices interacted with the disembodied voices of subscribers in telephone exchange systems. All of these encounters required careful supervision, technical manipulations, highly specialized knowledge, awareness of public expectations, and the management of public frustrations and demands. In these respects the labor of telecommunications workers was aligned with that of other workers, past and present, engaged in what has variously been described as emotional, intimate, caring, or affective labor.[30] To apply this insightful line of enquiry to past labor practices in the information industry—whether to illuminate the processes leading to our present moment or to properly distance past work cultures from current ones and thereby uncover alternative mechanisms of change—we need to distinguish the historical contexts out of which affective information service work emerged. Affective interactions between telecommunications workers and consumers—and between workers themselves—illustrate the extent to which competing ideals were manifested in communications systems and how human exchanges defined the parameters of information systems.[31]

Telegraphists, messengers, and telephone operators had to combine established forms of personalized deference, based on interactions between affluent subjects and domestic servants, with new demands for public accessibility, standardization, and expertise. These workers were thus central to shifting meanings about what "public service" meant and what it was worth.

GENDERING TELECOMMUNICATIONS

Gender was crucial to the ordering and imagining of telecommunications. The introduction of women to the telegraph service intensified administrators' and consumers' perception of telegraphy as cognitively disengaged and automatizing. Female telegraphists were the first women to join the British civil service and the vanguard of female clerical or "pink-collar" labor in Britain. These types of employment fundamentally altered work expectations and provided new opportunities for women as laborers, consumers, and public figures. However, the history of Victorian communications also exposes the deskilling of "feminized" labor as a result of technological development and social pressures.[32]

However symbolically potent in Victorian telegraphy—and foundational to historical narratives of women's advancement in the workplace —women telegraphists remained a minority presence within the industry. This was a manifestation of Victorian gender ideologies and social aspirations merged with industrial discipline. Administrators and engineers asserted gendered working parameters and hierarchies.[33] Men and women competed for resources and prestige.[34] These contestations were also evident in the arrangement of wires in metropolitan telegraph offices and beyond. Attempts to manage mixed-gender spaces often resulted in workers' agitation, which ultimately strengthened male claims to proficiency and caused employers to place constraints on women's labor. Telegraph offices were some of the first sites where women and men performed the same highly technical work, and the efforts of male telegraphists and administrators to resist this trend and maintain wage differentials reveal the profoundly gendered structure of the early information industry.

Another wave of technological innovation produced quite different results. As telephone usage increased among elites, female operators quickly came to dominate the telephone exchange's workforce. As an Edwardian telephone supervisor stated, "Telephony is essentially women's work." The perceived virtues and vices of the telephone rested on this assertion.[35] Female operators found themselves negotiating multiple boundaries between public utility and private interactions, and between networks of elite men and aspiring lower-class women. They enabled exchanges of all kinds while asserting their own claims to professional respectability.

SEX AND TELECOMMUNICATIONS WORK

For some telecommunications workers, sexual encounters, innuendo, and imaginative possibilities between themselves and information consumers were a direct consequence of the personalized service demanded of them. Concerns about the erotic potentialities of early electric communication systems were reflected in administrative attempts to monitor and direct workers' interactions with consumers. These concerns further underscored communications workers' struggles to claim authority and their own sense of value in their daily interactions.

A favorite anecdote among officials, often recounted by journalists in the 1870s, was a telegraphic romance. *Chambers's Journal* had perhaps the most vivid rendering of this tale: "Can the telegraph make love? ... Yes! Most emphatically." A Central Telegraph Office male operator in charge of the Berlin circuit had regular contact with his female counterpart in the new German capital, and "as time went on, these two began to know something of each other through daily telegraphic intercourse."[36] The double entendre confirms what Kate Thomas has identified as the imaginative sexual possibilities in the Victorian postal communications, a promiscuous system that "produces commutable relationships and intimate strangers."[37] This telegraphic flirtation occurred "during spare moments," as "they came to possess a mutual knowledge of each other's habits and character." They elaborated on their courtship with a combination of postal technologies: "Cartes-de-visite followed. Later on, to use the language of love, hearts were exchanged, electricity was made the slave of love, and finally the happy pair were made partners for life at the hymeneal alter [*sic*]!" For *Chambers's*, such instances of workplace telegraphic romance were many and manifest: "Certain love-code signals exist, known only to the parties most interested; and . . . it is perfectly possible for a sentimental telegraph clerk at A to transmit a kiss instantaneously to the lady who has charge at B, or—vice versa. I have seen it done!"[38] Flirtation, even electric embraces, were embedded in telegraphy's inherently (hetero)sexual operations, discernible to those familiar and expert with coded meanings.

However, the embellishments to this story perhaps belie the messages that GPO officials intended. The telegraphist couple represented a project of informational internationalism emanating from the center of the British Empire, a high-tech love story, and an example of properly channeled desire. At the root of this romance is a controlled relationship dependent on both imaginative possibilities and protective geographic separation. That the couple's attraction developed in "spare moments" accentuated the normal workings of business.[39] These parasexual electric intimacies led to conventional marriage and the end of the Berlin telegraphist's career.[40] Such an outcome ticked all the boxes of Victorian telegraphic progressivism.

The truly subversive message from this story was that telegraphists had discernible personalities. The marriage plot hinged on telegraphists' ability to develop "a mutual knowledge of each other's habits and character" while transcribing and transmitting the messages of others. The projection of individuated traces into the work of telegraphy ran counter to the construct of the passive, cognitively and emotionally disengaged automaton promoted by the GPO and embraced by the public.

Telegraph offices were rife with affective interactions, and so were telephone exchanges, where female operators had to manage male telephone subscribers' aural fantasies. On urban streets, delivering information was a strictly male endeavor, and this resulted in new possibilities for clandestine sexual practices associated with masculine street cultures. Telegraph boys added a new dimension to London's pederastic prostitution traditions. They fueled both the imaginations of men looking for "rough trade" and the anxieties of communications administrators, for whom telegraph boys represented the basis of a docile postal proletariat.

Administrators strove to promote the seamless flow of private information as evidence of public order. Yet unionizing postal workers, assertive female operators, and promiscuous telegraph boys enable us to perceive the exclusions and tensions inherent to Britain's telecommunications landscapes. State administrators emphasized the necessity of privacy in public communications, and they took seriously the role of telecommunications staff in policing the boundaries between private and public information. The exposure of networks of queer telegraph boys prompted a significant shift in the state's vision of the public and private realms and the extent to which privacy could be intruded upon in the name of public order. The 1889 Cleveland Street Scandal, which exposed telegraph boys' sexual interactions with aristocrats in a West End brothel, is an example of this new communications policing and its effects on the balance of power between competing authorities. The scandal has long been used as a peek into London's subcultural sex markets, but it is also a window onto an expanded, militant information monitoring network in London, one of whose main concerns was telegraph-boy misbehavior.[41]

INFORMATION SERVICES, SURVEILLANCE, AND CIVIC ORDER

Telecommunication workers were among Britain's first domestic targets of electric information surveillance. The first telegraphist strike in 1871 failed in part because London administrators had been listening in to organizers along the wires and had mobilized the GPO's internal policing division to eavesdrop on telegraphists' meetings throughout the United Kingdom. By the 1880s, concerns about the sexual activities of telegraph boys aligned with anxieties over other London insurgencies, namely militant Irish nationalism and labor union agitation. The expansion of the Post Office's internal surveillance amplified tensions between liberal doctrines of privacy and state oversight of communications. Clandestine information surveillance, stimulated by attempts to stamp out proscribed sexualities, continued to expand along the wires.

Telegraph boys also exemplified another remarkable transformation in the ordering of public and private spheres. Administrators took an increasingly firm hand in raising these young, not-so-self-regulating service providers. Whereas in the 1870s telegraph boys had been expendable afterthoughts, by the eve of the Great War they found themselves subject to mandatory schooling and were strongly encouraged to participate in GPO-sponsored activities outside working hours. They were also subject to increasingly thorough physical inspections and quasi-military rituals. Beneficiary institutions and martial forces coalesced to produce a reform culture that extended public interests into telegraph boys' neighborhoods, leisure activities, and social affiliations. The rise of the telephone and concerns over these young workers' future employment prospects collided with the GPO's paternalist policies, culminating in telegraph boys' prominent roles in "the boy labour crisis," a moral panic arising out of Edwardian perceptions that working-class male adolescence was a social problem with imperial consequences.[42] The educated, physically fit, well-drilled, patriotic, and docile public servant of administrators' imaginations symbolized the state's aspirations for a liberalism extended to working-class subjects. Displays of marching telegraph boys, carbines on shoulders, along major urban thoroughfares represented the apex of an orderly information environment. The Great War permanently changed the meanings of such displays.

Serving a Wired World draws on various texts, including literature, journalism, GPO association documents, and staff magazines, technical writing, police records, business archives, government reports, and administrative records. The bulk of my source materials come from two repositories: the BT (British Telecom) Archives and the Postal Museum (formerly the British Postal Heritage Museum and Archive). Such sources have enabled me to craft a bodied labor history: a cultural analysis at the confluence of labor and administrative practices bolstered by the histories of technology, liberalism, gender, and sexuality.

The ordering of the book is broadly chronological. Chapter 1 explores the influence of London's social and geographic landscape during the nineteenth-century "information revolution," the ramifications of nationalization on the telegraph service, the consumers the state's electric communications systems catered to, and the emergence of privacy concerns regarding the communications network. Chapter 2 develops my central claim that liberal demands for privacy underpinned the meaning, value, and conflicts inherent in telecommunications mediations. These ideological pressures, first apparent in

telegraphy, resulted in a deeply gendered transition that involved the redefini-
tion of public service during the later nineteenth century. Subsequent chapters examine distinct groups of workers. Chapters 3 and 4 go inside London's
Central Telegraph Office to explore the working regimes, cultures, disputes,
and aspirations of telegraphists, from their failed national strike in 1871 to
their unsuccessful attempts to acquire professional status by the fin-de-siècle.
Chapter 3 highlights the administrative logics that created gendered divisions in telegraphic work; chapter 4 focuses on telegraphists' own reflections
about their work and coworkers. Chapters 5 and 6 shift in both subject matter and analytical scale, with individuals as well as collectivities driving the
analysis. Case studies of late Victorian telegraph boys—their influence on
urban culture, their working lives, and some of their misadventures—involve
deep forensic readings of sexual crime investigations and a consideration of
the different discursive pressures apparent in legal and postal state archives.
Chapter 5 focuses on the sexual economy of telegraphy, and Chapter 6 further elaborates on the relationship between postal surveillance and sexual
scandal. Chapter 7 follows telegraph boys into the early twentieth century
and examines the increasing regimentation and militarization of their working lives under the auspices of new liberalism. The final chapter explores the
labor innovations and continuities telephone operators faced as they mediated connections and conversations between elite consumers.

In the epilogue, I briefly explore the symbolic value of telecommunications work in early twentieth-century political uncertainty and dissent. From
telegraph-boy impersonations in the music hall to suffragettes' infatuation
with information technologies and the significance of the postal infrastructure during the 1916 Easter Rising, telecommunications workers were
inscribed in attempts to challenge the current political order.

Today, the fortunate among us are surrounded by invisible labor managing our own flows of goods, money, well-being, and information. I write this
while trying to ignore text messages, email alerts, and the latest binge-worthy
series recommended by Netflix, based on my viewing history. An Amazon
box has just arrived on my doorstep, and I had a fleeting glimpse of one of the
thousands of people who work behind the scenes to make my privileges possible. Amazon and other corporations aim to remove even this glimpse: the
vision of drone delivery promises a service seemingly devoid of human
intrusion.

Like the Victorians and Edwardians in this book, we struggle with balancing convenience and privacy, service and silence. Pulled between ideological

instincts that privilege personal autonomy and our expectations of the services due to us as informed subjects and desiring consumers, many of us now live in a strange paradigm: we willfully give away all kinds of information about ourselves in the name of efficiency, yet we feel outrage when we discover that powerful external forces have access to intimate details of our lives. The ascendancy of big data, perhaps usefully imagined as the era of mass intimacy, is manifest in our homes, workplaces, landscapes, politics, yearnings, and wage scales.[43] This book explores an earlier iteration of these contradictions and their effects on a workforce.

ONE

Dispatches from Underground

FOLLOWING THE NATIONALIZATION of the telegraph system in 1870, London journalists described the outer and inner workings of Telegraph Street, the location of Britain's first state-run Central Telegraph Office. The street itself, known as Great Bell Alley before the Electric and International Telegraph Company set up headquarters there in 1859, was a small lane off Moorgate, near London Wall. Just a few blocks north of the Bank of England and the Royal Exchange, Britain's new telegraphic headquarters lay in the center of the global powerhouse that was London's financial district. According to an article in *Temple Bar,* the street itself was "by no means inviting, and those who have never penetrated its somewhat dismal recesses are little aware of the important part which it now plays, commercially as well as socially and politically, in the 'story of our lives from day to day.'"[1]

The article employed a rhetorical device common in Victorian discussions of telegraphy: a contrast between the all-encompassing, global ramifications of wired communication and its enigmatic, closed-off, and slightly forbidding internal workings. The telegraph network, that "sensorium . . . the nervous system of Empire," was everywhere, yet difficult to fully access or comprehend. Noting "the 'Strictly private' which meets our view the moment we enter," the reporter observed: "A portion of the pavement is 'up,' and over a hole . . . partly to shelter the workmen, and partly to hide from view their mysterious operations—a canvas tent of not the most handsome proportions."[2] *Temple Bar* painted a vaguely ominous picture of what was taking place across London. The General Post Office (GPO) had decided to route London's telegraph lines underground, both to protect the wires and to remove the poles and lines that clogged London's streets and skyline. At least, that was the aim. Despite its image as a city of increasingly ordered mobility,

London in the late nineteenth century was a cluttered network of railway construction sites and road-widening projects. Workmen engaged in "cut and cover" tunnel and trench construction perpetually deferred the promise of easy urban mobility.[3] In *Temple Bar*'s depiction, they were also perpetuating telegraphy's "mystery": shielded by rough canvas and laboring men, the system lurked underground, in the private recesses of public thoroughfares.

Telegraphy's multiple layers of opacity, from the science of electricity, Morse code, and underground wires to its high cost and its affluent users' various practices of encryption, reflected its social utility. Its visible elements included established class, gender, and imperial hierarchies, and while some high-minded reformers envisioned a democratized (yet profitable) system of ever-increasing knowledge accumulation and social uplift, telegraphy's fiscal priorities dominated the system's design and implementation. Nationalization of the telegraph network was effected by an alliance of influential groups who wanted the state to protect the system from market uncertainties. Like previous technologies that spurred Victorian state intervention, telegraphy encapsulated liberal aspirations: the ever-increasing mobility of goods, money, people, and information. The imperial metropolis became a global electric information hub, with nodes that, as Chris Otter has noted of other "liberal objective" systems, were "stratified and knotty," connecting socially and commercially powerful constituencies.[4] Journalistic attempts to elucidate telegraphy's mysteries were exercises that represented modern urban life to affluent consumers as coherent, knowable, and aspirational. It was important, however, that many aspects of electric information remain mysterious, in order to assure those consumers that the private discourse being transcribed in the nation's telegraph offices was protected. Many of telegraphy's consumers embraced codes and ciphers to further safeguard their messages. A crucial characteristic of nationalized telegraphy for the liberal project was that the system did not scrutinize the millions of messages sent along the wires.

ENVISIONING TELEGRAPHIC NETWORKS

By the 1860s, physiological metaphors for telegraphy were clichés depicting Britain—and London in particular—as the heart and brain of a global operation. *Temple Bar* asked its readers to imagine the wires as "the veins . . . which convey the electric fluid from the main arteries of communication to the very heart of the telegraphic system, and from the heart to the extremities of civilization itself."[5] The metaphor of the circulatory system represented a visible, vital, orderly flow whose workings Victorians had more fully discovered. For another journalist, the nervous system was a better analogy than the circulatory system: "The complete web of mysterious nerve-fibres which spring from the central ganglion of an animal . . . giving and taking intelligence from one to the other, is obviously for the creature what the telegraph system is for the Earth. Telegraph lines are the nerves of the world."[6] According to the historian Iwan Rhys Morus, this was a common association: "Both were systems that seemed to transmit intelligence instantaneously," and both were involved in regulation.[7] Mid-Victorians embraced this technomedical fantasy of imperial order, celebrating the telegraph "for its capacity to make their world smaller and more immediately manageable."[8]

Originally conceived as a subsidiary technology for railway operation, telegraphy had developed with the railway companies in the 1830s and 1840s, and the spread of wires throughout Britain followed the train routes. Its first transnational manifestation in 1858 was short-lived—the Atlantic Company's transatlantic cable lasted less than a month before breaking—but seven years later, telegraph wires directly linked the Atlantic British Empire via western Ireland and Newfoundland. By the 1860s all major British urban centers were connected either by railway telegraphs or by one of five private telegraph companies.

In 1860 London's internal telegraph market was effectively taken over by the District Telegraph Company. The Electric and International Telegraph Company, the largest of the national networks, had installed over fifty thousand miles of wire by 1868.[9] The "Electric" and its competitors charged rates based on the number of words transmitted and the distance covered. There was uneven collaboration between the companies, which consumers increasingly railed against as telegraphy's importance increased.

As a result of telegraph expansion, over three thousand telegraph stations were opened for public use throughout Britain and Ireland, ninety-five of which were in London.[10] The rest were clustered in the other large cities, generally in or near railway stations. By the 1860s, millions of telegrams were being sent every year. Telegraphy had become essential for government officials, industrialists, bankers, merchants, and journalists.[11] The private companies defended their high rates in terms of exclusivity, explicitly catering to state actors, business networks, and cultural elites rather than the masses (gamblers being an important cross-class exception). The telegraph might have gone global, but direct access to electric knowledge depended on proximity to wires and the ability to pay for telegrams, which were a rare or emergency expenditure for the vast majority of British and imperial subjects.

NATIONALIZATION

Those who could afford telegraphy often sung its praises and complained about it in the same breath. In the later Victorian period, commentators still evoked the quasi-mystical capacities of electricity to keep the Empire informed, regulated, and cohesive, but grandiose descriptions of the dazzling speed and civilizing powers of telegraphy increasingly served as preambles to frustrated criticisms of Britain's current network. Articles in the *Times* during the 1860s regularly complained about "ridiculous" and "costly" errors committed by private telegraph companies.[12] Observers bemoaned the exorbitant and complicated rate system, the inefficiency and unreliability of transmissions, and the inconvenient locations of telegraph offices. As early as 1854, commentators demanded some form of government intervention to untangle the mess of private wires.[13] Nationalization of the telegraph network under the postal system gained traction as a viable remedy even among those who usually opposed any government intervention in industry.

Reformers argued that the telegraph was the younger sibling of the postal system, which had enjoyed a period of successful reform and expansion. The penny-post innovations of the 1840s, introducing flat rates and the prepaid stamp system, had revolutionized the British public's relationship with letter writing; by the 1860s postal reforms proved fiscal successes as well. The GPO improved communication across the nation and empire and remained a valuable source of revenue. Early experiments with private telegraph company interconnectivity had proved expensive and unpredictable. Influential figures, including the political economist William Stanley Jevons, argued that under the auspices of the GPO, a nationalized telegraph network would be cheaper, faster, more accessible, and more accountable than the private systems.[14]

In rhetoric evoking the civilizing power of imperial communications, a group of powerful business and state representatives fueled the push for nationalization. Commentators repeatedly invoked metaphors of the "web," "nervous system," and "arteries" of empire in celebrating telegraphy's potential. These metaphors almost invariably relied on an implicit logic of control from a powerful center. News organs were almost universally in favor of nationalization, as the government had promised generous subsidies for news cables in order to maintain the competitiveness of the British press.[15]

Nationalization's adherents further argued that Britain's reputation as a world power was at stake if its telegraph system continued to lag behind the state-run systems on the Continent. Frank Ives Scudamore, second secretary of the GPO and the chief administrative architect of nationalization, published statistics-laden reports of the private companies' shortcomings and the success of nationalized European services.[16] The *Pall Mall Gazette* cited Scudamore's figures to argue that the success of nationalized Swiss and Belgian systems made it "quite clear that England, with its immense commercial engagements, its wealth, its social activity of every kind, must have incomparably greater need for quick intercourse by telegraph than the Belgians or the Swiss."[17] Besides imperial chauvinism, there were other powerful ideological prompts at work in the telegraph "debate." As the *Pall Mall Gazette* asserted, the ubiquity of the telegraph represented progress: "quick intercourse" was now a prerequisite for Englishness.

The parliamentary bills that transferred the wires to the Post Office were passed a year after the Second Reform Act, which extended suffrage to 1.5 million men. C. R. Perry has argued that underlying some telegraph reformers' rhetoric was a belief that a more accessible telegraph system would foster the spread of knowledge and thus improve British society. With respectable urban working-class men casting ballots in parliamentary elections, a small but well-connected group of administrators thought it all the more important that greater numbers of subjects be properly informed.[18]

These interests met with little resistance, even when it became clear that state telegraphy was a much more expensive endeavor than the penny post or the recent GPO savings bank scheme. Scudamore had predicted that with an initial expenditure of just over £2.5 million, the state could acquire all the wires, dramatically expand the system, reduce telegraph tariffs, and swiftly turn an annual profit. He proposed a flat rate for all domestic telegraphs: twenty words for one shilling, with free delivery in cities and within a three-mile radius of the post office in rural areas. His figures encouraged many prominent public figures, including economists like Jevons, bureaucrats like Edwin Chadwick, the politicians William Gladstone and Benjamin Disraeli, Charles Dickens, and respectable commercial associations such as the Edinburgh Chamber of Commerce, to support nationalization. As government negotiations with the private companies progressed, the buyout figure rose from £2 million to over £6 million, with most telegraph companies receiving twenty years' worth of projected net profits rather than the value of their current shares. A number of other concessions further compromised the government's future telegraph revenue. By the time the private companies officially ceded their wires to the GPO on February 4, 1870, telegraphy had already been transformed from a private enterprise into a public and imperial necessity in the minds of British legislators, commentators, and consumers.

TELEGRAPHIC LONDON

The cityscapes of the latter half of the nineteenth century promoted particular forms of urban mobility as civic virtues.[19] Unsightly vestiges of bodily and commercial activities were channeled indoors and underground, enabling those who made proper use of the city to avoid having their thoughts and bodies distracted or tainted by the unpleasant side of human commerce.[20] The architects and promoters of these environments relied on shifting distinctions between public and private. The language of inclusion and exclusion, inside and outside, concealment and revelation continually manifested itself in Victorian descriptions of the urban experience, as did bodily metaphors of circulation and flow. The unfettered movement of electric communications became a distinctive aspect of the modern civic circulatory system, illustrating the interplay of the social and the material in rearticulating who was included, who was excluded, and who maintained boundaries in the telegraphic city.

Just as the brain controls the nerves, so a central regulating body was needed to order the telegraph wires; and if telegraph wires were the regulating nerves of the imperial body politic, London was its brain stem. Not only were more telegrams sent to, from, and within London than anywhere else on earth, but the majority of the world's telegraph cables were manufactured there as well. By 1870, the Silvertown Works in the East End of London—on the north bank of the Thames in the modern borough of Newham, east of the Isle of Dogs—dominated the world's telegraph-cable industry.[21]

In the first year of the nationalized service, the scale of the GPO's urban presence increased dramatically. The post office hastily set up over three hundred additional stations in greater London alone.[22] GPO wires spread rapidly throughout Great Britain and the Empire. By 1875, the number of British telegrams sent annually had doubled.[23]

Scudamore and the postmaster general crowed about this remarkable expansion in services.[24] They were particularly proud that the telegraph's remarkable growth rate was attributable to centralized management. The old companies had all used London as a hub, but centralization was fundamental to the new system. Virtually all provincial and international transmissions, regardless of location, were routed through London. Telegrams from Dublin to New York, Penzance to Cape Town, or Brighton to Portsmouth went through Telegraph Street.

GPO administrators had anticipated that the exponential growth of offices, cables, and trunk lines would require a much larger headquarters than the Telegraph Street building. In 1869 foundations were laid for a new central office at the heart of the nation's mail network, St Martin's-le-Grand. Located in the City of London and just north of St Paul's Cathedral, St Martin's-le-Grand had been the GPO headquarters since 1829. An early Victorian example of civic improvement, the building was an imposing neo-classical structure fronted with grand Ionic columns. The site was deliberately chosen to clear out the prostitution market that had thrived in the area in the eighteenth and early nineteenth centuries.[25] The internal design of the building paid tribute to Jeremy Bentham's panopticon: detectives surveyed the mail sorting floor from a six-sided observation booth.[26]

The new Central Telegraph Office was likewise carefully planned to maximize productivity through the regulation of space. Completed in 1874, it was a massive four-story edifice facing GPO headquarters from the western side of St Martin's-le-Grand. Its exterior, of Portland stone and granite, gestured aesthetically to the older Post Office. The journalist John Munro proclaimed, "London is the metropolis of the world, and its Central Telegraph Station is justly the largest in existence."[27] He then plunged into a long description of the building's many rooms, galleries, mechanical innovations, and workers.

Telegraphy, like other electric technologies that emerged in the nineteenth century, remained a mystery to most consumers. Electricity had lost some of its novelty by the 1870s, but it still compelled writers to resort to a set of more concrete, historically situated analogies. When Victorian commentators wanted to explain telegraphy, they often contrasted its mysterious inner workings with its ubiquitous outer presence. The seemingly effortless public manifestation of London's telegraphy network was juxtaposed with the hive of hidden activity and labyrinth of underground wires that made it function. In *Temple Bar*'s description of the building, the reporter followed the "bloody entrails" of the telegraph wires up through a cellar and into the provincial instrument galleries, where readers were confronted with "curious arrangements of brass knobs and screws," and "450 different wires" along with telegraphy's technical jargon: "test boxes," "terminals," and multiple varieties of telegraph instruments with names like "Wheatstone Automatic" and "Morse Sounder."[28]

In this esoteric landscape, telegraphists, telegraph messengers, supervisors, and clerks, many of them women, went about their business. Another journalist highlighted the disorientating, even dehumanizing effects of the main instrument room, describing a sensory cacophony of "hundreds of minds . . . simultaneously conversing, some with tongues of steel, some with the clear sound of a bell, some again by means of piano-like notes, which spell the words letter by letter, although we have the clatter of all these sounds . . . hailing from distant western and northern cities, not a human voice is heard."[29] It was machines, not people, conversing. Far from dystopian, however, this rendering assured its audience that the network affected no human interest in the messages it conveyed.

Twenty years later the outer and inner workings of telegraphy still had narrative punch. In an 1891 special issue of *The Engineer* magazine titled "Our Postal Telegraphs," the workings of the Central Telegraph Office, to which a fifth story had recently been added, were laid bare. In highly technical prose and detailed illustrations, the magazine described the old and new office exteriors, central galleries, wall terminals, internal machines, and telegraph employees. The overall impression is of dizzying complexity, all encased behind the austere walls of a government building.[30]

The interior design of the building reflected social and professional hierarchies. In the days before elevators, the most convenient and prestigious spaces were those closest to the ground. The most important offices—the cable room, the foreign and colonial branch, and the offices of most GPO executives (who had all moved across the street from the now-antiquated mail building)—were located on the ground and second floors. The postmaster general and secretary had impressive ground-floor suites, across the hall from the presumably well-insulated, two-story boiler and well pumps room. The basement housed massive batteries and steam engines, along with low-ranking clerks' offices, the telegraph boys' and porters' kitchens, staff lavatories, and one intriguing area housing "secret messengers." The provincial and metropolitan instrument gallery occupied most of the fourth floor, along with the "racing and special events" section. A long side room, designated "Irish news," reflected the importance of monitoring political upheavals in Ireland.[31] Administrators enjoyed street views from their windows, while telegraph operators had to make do with occasional glimpses of the London skyline.

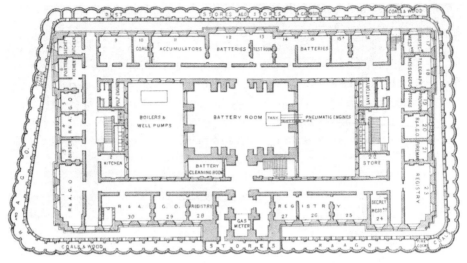

Basement floorplan of London's Central Telegraph Office. "Our Postal Telegraphs," *The Engineer,* 1891, 505. Courtesy of the BT Archives.

Beyond the Central Telegraph Office, London was being physically and mentally rezoned through the GPO's bureaucratic machinations. New stations were built to accommodate the higher speeds and volumes of communication. These were concentrated in areas associated with business, government, affluence and retail (Westminster, the City, the West End). Other areas (North London and the East End) were to varying degrees ignored. Social geographies of class were now calibrated by access to high-speed communications.

The GPO incorporated telegraph distribution into already established postal zones. London's postal area radiated out from St Martin's-le-Grand, stretching north to Whetstone, south to South Norwood, east to North Woolwich, and west to Hanwell. Central London was divided into the East Central (EC), West Central (WC), Western (W), Northern (N), Northwestern (NW), Eastern (E), Southeastern (SE), and Southwest (SW) districts. The massive E district encompassed Shoreditch, Whitechapel, Bethnal Green, the Victoria Docks, Hackney, Clapton, and Leytonstone.[32] The EC and WC divided at the City's boundaries: EC addresses began just east of Gray's Inn Road, ran southwest to the Temple and Fleet Street, east to the Tower and Bishopsgate Street, and North to the City Road. The WC included the Strand, Charing Cross, Trafalgar Square, Holborn, Bloomsbury,

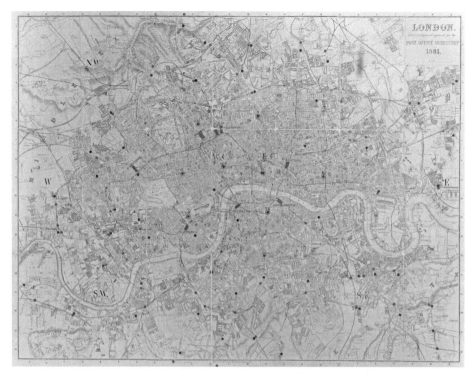

Map of London postal area, 1881. © Royal Mail Group, Courtesy of the Postal Museum, 2019.

and Covent Garden. The larger districts were further divided into central "town" and "suburban" districts. SW "town" areas included Whitehall and Buckingham Palace, and W "town" encompassed Piccadilly and Mayfair.

While tiny in relative area, the EC and WC districts had more telegraph stations than the E, N and SE districts combined. There were 44 GPO offices and telegraph receiving houses in the City by 1875, including 10 locations dedicated to "telegraph business only." The WC had 21 public telegraph locations. By contrast, the E district, notwithstanding its docks and markets, had only 15 telegraph-capable branch offices and receiving houses. SW had 19, including Parliament's exclusive lines. Mayfair and West End (W) residents had 29 telegraph offices and receiving houses to choose from.[33]

These numbers stayed relatively stable during London's telegraphic heyday. In the suburban districts, approximately 40 percent of post offices had telegraph equipment. By 1890, the number of telegraph stations and receiving houses in central London had declined, reflecting the growing dominance of the telephone in affluent areas.[34] In the EC district, the number of stations actually increased, even though many businesses rented private telegraph lines and were in the process of installing telephones.

THE INFORMATION METROPOLIS

In the first five years of nationalization, the GPO telegraph network grew exponentially. In London this growth materialized into hundreds of new offices, including a giant new headquarters, and thousands of rerouted underground wires that remade the civic landscape. On top of the considerable expenses of building construction, line installation, wire manufacturing, and digging up London's streets to install underground cables and pneumatic tubes, the GPO had made good on its pledge to connect unprofitable areas of the country to the metropolis, and hence to the rest of the globe.[35] Britain's other urban centers became lesser hubs in the telegraph system, and telegraph poles branched out from railway lines and along rural roads.

The entire system required constant maintenance and frequent upgrading. As a result, telegraph revenue quickly fell short of expenditure, and the telegraph service had to be supported by surplus revenue from the mail, the postal savings bank, and eventually the parcel service.[36] Within one year of the takeover, the *Pall Mall Gazette,* a great supporter of nationalization, had subdued its tone and remarked, "Whatever verdict may be pronounced on the telegraphic business of the post office, it is apparently impossible to assume that it has proved commercially a success."[37]

The GPO was still profitable overall, but telegraphy forced it to depart from the mid-Victorian doctrine that every post office department should be not only self-sustaining but also revenue generating. However, neither the postmaster general nor the chancellor of the exchequer was about to jettison this expensive acquisition. Most administrators reasoned that the telegraph network would pay for itself in the long term, just as the penny post had done. In the meantime, the GPO embraced its role as purveyor of a public good. Accessible, integrated telegraphy was more important than revenue. As the *Daily News* described the new system, "Cheap Telegrams have become a necessity of modern existence; and be they irksome or not, profits or no profits, the public must have them."[38] Other commentators reiterated arguments in favor of nationalization from the 1860s: improved domestic communications would perpetuate Britain's happiness and overall prosperity, and its overseas connections would enhance military and financial might across the Empire. State telegraphy, imagined in and emanating out of London, would be a civilizing engine at home and abroad.

The near-universal support for nationalization indicates general public trust in the Victorian postal network's handling of information. Fears of government spying through a state system were quickly brushed aside by commentators as the projected efficiencies of a public system gained enthusiastic media and cross-party political support. The handful who did complain—mainly railroad magnates concerned that the vogue for nationalization would extend to British rail services—evoked earlier instances of state spying through the GPO. In 1868 the Liberal MP George Leeman, a shareholder and future chair of the North Eastern Railway, reminded Parliament of the potential for increased government censorship and spying if the telegraph system was nationalized.[39] He evoked the Mazzini affair, a mid-Victorian GPO scandal sparked when officials intercepted and read the Italian nationalist's private correspondence.

Since its inception, the British Post Office had retained the legal right to open mail. From 1711, letters could be opened only with a warrant from a secretary of state. In the spring of 1844, the home secretary, Sir James Graham, exercised this privilege on Giuseppe Mazzini's letters while the Italian nationalist was exiled in London. After Mazzini revealed that his correspondence had been tampered with, a heated debate ensued in Parliament, and Graham was subjected to public fury and ridicule. *Grahamizing* flourished as a verb deriding "Continental" spying and censorship on English soil. The outcry stemmed the tide of letter-opening warrants, and for almost forty years the government worked hard to minimize mail tampering and to suppress any evidence when it opened correspondence. The right to search mail, however, remained (and remains) law.

Thomas Crook has posited that Parliament's tactic to reveal occasional letter opening, but never to justify it, allowed for spying to continue quietly in Britain once the public performance of anger had abated.[40] According to David Vincent, by "declining to communicate the control of communications," Parliament "reconciled the [public] confidence of liberalism with its fears."[41] This may explain in part why Leeman's dire warnings of telegraphic espionage fell on unconcerned ears in 1868. Pointing out the government's power to violate British liberal principles of individual privacy had no effect on a public in favor of a nationalized telegraph system. Leeman was ridiculed for scaremongering to advance his own financial self-interest.[42]

There is another possible explanation, however. As Vincent and others have highlighted, the idea of state surveillance, government "prying" into certain forms of private discourse, had explosive yet contradictory resonances for much of the century. Mid-Victorian Britons attempted to reconcile the sanctity of middle-class domestic privacy with demands for the exposure and transparency of public "problems." These tensions made questions and practices of authoritative discretion particularly crucial to orderly governance.[43] Coinciding with these trends was the explosive growth of commerce and fiscal services, whose discursive practices, as Mary Poovey has noted, depended on both the safeguarding and the timely disclosure of time-sensitive information.[44] Telegraphy's primary consumers—those working in the government, banking, and commercial sectors—were deeply attuned to practices of privacy, both in their livelihoods and in their homes.

The widespread indifference to nationalizing a system of information transmission that required human mediators to comprehend and transcribe private discourse can be attributed in part to elite consumers who were already used to managing privacy in relation to workers in all facets of their lives. The relationship of the telegraphic workforce to users' privacy is examined in greater detail in the next chapter. But telegraph users themselves relied on a number of strategies to protect the privacy of messages circulating in a public system.

TELEGRAPHESE

Telegraphic communication involved multiple forms of coding. Beyond the rendering of letters into visual and sonic patterns, the content of messages could be made opaque to the uninitiated. The ability to send telegrams, and, even more important, how to write them to convey the greatest amount of information using the fewest signifiers, became a yardstick of worldly acumen. For telegraphy's consumers, whose access to the most up-to-date information could promise financial windfalls, exclusive news reports, or a bet on a winning horse, speed and discretion were paramount.

From the 1840s, trading companies had printed code books for their employees and partners that provided telegram writers with word and number combinations that both concealed meaning and minimized word counts, and thus costs.[45] By the 1860s, generalized telegraph code books were marketed to the public, and specialized code books were developed for the banking, shipping, cotton, timber, and other industries.[46] One of the most popular general books, the *A.B.C. Universal Commercial Electric Telegraphic Code,* went through five editions by 1901. Its motto, "Simplicity, Economy, and Secrecy," found expression in exhaustive guides to ciphering telegrams with efficiency. Its coding mechanism used single words to represent phrases. "What is the freight and insurance?" became the single word "Forbear."[47] In the preface to the 1876 edition, the *A.B.C.* gave the following example to show how long and complicated messages could be whittled down to a few words:

> There is a favourable change in market in consequence of small supplies coming to hand. Telegraph cost, freight, and insurance Dutch crushed sugar, immediate shipment, payable one-third on shipment, two-thirds on delivery. Last parcel arrived in a very bad state, owing to bad weather at sea; have held survey, certificate by first post. Keep us well advised of sailings from your port.

In code, this became "Celebrity, Concommitant [*sic*], Subtile, Control, Humlah, Imagery, Parlor, Palmiferous, Aphamite, Wayside, Surname, Salve."[48] This example also speaks volumes about telegraphy's main consumers.

Telegraphic shorthand often drew on classical Greek and Latin. The code word for Glasgow General Terminus was "Agamemnon"; Portland, Oregon, was "Midas"; South African dry-salted hide was "Dryades"; and marmalade was "Erigone."[49] Some combinations must have elicited smiles in educated telegraph consumers steeped from an early age in Greco-Roman epics and Latin phrasing. Commentators often poked fun at telegraph users' cryptic tendencies and the word combinations that resulted. *Punch* lampooned the practice in 1870 and at the same time inserted a grim Latin in-joke: "Fenians' Telegram to their Friends: *Venimus, vidimus, victi sumus.*"[50] "We came, we saw, we were conquered" (an ironic inversion of Julius Caesar's laconic report of conquering Gaul) referred to attempts by Irish American Fenian nationalists to invade Canada and foment revolution against British rule. *Punch* was perhaps being doubly arch, as well-placed spies were reporting Fenian activities by telegraph to British and colonial officials, who suppressed the raids by 1871. Coded telegrams added another layer of mystery to the wonders of electric communication and reinforced existing networks of imperial control and commercial exchange.

TELEGRAPHIC PUBLICS

The cost of sending a telegram had decreased with nationalization, but at a minimum rate of one shilling for twenty words, it remained unaffordable for most people. As a consequence, class continued to mediate the social impact of telegraphy. For most Britons, a telegraph boy's appearance at the door almost certainly meant very bad news: the death of a loved one, demands for money, a court summons, or worse. In practice, telegrams often evoked fear rather than pleasure in the new system.[51] Victorian commentators often represented a telegram recipient's emotional response to be as telling a social signifier as dress or accent.

Unlike the general population, the press had relied on telegraph systems for years, and journalists exploited their familiarity with modern technology to cultivate a detached, knowing style of social observation. A truly modern metropolitan knew all about telegrams, and after 1870 the social demarcations of telegraph usage became even more apparent. Humorous anecdotes often caricatured those who were inexperienced in sending and receiving telegrams, and women were frequent targets. An 1876 *Chambers's Journal* article describes an elderly lady storming out of a post office "in high dudgeon" after realizing her message would be read by the operator. The same piece describes the author's "lady friend" apologizing for her telegram's grammatical mistakes, "as it was the first one that she had ever sent."[52] Such anecdotes cast the (male) reader as a telegraph consumer and thus "in the know," invited to smile at those not yet up to speed with London's technological progress. Telegraph consumption was gendered both in practice and in the public imaginary, a reflection of the masculine networks of trade, finance, journalism, and governance. British telegraphy allowed for privileged flows of discourse and elaborately coded, exclusionary modes of knowledge accumulation that helped preserve elite political control while presenting a veneer of democratic access.

The Public Service of Discretion

I, ___, do solemnly and sincerely declare that I will not wittingly, or willingly, open or delay, or cause, or suffer to be opened or delayed, contrary to my duty, any Letter or any thing sent by the Post.

Excerpt from the Post Office
Telegraphs Declaration, 1877

Probably most of the notes you are expected to carry might, with equal harmlessness, be communicated to you; but it will be better not to take so lively an interest in your mistress's affairs.

Beeton's Book of Household Management, 1861

AT NOON ON DECEMBER 8, 1871, just over one hundred of Manchester's telegraphists walked out of their GPO headquarters. Telegraphists in Liverpool, Bradford, Edinburgh, Glasgow, Dublin, and Cork followed suit. They were quickly replaced by temporary telegraphists sent up from London and by telegraphists stationed in London itself, waiting next to quietly rerouted lines. The GPO secretary, Frank Scudamore, had ordered strike organizers' telegrams—intended for transmission to other offices and to Britain's major press outlets the evening before the walkout—to be delayed until the action collapsed. Well-informed administrators exercised the Central Telegraph Office's power as the network's dominating institution and enforcer, capable of diminishing the vibrancy of telegraphic labor organizing outside the capital.[1] The rerouting tactics in London ensured a flow of information to officials and represented an innovation in British labor discipline: strikebreaking telegraphists were able to maintain the network without having to board a northbound train. Scudamore and his staff swiftly crushed Britain's first telegraphists' strike, the origins of which lay in a dispute between GPO officials and telegraphists over the nature of telegraphic work.

At the level of physics, telegraphy is the disruption of electric currents at formalized intervals. Morse code—the backbone of telegraphic communication by the 1870s—was a visual or sonic representation of these disruptions: it used patterns of long and short sounds (rendered on paper as dashes and dots) to represent letters. Telegraph operators' work entailed two principal tasks: transcribing incoming messages into language, and transmitting messages by tapping out dots and dashes on the key of their telegraph instrument, turning language into electric signals. This work involved unique cognitive processes: manual and aural dexterity to transmit and decipher signals, along with the perceptive and discreet management of a message's context, form, and content. Telegraphy necessitated a blend of competencies, and their value was ambiguous and open to interpretation.

For the nascent Telegraphists' Association behind the strike, at stake was whether telegraphists qualified as government clerks. In the parliamentary act nationalizing the British telegraph service, the state declared that "Such Officers and Clerks upon their appointment shall be deemed to be, to all intents and purposes, Officers and Clerks in the Permanent Civil Service of the Crown, and shall be entitled to the same but no other privileges."[2] Telegraphists interpreted their new role as civil servants in the traditional sense, with all the status it implied, which in mid-Victorian Britain meant recognition of telegraphy as a respectable profession.

For GPO administrators, in contrast, telegraphists were simply the latest members of "the manipulative grades," a category invented to distinguish the lowest caste of Victorian government office workers from gentlemen officials (and their pay and privileges). From the point of view of administrators, telegraphists worked more with their hands than with their heads, and telegraphists' wages, hours, and benefits were structured accordingly. Telegraphy became one of many GPO public professions aligned with private domestic service: physical, repetitive, unthinking, and often intangible labor performed for and subject to supervision by social superiors.

The two sides debated this question in terms of the nature of telegraphic communication and of workers' proximity to the information they mediated. Did transcribing messages make telegraphists discerning, honorable guardians of the public's privacy, or were they little more than extensions of the instruments they operated? The value of privacy was the practical and ideological parameter by which the value of telegraphic work was assessed.

The presence of women workers in the new telegraphic workforce was central to this debate. Following the strike and throughout the 1870s, journalists presented London's Central Telegraph Office, the "nerve center" of British domestic and imperial telegraphy, as a largely feminized operation, and this was beneficial for the sanctity of the public's private communication. As we are reminded by the parodied woman who left a post office in "high dudgeon" upon learning that her telegram necessarily had to be read to be sent, the public's trust in the telegraph system depended on its human infrastructure's disinterest in the words they transcribed. This is also why administrators and public commentators for the most part embraced women as telegraphists. By describing telegraph workers as bodily attuned mediators, and by harnessing female fingers and voices to telegraph instruments while concurrently relying on reassuring descriptions of the overwhelming busyness of urban telegraphy, popular renderings of telegraph work encouraged consumers to regard telegraphists as no more than marginal interlopers in their private exchanges. Such descriptions reflected and helped to establish a new type of marginal public servant, translated through women's labor, subject to the disciplines of privacy.

DISHONORABLE PUBLIC SERVANTS

When the selection process for the British Civil Service was reformed from a system of patronage to one of competitive examination in the wake of the Northcote-Trevelyan Report in 1854, William Gladstone, then chancellor of the exchequer, wrote approvingly that "one of the great recommendations" of the new policy

> would be its tendency to strengthen and multiply the ties between the higher classes.... [A]n essential part of any such plan as is now under discussion is the separation of work, wherever it can be made, into mechanical and intellectual, a separation which will open to the higher educated class a career and give them a command over all the higher parts of the civil service.[3]

From the beginnings of the merit-based civil service, its architects and supporters envisioned a set of educational and social prerequisites that would enable the elite order to maintain its close ties to the upper echelons of governance while employing a much more diverse administrative staff. In the view of David Vincent, this reassertion of the old order in the establishment of a multitiered bureaucracy was crucial for the development of "honourable secrecy" among government officials. Discretion about the state and public

affairs was repackaged as a burdensome duty and test of gentlemanly character. A civil servant's access to sensitive information, or state secrets, was a
mark of social elevation, a testament to and reward of well-developed powers
of discernment and disinterested observation.[4]

In the later Victorian period, grades of civil service work were deftly calibrated exercises in the maintenance of social power, and the post office was
at the forefront of this process. To ensure a supply of competent elites and
well-educated bourgeois administrators for Britain's largest but least glamorous government institution, GPO executives developed careful delineations
of postal tasks that positioned classes of workers in very different proximities
to the public's information, creating high- and low-value communications
service work. Honorable public servants oversaw the quotidian ones whose
daily tasks enabled the public's information flows.

Certain workers' interactions with ever-increasing numbers of letters,
parcels, and later postcards ensured their low socioeconomic status, producing the modern postman as a kind of information proletariat whose knowledge of access roads, addresses, correspondence habits, and even written
missives did not threaten the privacy-obsessed, GPO-dependent public.
Recent scholarship has productively addressed the imaginative possibilities
for GPO consumers in asking, "[What] happens when a postbag bulges with
the communication of *all* sorts, communication unified by engines of the
national Post Office?" To paraphrase Kate Thomas, the democratic promiscuity of the Victorian postbag opened up connections of all sorts, allowing
for a blurring of social boundaries and of public and private life.[5] For postmen, their necessary proximity to this type of promiscuity led to their socioeconomic stagnation. They emerged in the later nineteenth century as icons
of an inclusive state, but low-paid ones who understood their work through
narratives of decline.[6]

In their comprehensive histories of the work regimes in the British post
office, Martin Daunton and Alan Clinton chart its byzantine wage divisions
and ranking systems, including "established" positions that offered pensions
of varying amounts and "unestablished" positions that provided no benefits.
Every position, from the GPO's chief executives down to temporary postmen
and cleaning women, comprised many salary levels. Postal administrators
determined job duties and wage scales on the basis of perceptions of social
rank rather than on economic value, likely in order to mitigate threats of
collective unrest.[7] For Daunton, the most fundamental labor organizing
principle at the GPO was the division between indoor and outdoor occupa-

tions: "A clear line was drawn between the duties of the postmen and the indoor staff, between the uniformed outdoor workforce and the higher status white-collar indoor occupations."[8] This distinction had substantial emblematic and material consequences. Inside the GPO offices, additional discretionary regimes diminished the prestige of information mediation work while enhancing that of other types of labor.

The most revealing of these distinctions was that between mail sorters and mail deliverers. The sorters, working indoors in plain clothes, were paid considerably larger wages than the postmen, who wore uniforms of GPO blue, a symbol of both the dependability of the service and the wearers' subjugation to state discipline. As Patrick Joyce has noted, the postman of the latter half of the nineteenth century further embodied the systematization of state communications through "routine, dependability, and visibility."[9] Rituals such as the "postman's knock" developed at the interface of the public system and private residences. The uniformed postman, among the most public of public servants, may have represented an extensive and secure communications regime, but his wages, dignity, and even the quality of his uniform had decreased as the post office expanded.

Mail sorters, anxious to maintain their status, strenuously maintained that sorting the mail was much more intellectually challenging and respectable than delivering it. Despite arguments that combining sorting and delivery duties would be more efficient, GPO administrators concurred to a point. In urban offices, sorters were recruited from a "better class" of young men than postmen (many of whom had been ex-servicemen and, once GPO telegraphy was established, telegraph boys). But sorters never achieved status equal to the lower GPO clerical grades, which were mostly drawn from educated middle-class and elite young men.[10] The mail sorters and postmen developed separate associations that often vied with one another. The sorters attempted to align their interests with those of larger civil service organizations; the postmen looked to the trade unions. As Alan Clinton gloomily noted in his trade union history of the Post Office, this "snobs inferno" prevented the GPO staff from playing an effective part in the Victorian labor movement.[11]

Sorters' sequestered work and indirect proximity to the public's letters also mattered to their status in terms of the discretionary value of their tasks. Having access to the envelopes of millions of letters directed their energies to the form and destination, not the content, of private communication (though postcards soon offered a loophole). Their anonymous channeling of the mail was generally nonthreatening to a privacy-obsessed public, their knowledge of mail routing indicative of modern postal efficiencies rather than state surveillance. Telegraphists, as office workers, should also have benefited from the cachet of this orderly, educated, and discreet work regime, but the value of their labor was downgraded, despite certain advantages, because they were too close to the information they were responsible for.

Defining GPO Telegraphy

When telegraphists joined the post office, they attempted to position themselves above the sorters in the complex indoor hierarchy.[12] Henry Swift, an Edwardian chronicler of postal workers' agitation, noted that the telegraphists transferring from the private companies to the GPO in 1870 were "often men of birth and education ... an independent, Bohemian lot."[13] At first, GPO telegraphists' annual wages were higher on average than those of sorters—£71 and £59 respectively—but the complex ranges of job classifications and salary grades meant that most male telegraphists were paid similarly to or less than sorters for most of their careers.[14]

Disappointed in their hopes for high-status clerk positions, telegraphists engaged in various forms of agitation. They took full advantage of the potential for high-speed, coded, nationwide networking on the job. During the fall of 1871 a "Telegraphists Association" began to take shape in Scottish, Irish, and northern English urban centers; it reached out to telegraphists across Britain and resonated in the capital. By November 30, however, telegraphists had stopped openly discussing agitation through the telegraph network. They suspected (correctly) that their telegrams were being "Grahamed."[15] Administrative correspondence reveals that the telecommunications replacement of this mid-Victorian term for state spying had entered common currency: "It appears they have discovered that the wires are being tapped which will account for their silence."[16] Officials in London had secretly reversed the Manchester line through the Central Telegraph Office in London to keep tabs on the leaders of the Telegraphists Association and its growing influence. They had also mobilized the internal security department of the GPO, known then as the Missing Letter Branch, to observe telegraphists' after-work meetings and read their pamphlets. Scudamore, orchestrating counter-agitation efforts from London, readied one of his undersecretaries to send Thomas Jeffery, head of the Missing Letter Branch, up to Manchester with a team to "watch the men. ... Meanwhile I want you, while watching as many wires as you like, to keep as much in the background as possible."[17]

Astute enablers of British media, the telegraphists had planned to announce the strike through prominent press organs and distributors. But shortly before midnight on December 7, Scudamore delayed the Telegraphists' Association's telegrams to the *Times,* the *Daily News,* the Press Association, and the Central News. When he acknowledged doing so, public outcry was swift. The *Daily News* protested against the "arbitrary and unjustifiable conduct of the London authorities," and this opinion was widely shared.[18] The Tory *Saturday Review,* while condemning the striking telegraphists, opined that "it is well that Mr. Scudamore should be reminded on the first occasion that it is not the business of his department to think, but to forward messages with despatch."[19] Scudamore was subsequently ordered to justify his actions to Parliament and duly received official censure from the postmaster general. Supporters, however, argued that his acts were a matter of in-house discipline rather than of information censorship by the British government. Public criticism died down after the reprimand, and for the rest of the decade, anxieties about GPO electric spying and censorship were expressed obliquely, often through enthusiastic depictions of discreet female telegraphists.

Telegraphists' attempts to demonstrate their value by disrupting press cables and private correspondence barely registered, because GPO officials had taken measures to ensure a seamless telegraph operation during the walkout. In the wake of the failed strike, those still committed to achieving clerk status backed away from trade-union tactics. GPO telegraphists would not strike again until after World War I. Not only had striking proved unsuccessful, but it was tainted by association with the working class. Reform through petition and negotiation became telegraphists' only imaginable strategy for attaining middle-class professional salaries and status.

Aspiring telegraphists found a realistic goal to rally around in 1874, when Sir Lyon Playfair's Civil Service Commission advocated the establishment of a new "2nd Division Clerk" position across the Civil Service. With an annual starting salary of £80 this designation was, according to the commission, for "inferior" office work, "mechanical and monotonous labour" from which men of "responsibility, discretion, and power to direct work" should be shielded lest "they degenerate to mere machines."[20] From the telegraphists' perspective, however, the clerical title and salary range represented a step up from the "manipulative" employment strata they occupied at the GPO and would symbolically divorce them from the Post Office's manual work of information circulation.

In reclassifying positions to the new clerical grades, administrators negotiated separately with representatives from different job categories and played them against one another. When, for example, administrators dispensed with the position of "telegraph clerk" in favor of "telegraphist and sorter" in 1878, furious telegraphists distanced themselves from the sorters, who perceived the new designation as a step up. Telegraphists' demands to be treated as "true" civil servants were manifested in the establishment in 1881 of the deliberately named Postal Telegraph Clerks Association, whose members pushed against "the obnoxious designation of sorting clerk and telegraphist."[21]

Administrators' attempts to amalgamate telegraphists and sorters were part of a larger strategy to assert the purely manual nature of telegraphy. During an exchange on GPO staff recorded in the discussions of the Select Committee on Post Office Telegraphs in 1876, Playfair likened a telegraphist to an "ambi-dexterous monkey."[22] On one level this process reflected, as Patrick Joyce has argued, the GPO vision of an interchangeable "technical" workforce, taking "the Post Office into self-regulation, supposedly beyond the vagaries of human frailty."[23] In 1876 provincial GPO offices began training "learners" in both telegraphy and sorting duties. That same year the select committee inquired into whether telegraphists should receive some basic engineering and electrical training so that those posted at small village stations and privately run urban receiving houses could perform maintenance on their machines and batteries, and, if time allowed, do basic repairs on the outside wires.

The idea behind this policy was to reduce the number of GPO electricians and the cost of their long-term, pensioned employment. It was inspired by measures taken in the imperial telegraph networks in South Asia. Following the Indian Uprising in 1857, to prevent appropriation or sabotage, British and European telegraphist recruits took over the tasks of instrument, battery, and line repairs from indigenous telegraphists, who were thenceforth limited to transcription duties in offices overseen by white supervisors.[24] In Britain, however, the idea of the GPO telegraphist as engineer and system enforcer was shot down on the grounds that in many small post offices and receiving houses "the available staff is a young girl." It was "obviously out of the question that the work of washing batteries, cleansing them, and so on . . . could be carried out at such an agency."[25]

Women's incorporation into British telegraphy had a number of effects, one of which was to prompt a clearer delineation of telegraphists' duties. In 1870 2,400 women were recruited as telegraphists across the British Isles. The

1871 strike led to an increase in the number of female telegraphists and likely accounts for their brief domination of the London Central Telegraph Office telegraph staff in 1874. Their increasing presence ensured that telegraphists remained operators rather than mechanics or electricians. This trend led telegraphists to focus their efforts on redefining telegraphy as a skilled profession in itself, while limiting the kinds of intellectual leverage they could apply. Gender subtly defined the terms through which telegraphists could classify and champion their work.

The entry of women into GPO employment led to the emergence of the dual role of "counter clerk and telegraphist," further troubling the inside/ outside employment divide. These workers were trained both in telegraphy and in dealing directly with the public: selling stamps, handling parcels, and receiving telegrams at post offices and at GPO counters in privately run receiving houses. As a substantial part of this workforce, women became highly visible symbols of the new GPO services on offer.

In 1881, "dual training" in telegraphy and sorting became standard practice outside London, and the following year amalgamated pay scales and "dual qualification" became standard practice for the capital's workforce. The pay scales remained in place, but interchangeable work duties did not last. The Central Telegraph Office ignored these orders, and other large provincial offices quickly backed away from switching telegraphists and sorters when it became apparent that the intricacies of both tasks were hard to sustain if not practiced constantly.[26] Except in smaller offices and village post offices, the interchangeable technotron remained a fantasy (and even in these environments, the individuated daily interactions between GPO staff and a more tightly knit public tended to work against the depersonalization of postal workers). Women were increasingly those who most closely approximated this role.

Telegraphist agitators consistently framed their work as skilled and often drew attention to the scientific acumen required. A pamphlet produced by the Postal Telegraph Clerks Association (PTCA) in response to the dual training and salary regimes instituted in 1882 noted that telegraphists "attend science classes, and bought the necessary books for scientific study."[27] In 1885 a contributor to the PTCA's affiliated journal, *The Telegraphist,* argued that "the Telegraph Service may now be classed as a profession, and its claim is indisputable the moment the necessary clerical labour attaching to it is supplemented by a knowledge of the science of electricity." He went on to observe, "Every day sees the introduction of finer and more complicated instruments, and the knowledge which is necessary for clerks in charge of the best class of apparatus, is such as to place him entirely above those engaged in ordinary clerical pursuits."[28] Here telegraphy is represented as a specialized informational vocation not just equivalent but superior to clerical labor.

In addition to highlighting the scientific understanding, technical expertise, and attention to detail required of telegraphists, the PTCA literature emphasized discernment, public responsibility, high levels of general education, and discretion. The telegraphist was "never free from a sense of grave responsibility, because there pass through his hands many messages of vital importance." The "peculiar nature" of the work "demands great tact, discretion, and promptitude, constant application, and distinctive training and experience."[29]

In their petitions, telegraphists highlighted their active engagement with press cables: "In order to deal with press work satisfactorily, a knowledge is necessary of the names of public men, of current events, and of political questions, &c." Such "good general knowledge of foreign intelligence, and of the current topics of the day, political, financial, social, sporting," was "especially needed on those busy Parliament nights when the latest intelligence had to be supplied to the press with such dispatch, and blunders are likely to prove so embarrassing."[30] Telegraphists relaying news cables had "frequently to translate faulty signals and to discover their meaning through entire paragraphs of press work by the exercise of their reason," and to compensate for the slapdash work of some reporters whose "indistinct and at times almost illegible handwriting . . . would make it almost impossible for their copy to be used." According to a senior telegraphist at the Central Telegraph Office in 1889, the work of transcribing press cables "approximates very closely to that of the subeditor of a newspaper in the variety of subjects brought under their notice, and with which they have to deal."[31]

From subeditor to stockbroker, GPO telegraphists also had to "be thoroughly conversant with the names and prices of stocks, and the frequent changes of the markets," a necessity for the "speed and perfection of transmission" of the Stock Exchange lines, "which can be readily understood as regards business connected with the greatest markets of the world." London's Central Office telegraphists were "expected to have a knowledge of the French and German languages, [and] Foreign Service Work, to detect irregularities in all Foreign Companies Telegrams."[32] A telegraphist's "knowledge of public men and events" had to be "universal. . . . Business transactions of every conceivable nature pass through his hands. . . . [He] should be familiar as he must be with home and foreign political events, all descriptions of sport, and numerous other matters, in order to render efficient service."[33] In their demands for greater pay, telegraphists represented themselves not just as mediators but as informed interlocutors of imperial commerce.

Refusing to be subject to their machines, telegraphists also fought to retain their position as finely attuned controllers of circuitry, insisting that their keys and sounders were intellectual tools rather than signifiers of an automatizing process. Telegraphists sometimes referred to themselves as "manipulators," creating a different meaning for the term than that designated by the civil service hierarchy. It was an acknowledgment that their work was a type of informational craft. At the very least, they wanted recognition that "a rapid and true transmission of telegrams, most of which are highly important, and many of which are written in code or in a foreign language, is better work and deserves better pay than that of the sorting of letters."[34]

Administrators were occasionally of two minds about telegraphists. When contemplating updating pay scales in 1892, Robert Tombs, the central office controller, went back and forth over the relative responsibilities of sorters and telegraphists, noting that "there is no money responsibility in working a telegraph instrument," but on the "question of confidence," telegraphists "see the contents of telegrams, whereas the sorter does not see the inside of a letter," and therefore "in that respect the responsibility of the telegraphist is greater."[35] However, direct access to the public's correspondence, no matter how expertly managed or rendered, never resulted in greater privileges for GPO telegraphists. They, like postmen and sorters, were part of the vanguard of a vast new public information service in want of honor. Telegraphists were unique, however, in that they were the first modern workforce in which women practitioners both helped sell the service to a privacy-fixated public and symbolically contributed to the devaluation of the work itself. The female telegraphist redefined the meaning of public service.

WOMEN'S TELEGRAPHIC MEDIATIONS

The telegraphists' strike in 1871 occurred as telegraphy became publicly associated with female labor. Women occasionally appeared in the press coverage of the strike. In the *Spectator,* for example, they were depicted as loyal government workers, though not to the point of tolerating sexual harassment: female telegraphists "unfortunately for their own interests had not learned the art of Striking," but when hastily trained soldiers replaced telegraphists dismissed for striking in Cork and Dublin, this arrangement resulted in "a furious remonstrance from the female clerks, who at last refused to work in company with the poor men."[36] Administrative correspondence confirmed that the women operators were "dissatisfied" with the "loose" antics of the soldier-strikebreakers. To prevent disruptions of telegraph work caused by soldiers' "stares," the Irish GPO secretary "arranged that the soldiers shall be employed only between 8pm and 8am, ie. during the time the females are not on duty."[37] Internal memos also reveal that in Ireland, at least, women held a range of views on the strike: while "many" supported men in the Dublin walkout, many others stayed on duty there and elsewhere, and a telegraph "instructress" from Limerick, along with her "advanced pupils," joined the soldiers as strikebreakers in Cork.[38]

Back in London, visions of striking men were eclipsed by the increasing number of women in the telegraphic workforce. When telegraphy was nationalized, approximately 300 of the existing operators in London were women.[39] By 1872 women made up 44 percent of the system's workforce, and in 1874 the Central Telegraph Office's staff consisted of 700 women to 500 men. A year later, just under half of the 1,400-strong London Central Office telegraphic workers were female.[40]

The GPO actively encouraged the impression that women dominated telegraphic work at the Central Office, and media portrayals of telegraphy in the 1870s lingered in fascination on the female staff. *Temple Bar*'s report on London's first Central Telegraph Office noted that "the instrument room was "one of the most curious sights in the metropolis," and "stranger still, the [telegraph] manipulators [were] all women."[41] The *British Quarterly Review*'s article on London's new Central Telegraph Office in 1874 opined that beyond the complexity of instruments, circuitry, and pneumatic tube system, "the great feature is the prominence given to female labour."[42] Women's abilities, pay rates, meals, hours of work, and demeanor were widely commented upon. The writer Anthony Trollope, a former postal surveyor, acknowledged a gendered myopia in his 1876 representation of London's female telegraphists in *Good Words:* "The stranger . . . will think a great deal more about the young women than the telegraphy. . . . Even those prolonged iron spouts [pneumatic tubes] . . . did not interest me much, because they were waited on by boys and not by young women."[43]

Novelty and titillation aside, sympathetic journalists adopted a number of different economic and cultural scripts that incorporated female telegraphists. Susan Shelangoskie has argued that lower pay for young women employees contributed to the GPO's reputation for both social utility and efficiency, especially as telegraph expenses began surpassing projections.[44] Celebrating the increased opportunities for respectable, white-collar employment for women at the telegraph office became an important public relations maneuver, a mark of the GPO's progressivism and social responsibility, especially after it became clear that the nationalized telegraph network was operating at a loss. Women's low wages, their supposedly short-term and nonpensioned employment, and their propensity to undermine male union organizing made them perfect additions to the GPO workforce, and at the same time their employment provided young women with opportunities to internalize dutiful service in preparation for the married life awaiting them after their stint on the wires.[45]

Many commentators emulated Trollope's paternalist mode of Victorian modernity in focusing on women telegraphists' disciplined work. But female telegraphists also became crucial components in the GPO's assurances to the public of the protection of private information. Women's employment in the telegraph network reinforced existing models of cross-class, cross-gender labor.

Domesticating Public Service

Telegraph consumers and administrators were overwhelmingly members of the servant-keeping classes. Affluent Victorians' reliance on and close proximity to domestic workers was one of the crucial determinants of the cultural meaning and value of telecommunications work in the nineteenth century. This may seem an incongruous assertion on the face of it: domestic service does not usually feature in histories of modern technologies except as a diminishing social reality, as electric irons, refrigerators, and vacuum cleaners pushed maids out of most private households. The telegraph, along with typewriters and telephones, paved the way for "pink collar" clerical labor, respectable work outside the home for aspiring women. Both recent scholarship and a resurgence in paid domestic labor have poked holes in these twentieth-century stories, but nineteenth-century commentators also compared the drudgery of domestic service with social opportunities afforded by new technologies. When the American journalist Elizabeth Banks wrote about her experiences posing as a maid in 1890s London, she observed that for the young urban women she encountered, domestic service represented the denial of independence. "Everywhere I heard that word. It sounded above the clickety-clack of the type-writer. . . . I heard it in the clink of the barmaid's glasses; it mingled with the ring of the telephone-bell, the whirr of the cash-machine, and the refrain of the chorus girl. The telegraph-operator murmured the word as she took down the letters of various messages."[46] Telegraphy attracted young women and men from the lower middle classes—in other words, from families who could just afford a female servant and whose female members had narrowly escaped going into domestic service themselves. Telegraph operators, like other office employees, imagined that their work situated them above the working classes. It was understood in terms of modern opportunity and upward mobility (despite the GPO's intransigent taxonomies), diametrically opposed to the drudgery and hierarchical rigidity of domestic work.

Yet domestic service and telecommunications are not just mutually constitutive as oppositional or successional labor forms: they also represent points on a continuum in the valuation of certain forms of work. The connection lies in the management of privacy, and in why performances of discretion mattered so much to Victorian notions of respectability and the political order. Telegraphists' intimacies with private communication had to be interpreted positively by a public obsessed with personal discretion. And in the later Victorian era, gender was an increasingly important factor in the valuation of the public work of discretion.

The ubiquity of domestic servants in nineteenth-century Britain cannot be overstated; neither can the value of their work to the production of respectability. From the dozens of liveried staff at country estates to the "essential" staff of four in upper-middle-class houses, from the housekeeper in middle-class Londoners' flats to the huge numbers of charwomen and young maids-of-all-work or skivvies who represented the majority of domestic laborers by the end of the century, servants were essential to the comfortable and orderly Victorian home.[47] They provided the material necessities required for genteel respectability, forged with a combination of self-discipline, mental labor, and social duty. Domestic servants ensured that their employers could engage in the kinds of cognitive and performative work that mattered in the accrual of this liberal "character," and this process began at home.[48] It was manifested in clean curtains, scrubbed thresholds, polished boots, and coiffed hair; in the maintenance of social networks; and in the domestic hierarchies of men and women, parents and children, and employers and servants that assured moral discipline and social cohesion. For respectable men, the domestic work done to and around them was as essential to the performance of character as what they did for financial gain, their spiritual commitments, and how they were regarded by their peers. For respectable women, the task of overseeing rather than performing domestic work was vital to the harmonious household.[49]

With the material trappings of character went the mental discipline of knowledge accrual. Managing the challenges of the public sphere—business dealings, heterodox religious, scientific, and theoretical ideas, appropriate social activities, public policy, governance, and moral action—required a dispassionate, cultivated mindset.[50] The ideal Victorian subject read widely, listened impartially, asked the right questions, and came to his own conclusions without coercion or prejudice. Such mental rigor necessitated seclusion. For respectable men, the private study was one of the many requisites of Victorian bourgeois domestic propriety. Here the paterfamilias could escape both the world and his family in order to better them. That room was tended by a young working-class woman, though such reliance could have pitfalls: the writer and popular anthropologist Andrew Lang joked to his readers about how his maid disturbed his train of thought while she cleaned his study.[51]

Public reputation was built in part on the ability to sequester less virtuous acts or connections in private spaces and networks. As Deborah Cohen observes, "For the Victorians ... privacy meant keeping people out of one's own business; the domestic fortress was privacy's stronghold. . . . Secrecy was privacy's indispensable handmaiden, for the various sorts of shame that could be visited upon families ... were catastrophic, subject both to legal disability and to social scorn if they became known."[52] The Englishman's castle was breached as a matter of course by servants, and managing their necessary presence in respectable Victorian family households was a fraught, much-discussed subject.

If domestics were essential to Victorian respectability, they could also undermine it. The efforts to which Victorians went to segregate servants in their homes—the proliferation of back stairways and servants' hallways in wealthy families' residences, for instance—are indicative of their anxieties about what servants could see, hear, and do. Brian McCuskey has argued that the proliferation of spying servants in nineteenth-century fiction was indicative of these concerns, "fix[ing] the middle-class family as the center of the servants' attention and affirm[ing] middle-class secrets as worth possessing."[53] Attentive servants could easily become inquisitive ones.

Servants often performed crucial rituals of privacy, such as mediating the elaborate system of personal card exchanges that heralded visits between members of elite households. Genteel men and women established meetings in private homes by first leaving a visiting card with a servant at the entrance (usually on a special tray on which the servant would subsequently deliver the card without ever touching it). The many elaborations of this ritual are reminders of the importance attached by affluent families to social and spatial discretion, and the role of servants in enabling these processes.

Both bodily intimacies and informational ones provoked anxieties. Mrs. Beeton's advice concerning maids and valets captures the high value of discretion in these relationships: "The valet and waiting-maid are placed near the persons of the master and mistress . . . the confidants and agents of their most unguarded moments, of their most secret habits. . . . All that can be expected from such servants is polite manners, modest demeanour, and a respectful reserve, which are indispensable."[54] Affective bonds based on trust could be forged, but the establishment of such trust elevated the servant to . . . a better servant.

Employers deployed varying strategies to manage privacy and domestic work. One was to ensure that servants were fully occupied with domestic chores in order to keep them from taking "too lively an interest" in their employers' affairs. Servant manuals portray female domestics as less rational and more prone to distraction, requiring particularly firm discipline to keep their minds from wandering in nonproductive, even sexually dangerous, directions. Margaret Beetham has elaborated on the fraught subject of domestic servants' reading habits, noting concerns that working-class women's proclivities for "poisonous" popular texts threatened the orderly, virtuous home.[55] The exponential growth of print was another manifestation of a Victorian information age, and not always seen as cause for celebration. Channeling flows of information (newspapers, magazines, books, letters, telegrams, and secrets), ascribing legitimacy to certain types of information mobility and negating others—especially in the name of privacy—were signs of, to quote David Vincent, the deep "trouble" Victorians felt about people "reading what was not meant for [their] eyes."[56]

This digression into domestic service work makes a simple but essential point: telegraphy's administrators, consumers, and admirers were used to social inferiors, particularly young women, having intimate access to their personal lives and private utterances. These arrangements provided a model for accepting and valuing the work of information mediation in telegraphy. This attitude even overtly materialized in the GPO itself. "What sort of conscience had the Country Postmaster who lately engaged a female Telegraphist at the magnificent salary of 5s. per month?" began an indignant editorial in the GPO telegraphists' monthly *The Telegraphist* in 1886, protesting against the conflation of GPO duties with domestic ones in small offices. This offending Postmaster "expected the young lady to send and receive telegrams, sell stamps, issue money-orders, serve grocery and tobacco, clean her bedroom, make her own bed, and assist in the housework, which included firelighting, sweeping, dusting, and potato-peeling!" This was not exceptional: "Another requires a 'domesticated clerk' ... who does not mind mending stockings or nursing babies when not required for telegraph or postal work!" This made the writer "long for the day when every telegraphist will only be expected to perform telegraph duties, and when the work of Her Majesty's Post-Office will not be mixed up with sugar, salt, lucifer matches, rags, bones, and tobacco."[57]

Reservations about telegraphy's necessary transparencies led to the telecommunications equivalent of servants' back stairs, whose purpose was as much about maintaining the illusion of disinterested workers as it was of keeping them (mostly) out of sight. The elaborate telegram code books produced by commercial traders combined cost efficiencies with business rituals of secrecy. Many London-based enterprises and a handful of private homes heavily reliant on the telegraph rented lines from the GPO and employed private telegraphists (usually recruited from the GPO), whose proximity to the in-house intimacies of their employers' of wired discourse could also have prompted ever more elaborate codings. Whether out of distrust of telegraphists, or a wish to reassure their shareholders, or as pleasurably exclusive acts of professional grandiosity (or various combinations of all three), coded telegrams in the world of trade and finance were a mainstay of nineteenth-century telecommunications.

Mediating Bodies

The relative bodily presence, or absence, of telegraphists further ensured discreet networks. Frederick Ebenezer Baines, a retired telegraph administrator, described the labor performed in the updated main telegraph instrument gallery in 1895 in terms of hyperactive wires, sounders, batteries, instruments, and pneumatic tubes while downplaying the role of the operators: "the noisy hum" of telegraph sounders and the "continual popping" of pneumatic tubes dominated this "orderly" spectacle.[58] Such a description minimizes the involvement of humans in the transmission of messages.

Other public commentators, rather than ignoring workers, focused on the particular aptitudes of women telegraphists. "The delicacy of their fingers" made young women proficient operators. Because of their "finer sense of touch" and "deft fingering" of instrument keys, telegraphy was "a work in which feminine hands are peculiarly adapted."[59] Many observers remarked how similar telegraphy was to playing the pianoforte, a staple of bourgeois feminine accomplishment. Underlying these tropes were gender ideologies that insisted on a distinct female physiology.[60] Women's acutely sensitive nervous systems were responsible for not only their greater physical dexterity but also their emotional awareness, which made them well suited to the management of others' needs and dialogues.

At the same time, women's sensitive bodies were disposed to passivity, automatism, and unconsciousness. Jill Galvan has traced the growth of telegraphic and telephonic networks alongside the Anglo-American craze for spiritualism, arguing that "human-mediated exchange became especially visible as a category of communication" in the latter half of the nineteenth century. Women "were exemplary go-betweens because they potentially combined the right kind of presence [sensitivity] with the right kind of absence [passivity and automatism]," thus fostering communication both along the wires and beyond the grave while allaying anxieties about interjecting or listening in on the dialogues of others.[61] Women's entrance into telegraphy, typing, stenography, and other clerical work was acceptable to the public in part because authoritative perceptions of femininity affirmed that communications were better channeled through women.

Female clerical workers functioning as mediums—and vice versa—have garnered much recent attention.[62] From Charles Dickens to Bram Stoker, Victorian fiction offers multiple examples of women as conduits of male or spiritual writing, thoughts, and desires.[63] Likewise, women's "sensitive, deft" fingers perfectly accommodated telegraph keys; their "patience with attention to small matters" was, according to Frank Scudamore, "essential to the well-working of a telegraph office."[64] The periodical *Capital and Labour* further attributed feminine telegraphic proficiency to operators' "watchful eyes and ears [which were] quick to observe, and swift fingers . . . waiting to write down and transmit the varied tidings."[65]

The feminine voice, too, was an asset to telegraphy. The fear that undisciplined, gossipy females in rural telegraph stations would expose a telegram's contents to one another and the public was occasionally expressed. An article in the *Edinburgh Review,* for example, commented: "We know that it is rendered a misdemeanour to divulge the nature of a telegram; but whoever heard of any law that was capable of shutting a woman's mouth when she wished to open it?" But this comment was preceded by an affirmation of privacy in city telegraph networks, where "we are too far apart, and our affairs are not localized enough to interest the telegraphic clerks in our private matters."[66] Among female telegraphists working at London's Central Office, the troubling feminine propensity for talking was effectively channeled into Morse code. According to the *Englishwoman's Domestic Review*'s description of women's training at London's Postal Telegraphy School,

> It is somewhat significantly declared—perhaps as a delicate hint to the ladies—that "talking will not, under any circumstances, be permitted among the learners"; but it is consolingly added that "indeed, there will be no necessity for talking, as every learner will be provided . . . with an actual telegraph instrument in connection with some other instrument, and in the hands of another, so that each may speak to the other *without the use of the voice*."[67]

Telegraph training both took advantage of and disciplined young female workers' sociability. "According to the rules of the service," noted an article in *Bow Bells,* "the swifter they talk the better; but it must be done in silence with some unseen correspondent at the extremity . . . of the kingdom—a necessary condition in order to ensure attention and accuracy."[68] Anthony Trollope noted in his visit to the Central Telegraph Office in 1876 that the women's voices were reduced to "a low hum, very pleasant to the ear."[69] Silences, whispered necessities, and the sensitive mediation of the messages of others ensured observers that that the information relayed through female telegraphists remained unaltered and discreet.

The *Edinburgh Review*'s misogynist aside implies that networks were more private in urban centers because telegraphists did not have personal knowledge of individual users or their circumstances. The "hive" of "ceaseless activity" invariably commented upon by reporters also reassured telegraph consumers that telegraphists had neither the time nor the mental capacity to pay attention to individual messages.[70] The unrelenting pace of metropolitan telegraphy, like the work piled on housemaids to keep them busy, enforced discretion.

Most commentators celebrated these processes. For the *Illustrated London News,* the Central Telegraph Office was a "cheerful scene of orderly industry . . . not the less pleasing because the majority of the persons sitting here are young women, looking brisk and happy, not to say pretty, and certainly quite at home."[71] On a slightly more condescending and contradictory note,

Temple Bar opined: "It is certainly no unpleasant sight to see these young women doing the work of the world, proving that they are capable of thoughtful labour, and trustworthy in circumstances of great pith and moment. It is discovered at last that the sewing needle is not the only instrument they can master." In a gesture towards telegraphy as "thoughtful labour," the magazine acknowledged the mental capacity at work in this world of feminine information mediation. The author went on, inevitably, to announce that women "make capital manipulators, the delicacy of their fingers seeming to point out to them the telegraph as a suitable means of employment."[72]

To the public, the women in London's GPO telegraph offices were generally seen not as a threat but as a perfect fit. Consumers and administrators employed tactics that reduced the potential for indiscretion in the transcription of private discourse. The perception of female telegraphists as sensitive, physically attuned, busy transcribers, whose services brought them into proximity with the confidential thoughts of elite strangers, gendered the labor of discretion in a new way. Victorian practices intended to ensure the discretion of young working women were adapted from the home and incorporated into modern information work. Telegraphy was represented as a routinized process rather than an intellectual challenge, as physical rather than mental labor— the constant references to women's fingers signaled where the true value in telegraphy lay. The public's private information was secure because women were the perfect vessels to mediate words without thinking about their meaning. These mediums would not affect the message.

So confident in women's discretionary capabilities were commentators that many reported favorably on an even more sensitive duty performed by the Central office's female staff: checking the contents of telegrams for errors in messaging. *Temple Bar*'s article "Telegraph Street" reassured readers that this process, "performed by an efficient staff of sharp intelligent young women, . . . is really confined to the placing of a consecutive number on each message, and to the filling-up of such 'official' particulars as may have been omitted by the often hard-pressed receiving clerk." No editorial tinkering occurred, as "for obvious reasons, we think any such telegraphic censorship . . . would be unwise and objectionable in the highest degree." Once women screened the messages, men ensured that they went to the appropriate destination: "The 'handing-over' duty, in which considerable geographical knowledge and long experience are necessary, is performed by the male staff."[73]

Male operators receive fairly short shrift in public depictions of telegraphy. In their coverage of telegraphists' agitations, journalists focused on male organizers, and the literary critic Richard Menke has identified a handful of stories from fin-de-siècle fiction that feature male telegraphists navigating an imperial "realm of electric adventure."[74] John Munro's depiction of the Central Office in *Time* mentions "between the damsels an idle youth, who looks as if he could easily handle a bat with as much ease as a signaling key . . . reclining easily in his chair, until the moment arrives when the sharp click of his instrument shall warn him that a message is coming."[75] As both Morse coder and cricket player, this young man is presented as skillful and virile, reminding readers that telegraphy could still be men's work. However, this is a rare glimpse. In contemporary sources, male clerks are almost always mentioned only in relation to women, in contexts such as task specialization and hours of duty, where once again traces of concerns over privacy lingered.

On the one hand, the gendered division of labor described in *Temple Bar,* with women checking telegrams for errors and men sending them to their proper destinations, adhered to conventional scripts: women performed routine clerical ordering, while men made decisions. On the other hand, this arrangement ensured that men were a step removed from the message's contents. *Capital and Labour* observed that during the night shifts in the Central Office, which consisted solely of male telegraphists, "private messages are then but few; the chief employment being furnished by the newspapers."[76] Men's "greater powers of endurance" were a common justification for their handling of press transcriptions, but their limited access to personal telegrams was an unspoken advantage of this arrangement.[77]

London's Central Telegraph Office, the "nerve center" of British telegraphy, emerged as a feminine operation in the early era of nationalization. Female telegraphists' proximity to private information appeared unthreatening: women's nerves were particularly suited to attuned, passive channeling, their fingers conduits for the thoughts of others, their voices productively muted and channeled into the transcriptions of telegraphic coding. Women's attentiveness to "little matters" in the ever-expanding vastness of British imperial telecommunications kept them tied to the mediating tasks at hand, with no spare mental capacity for distraction or reflection. Administrators favored depictions of these diligent maids-of-all-informational-work over those of male telegraphists, who were only fleetingly mentioned in glowing press exposés. This amounted to the telegraph-consuming public's acceptance of a new kind of public servant, displaced from the elite model and its vaunted civic humanist overtones, and reinscribed with long-standing devaluative meanings associated with domestic work. This mundane public servant was kept at arm's length from professional associations—and the kind of salaries that went with elite civil service appointments—because their value lay in maintaining close proximity to private utterances which little affected them or the message. Women excelled at telegraphy because their imprint was immaterial.

Inversions of this passive role of course remained an imaginative possibility and a means of exploring the some of the fragilities inherent to the social order. The protagonist of Henry James's *In the Cage* (1898) is a nameless female telegraphist with acute sensitivities, "a whimsical mind and wonderful nerves," who works behind a partition at a Mayfair receiving house. Bored by her work and her unexciting marriage prospects (her fiancé is a clerk named Mr. Mudge), she channels her gift for "sudden flickers of antipathy and sympathy, red gleams in the grey, fitful needs to notice . . . and odd caprices of curiosity" to her own ends.[78] The telegrams of one "memorable lady" set her on an imaginative collision course with this customer's lover: the narrative hinges on a public encounter between the telegraphist and the male aristocrat on a London park bench.

A number of literary critics have argued for a queer reading of *In the Cage,* some claiming that the protagonist's ability to perceive, facilitate, and then reveal her customers' illicit affairs reflected the fin-de-siècle's concerns about homosexual scandal.[79] I do not disagree, but my point here is that such fantasies, with their inherent titillations and threats, were always about the power of consumers. The nameless telegraphist of *In the Cage* is ultimately a cipher for the telegram-sending public and its obsession with its own correspondence. *In the Cage* is a particularly rebellious exploration of the ideological pressure exerted by discretion.

Telegraphists frustrated with their liminal status as less-than-honorable civil servants sought acknowledgment that their work required intellectual discernment and technical acumen. Their insistence that they were engaged with the content, not just the form, of the public's communication put them at odds with an administrative order and a consuming public that did not want cognizant evaluators of telegraphed information. Female labor was crucial to the public imaginary of an unobtrusive system: the GPO female telegraphist came into being at a moment when long-standing models of female domestic service fused with the implementation of ever-lower strata in the new civil service. The cumulative effects of these cultural forces on the women and men performing telegraphic work was substantial: privacy curtailed their professional aspirations.

THREE

Gendering the Central Telegraph Office

THE VARIOUS HISTORICAL RECORDS describing the women and men who worked as GPO telegraphists during the late Victorian period reinforce a narrative of male grievance redressed somewhat through organizing, and of female integration and compliance. According to most public sources, male telegraphists faded into the background as female telegraphists took center stage. Women remained prominent into the twentieth century, celebrated as both discreet information conduits and forerunners of female advancement in the civil service as a whole. Following the GPO's successful experiment with female telegraphists, by the mid-1870s, women were employed in the savings banks, the Returned Letter Branch, and the Clearing House Branch. These positions, however, were intended to attract "gentlewomen of limited means, daughters of officers in the Army and Navy, of civil officers of the Crown, of those engaged in the clerical, legal, and medical professions, of literary men and artists."[1]

GPO officials, reflecting deeply ingrained notions about the advantages and drawbacks of sexed bodies, delegated tasks and designed office circuit layouts in attempts to effect a seamless service (including the mitigation of labor tensions)—with varying degrees of success. Administrators shrewdly incorporated the trappings of respectability in inhibiting telegraphists' rise up the grades of the civil service. The perceived dangers of urban darkness and female mobility further calibrated GPO telegraphy's work regimes. One of the many effects of this process on telegraphy in London's Central Office was the creation of high-status circuits catering to the state, international trade, sporting life, and imperial business, and low-status circuits serving local and provincial consumers. These distinct telegraphic orbits were connected with different types of telegraph instruments, operated by differently gendered telegraphists.

During the buildup to and aftermath of the telegraphists' strike in 1871, the GPO channeled female respectability in a seemingly paradoxical direction, employing bourgeois attributes to negate workers' claims to higher wages. In a report "on the reorganization of the Telegraph System" in 1871, Frank Scudamore laid out plans for recruiting and policing cheap labor, in which he envisioned a central role for female telegraphists: "The wages, which will draw male operators from but an inferior class of the community, will draw female operators from a superior class. . . . [They] will, as a rule, write better than the male clerks . . . and where the staff is mixed, the female clerks will raise the tone."[2] He elaborated on these assertions the following year: "It raises the tone of the male staff by confining them during many hours of the day to a decency of conversation and demeanor which is not always to be found where men alone are employed."[3]

Some male telegraphists agreed. Looking back from 1887 to the introduction of female staff, a correspondent to the GPO telegraphists' news organ, *The Telegraphist,* noted, "Time was when the bibulous propensity was so strong amongst the male clerks, that it was no uncommon thing for thirsty grinders to send out a boy for their liquor and consume it within the office precincts." Women's entrance to telegraphy had, "I am glad to say, raised the tone of the staff above what it used to be in the old days, when Bohemianism was so rampant."[4]

The respectability politics at work in telegraph offices were not straightforward windfalls for telegraphists, or "grinders," as they called themselves in office slang. This mutually supportive world of sober diligence and heterosocial propriety also suppressed other potential problems arising from low-paid male staff. As a journalist noted, "It may be taken for granted that you will always be able to draw from a better class of females than males for employment of this kind, that they will be satisfied with smaller pay for their work and will be less likely to combine for any disaffected purpose." Women's willingness made them more productive workers than men: "You will get, as a rule, that patience with and attention to small matters from females which men never can be trained to exercise cheerfully and without a grumble, and which are so essential to the well-working of a telegraph office."[5] Telegraph instrument operation, once the exciting and exclusive purview of bohemian men, had become the routine work of women.

Journalistic accounts portrayed businesslike interactions between male and female workers. Their inclinations to talk were channeled into their work, and when they did communicate, it was in subdued, discreet words and voices. Female telegraphists' civilizing presence, combined with their receptive passivity, made for an efficient, harmonious, and secure workplace. At wages that started at a third of those of men, they were an asset to administrators facing the spiraling costs of the network. Women also kept pension costs in check because "they will solve these difficulties for the department by retiring for the purpose of getting married as soon as they have the chance."[6] This assumption became policy in 1875, when the GPO officially forbade married women from working. The GPO developed feminized labor efficiencies by relying on respectable female telegraphists to tackle growing deficits, civilize the workplace, and suppress potential labor unrest while maintaining its public image.

TELEGRAPH WOMEN

"Telegraphy, . . . as we all know," a telegraphist wrote in 1887, "is not exactly the romantic occupation as it is viewed through the roseate spectacles of the casual visitor."[7] Telecommunicative fantasies, including accounts by eyewitnesses who exposed the "inner workings" of the network, lingered on women operators with fascination. Media and fictional renderings of female telegraphists tended to endow them with middle-class associations, but an 1879 survey of fifty senior female London telegraphists shows that they came from a broad cross-section of urban society. Just over half came from solidly middle-class families, with fathers who were merchants, doctors, lawyers, and government officials. But 32 percent had servants, police sergeants, and engine fitters as fathers, and another 12 percent had fathers who labored as builders, warehousemen, and carpenters.[8]

Women telegraphists' varied backgrounds resembled those of their male counterparts in London.[9] Their social stratum was also similar to that of the growing body of female teachers working at London's primary schools. With childhood education made compulsory in 1870, teaching became another of the respectable, lower-middle-class occupations that, as Dina Copelman observes, "required education and . . . some form of advanced training, which distinguished them from working-class women."[10] Set between unskilled labor and middle-class mores that restricted women's work, this stratum of women expected to earn wages until they married.

Arthur Munby's observations about a "bona fide female city clerk" in 1863 likely resonated with female telegraphists' experiences. Munby met, danced, and drank with a twenty-two-year-old City copyist at Caldwell's Dancing Rooms in Dean Street, Soho. Afterward he walked her home, all the while marveling at her "air of calm equality":

> [She] was ready to talk and dance with Severn and myself without any introduction; to make me her companion homewards, and to chat freely with a stranger about her work, her dress, her daily ways.... [S]he did all this ... out of a kind of manly frankness and affability.... She was a city clerk, and moved among men as other city clerks would.[11]

Munby's keen interest in the "modern girl" provides a window into the heterosocial environments in which female telegraphists moved. Their work required them to commingle with men and commute through city streets, and their wages, though small, enabled them to participate in leisure activities such as dancing, concerts, the music hall, and department-store shopping. Most female telegraphists lived with other family members, but some shared lodgings and pooled domestic resources with fellow telegraphists and other working women.[12] Such circumstances allowed female friendships of all kinds to flourish. Telegraphists, teachers, typists, and other office workers made up the vanguard of respectable women's labor in the 1870s, their work and pleasure patterns setting the stage for the "New Woman" trope of the fin-de-siècle and shifting modes of sociability between men and women.[13]

Bodied Circuitry

From the beginning of women's telegraphic labor, GPO policies governing task delegation, spatial organization, and working hours ensured that men and women's work remained distinct.[14] Unlike female typists or stenographers, women telegraph operators only briefly outnumbered their male counterparts in London. In the provinces, men dominated larger telegraph offices, while women staffed small post offices and receiving houses, performing telegraph duties alongside selling stamps and conducting other counter business with the public.[15] Male telegraphists' demands for professional status and administrators' perceptions of gendered labor meant that the most "important" telegraphic labor was assigned to men. Assumptions about the shortcomings of female strength, endurance, and technical know-how made male workers indispensable in telegraphy's global hub. These gendered divisions of labor provided justification for the higher wages paid to male telegraphists, who grew increasingly defensive about the pay gap during the late Victorian period, and gave them pretexts for demanding further concessions.

Gender divisions at the Central Office began, predictably enough, at the start of telegraph training. Applicants between the ages of fourteen and eighteen were accepted at the GPO's School of Telegraphy in London, provided they passed the telegraphists' civil service test, with an emphasis on arithmetic, handwriting, and geography, and the doctor's examination, which focused on hearing and eyesight. (Men's chest diameters were also measured to ascertain overall health; women were exempt from this particular measure of fitness.) In the latter half of the nineteenth century no explicit hiring exclusions based on ethnicity or race were recorded in administrative records (this would change at the turn of the twentieth century, when the GPO stated that all recruits must be "British born").[16] Although classes were segregated, men and women received similar telegraphy training. The male "learners" were also given "technical instruction of the simpler kind." Trainees learned to operate at least four different kinds of telegraph instruments: the Morse printer, the Wheatstone Automatic, the Bright Bell sounder, and the Morse sounder. In addition, women were taught how to use the increasingly obsolete single-needle apparatus, which was considered too "effete" for men.[17] By the late 1870s, the Morse sounder dominated Central Office operations, and other machines that did not require comprehensive training in Morse code, such as the ABC, came into use in rural stations.[18] Instructors monitored the learners' progress, and candidates unable to achieve satisfactory transmission speeds faced early "weeding out." After six weeks of instruction, successful learners received weekly stipends of seven shillings and began shifts on less busy lines at London offices. After another three months, learners advanced to the status of third-class telegraphist.

In the 1870s third-class male London telegraphists, who made up about half of the Central Office's male workforce, started at twelve shillings a week (£31/4 annually) and advanced to sixteen shillings a week (£41/12) after "becoming qualified to take solo charge of a moderately busy circuit."[19] After a year at this level, they advanced to an annual salary of £45, which rose in yearly £5 increments to a maximum of £65. After six years of work at the Central Telegraph Office, men could advance to the much more exclusive second class, which topped out at an annual salary of £90 over another four years' service. About half the third-class telegraphists made this grade. The highest rank of male telegraphist, of whom there were only 57 out of a staff of over 1,400 at the Central Telegraph Office in 1879, could make £160 annually after approximately eighteen years of service. This brought them into the lower ranks of the middle class.

Above the three classes of telegraphists were three supervisory grades: senior telegraphists, assistant superintendents, and superintendents. Again, the supervisory grades accepted about half of those who had made it this far. Provincial telegraphists earned considerably less at all grades. Above this level, the assistant controllers and senior superintendents, culled from the clerk grades, started at £220 per annum, with the department's controller earning an annual salary of £850.

Female telegraphists had a similar hierarchy, though their monitors were "supervisors" and "matrons." The gender gap in wages was significant. Third-class female telegraphists started at eight shillings a week compared to the men's twelve, and this discrepancy widened as men and women rose through the telegraphic ranks. Senior female telegraphists made a maximum of £75 a year, less than half the salary of their male counterparts.[20]

The classification system, with its wage caps and limited promotional opportunities, made postal telegraphy a fairly high-turnover occupation: up to a third of young men left the GPO after a few years' service to work for the private overseas cable companies or switch careers altogether. According to contemporary GPO reports, a female telegraphist's career lasted six years on average, with the majority marrying out of the service in their mid-twenties. The promotion system was a constant source of anger and target for reform by telegraphist organizers. It was also one of the most toxic sources of resentment between male and female telegraphists: the male staff at large offices in London and the provinces regularly complained that their senior positions were limited due to senior women's positions. While the majority of female operators left the GPO when they married, substantial numbers of single women remained in the service. Those who stayed on might receive more promotional opportunities and higher wages than men in the second- and third-class rankings, a situation that routinely prompted petitions to supervisors and, by the 1880s, when telegraphists began to organize, delegations to the postmaster general.

Male and female operators were expected to demonstrate equal competency on all types of telegraph apparatus, but their responsibilities in the first decade of nationalized telegraphy differed in notable ways. Women controlled the metropolitan and domestic wires connecting areas near London, while men took care of more distant provincial circuits, international cables, news dispatches, and special-event messaging in the Central Office and at mobile telegraph stations set up at racetracks and other sporting events.

This neat demarcation of separate spheres emerged out of a perceived need to protect the service from the temperamental female finger. Some engineers at the Central Office believed that too light a touch on the telegraph key could result in a muted or lost signal along the wires. Henry Fischer, the Central Telegraph Office's controller in the first two decades of GPO telegraphy, maintained that a firmly tapped-in signal had a much better chance of reaching its final destination, and therefore men's tapping abilities were superior to women's.[21] As a result, female telegraphists in London were relegated to transmissions along shorter circuits, while men controlled long-distance and international wires. Administrators were even dubious that women could transmit clearly to Manchester, Liverpool, and Leeds.[22]

Ironically, while these work arrangements were being put into place in London, engineers in the field were discovering that reliable long-distance transmissions depended not on the firmness of a telegraphist's initial signal but on more sensitive relays.[23] At the Central Telegraph Office in London, however, the supposed deficits of female bodies became further justification for male telegraphists' higher salaries and task specialties, though a female telegraphist in the 1880s offered a different perspective: "The truth is, we do not go bouncing about smashing keys &c., but do our work quietly and conscientiously."[24]

London's Central Telegraph Office was organized according to Fischer's gendered assumptions. Women mostly worked on the east side of the top floor, running the metropolitan wires, while men occupied the other gallery spaces. In the central provincial gallery, men and women could sit next to one

View of the Central Telegraph Station's provincial gallery, 1874. *Illustrated London News,* December 12, 1874, 569. Courtesy of Mary Evans Picture Library.

another, depending on the routing of provincial circuits. Men ran the news wires, parliamentary dispatches, and the Racing and Special Occasions Section, as women's ability to relay multiple circuits and long dispatches was also suspect. Male telegraphists defended this ordering on grounds of both physical strength and intellect: as a male telegraphist complained, women's "want of acquaintance with current topics, politics, markets, sporting, &c., renders them more liable to the commission of errors."[25] Mastery of content was a key component of telegraphists' pitch to administrators for their profession's intellectual nature, and male telegraphists also used these arguments to distance themselves from women.

This ordering intersected with the vertical spatial hierarchies already established at the Central Telegraph Office (see chapter 1). Low-ranking male workers inhabited the basement; office clerks, executives, and chief engineers had the run of the ground floor; female telegraphists occupied the east wing of the top floor; and male telegraphists dominated the rest of the space, with a mixed-gender zone in the provincial section. As virtually all British and international telegraphic traffic was routed through London, male telegraphists' fingers were on the pulse of global communications circuitry.

Men and women at different telegraph instruments. The women portrayed operate a single-needle and an ABC machine. Men operate the latest Wheatstone Automatic, Hughes Printer, and Direct Writer. *Illustrated London News,* November 28, 1874, 504. Courtesy of Mary Evans Picture Library.

By the late 1880s, concerns about women telegraphists' shortcomings had disappeared from administrative memoranda, probably as a result of advances in relay technology and decreasing numbers of interrupted circuits (though the tendency to blame women operators for technical deficiencies would return as telephone networks proliferated at turn of the century). In large urban telegraph offices, gender stratifications determined not only work regimes but also staff grievances. When new telegraph technologies such as the multirelay duplex and quadruplex instruments appeared in offices, male staff were put in charge of them. The new machines were deployed for the more prestigious telegraphic business already assigned to men: press cables, government wires, and international trade. Male telegraphists also staffed the mobile telegraph stations set up at sporting events, as female telegraphists were not permitted to work outside GPO offices and officially sanctioned receiving houses. The politics of respectability dictated that women telegraphists should not directly interact with the public where sports and the attendant betting were the main focus of business.

Even within offices, women's involvement with racing circuits provoked hostility. A short-lived experiment assigning some women to handle racing circuit lines was discontinued in early 1885, prompting a gloating male telegraphist to comment sarcastically in the *Telegraphist,* "We live in stirring times. The latest reform at TS [code for the Central Office, a holdover from its former location on Telegraph Street] is the annihilation of the female racing staff, who are to 'go back to the place from whence they came' . . . This is indeed agonizing news. It is indeed cruel. It is awful. It is too dreadfully much."[26]

His parting shot, "And after all those pleasant little tetes-a-tetes, and after all that nice crochet-work!" while sneeringly misogynist, was not wholly inaccurate.[27] Because they staffed the less busy circuits, women telegraphists could experience more down time than men in large offices. Especially in the early evenings, women were permitted to have tea at their stations and to read or knit, an activity that drew acerbic commentary. The *Civil Service Gazette* asserted that while women operators were "reading or knitting," their male counterparts were "endeavoring in every possible way to gain a knowledge of their craft."[28] A woman writing to the *Telegraphist* countered, "We cannot all attend to the broken wires, neither can we all be furnished with an item to write up; therefore are we all to be condemned because we improve the shining moments rather than sit gazing vacantly around with hands in pockets like our brethren?"[29] Knitting while the lines were quiet was "improving" rather than frivolous, a feminine telegraphic efficiency incomprehensible to many male operators and observers.

Female telegraphists were never entirely sequestered from men. While they sat at desks engaging with their Morse printers, sounders, Wheatstone automatics, or single-needle apparatus, they would have been surrounded by male as well as female superintendents, to say nothing of a constant stream of telegraph boys running messages and errands from one gallery to another. In an 1891 article on the updated Central Telegraph Office, *Chums,* a popular boys' magazine, provided a striking description of the embodied process by which a message from Margate was passed to "Victoria Street, Westminster": "Close to where we stand is a female operator. . . . As soon as the message is complete, it is placed in a wire cage at the end of the table. It is immediately noticed by a sharp-eyed boy, who seizes the paper, reads the address, and hurries to the stairs." The reader then follows the telegraph messenger "to the top floor, where he threads the centre gangway, turns down a side passage between two tables, and hands the form to an operator at an instrument labeled Victoria."[30] *Chums* invited its young male readers to imagine themselves as telegraph boys in this pattern of movement, in which women sat and passively received messages from the metropolitan wires, while boys enacted the flow of information by navigating their way up stairways and through passages connecting various departments.[31] The magazine failed to mention male telegraphists or the post office supervisors who would have patrolled the floors. In its world devoid of adult men, *Chums*'s telegraph office has boys running the system while immobile women remain subject to their machines.

The effect of all these practices was the gendered division of telegraphic work: the international versus the local, the public versus the domestic, the glamorous versus the pedestrian, the quadruplex versus the single needle, the male versus the female telegraphist. Such neat distinctions may seem predictable, but they offer staggering evidentiary reminders of the ideological power of the Victorian gender order and its multiple sites of production.

GPO supervisory culture reinforced these gender hierarchies. Male superintendents monitored all workers, whereas female matrons and supervisors had authority only over other women and boys—and, as with the racing circuits, experiments that altered these arrangements were met with furious resentment by the adult male staff.[32] Male and female telegraphists also had separate kitchens, lounges, and cloakrooms. At the Central Office the male telegraph staff set up a members-only dining club. Women, who were not permitted to leave telegraph offices during their shifts and were consequently obliged to purchase canteen food or bring meals from home, were not invited to join.

NIGHT DUTY

Certain moments in the workday forcefully reflected gender divides. One journalist commented that "it is not a little amusing to watch at 8pm, when the duties change, the constant stream of females out of the gallery by one door, and the opposite stream of males inwards by another."[33] This observation marked a highly contentious form of segregation at Central Telegraph Office and other large urban stations. Telegraphy was a twenty-four-hour business, but it was beyond Victorian comprehension that respectable women be permitted to work night shifts, especially in London. Female telegraphists worked eight-hour shifts between 8 a.m. and 8 p.m. Their male counterparts, in addition to working daytime shifts, had to perform night duty as a condition of their employment.

GPO officials were anxious to assure the public that women were not required to commute to work during the hours of darkness. London and other hubs, such as Liverpool and Manchester, were not safe for respectable women at night, and the GPO did not wish to shoulder responsibility for any nighttime harassment or assault of women telegraphists. Administrators also felt that it was simply not proper for women to labor after dark. There was something deeply unsettling about women's nighttime exertions for money. Anxieties about "public women" subtly guided GPO policy.[34]

Night duty was a major grievance for male telegraphists. Although night shifts were almost completely devoted to press cables, overseas trade, and other prestigious traffic, they undermined aspiring male telegraphists' notions of their own respectability. Night duty was onerous work without extra compensation, performed at inconvenient and professionally dubious hours. The GPO's refusal to pay additional compensation for night duty drew heavy criticism, as did scheduling practices that offered little recovery time for telegraphists switching from day to night shifts. Men argued that the frequent double shifts and disruption of sleep led to physical and mental exhaustion, weakening both their career prospects and the telegraph system itself. The exemption of women from night duty added to male resentment: men argued that their night-duty overexertions were the result of underemploying men in favor of women. Some male telegraphists argued that night duty justified the removal of their female counterparts altogether.[35]

These gendered conflicts came to a head in 1879 when MPs, feminist commentators, and sympathetic journalists noted with consternation that female employment at the Central Telegraph Office appeared to be declining. They had uncovered a policy first instituted in 1875, when Fischer began increasing the number of male telegraphists relative to the female staff. Fischer was both overtly skeptical of female telegraphists' capabilities and concerned about rising "grumblings" among the male telegraphists. Almost equal numbers of women and men were employed, but men took sole control of the wires at night, on top of their long-distance, international, news cable, new instrument, and mobile station duties. Many male telegraphists consistently worked fourteen-hour shifts with no overtime pay. Occasionally they had to work back-to-back night and day shifts. This situation was especially egregious in the summer, when male telegraphists had to run the mobile stations and racing wires. They were paid overtime for these shifts, but the working conditions were often unpleasant. (At Epsom Racecourse in the early twentieth century, for example, telegraphists complained that the instrument room "opens into a public urinal . . . the whole staff subjected to the unpleasant odours at times penetrating").[36] Such collisions of public services did not endear administrators to telegraphists.

The GPO's restrictions on women's work created a need for a larger pool of male labor, and Fischer duly restricted the number of women learners at London's telegraphy school. He also limited the number of vacancies for higher-paid female operators while increasing the number of higher-paid male positions. As a result, women's chances of promotion at the Central Office dried up. When this state of affairs became public in 1878, women's employment advocates, who had by this time assumed women's telegraphic labor was a fait accompli, lobbied on behalf of the long-serving women telegraphists still at the bottom of the pay scale and petitioned sympathetic legislators. MPs from the Liberal opposition questioned the postmaster general in May and July of 1879 on the "tapering off" of female labor and wages at the post office.

According to internal memoranda, some GPO administrators were sympathetic to the women's grievances. In spite of officials' calculations that most women would leave telegraphy to get married "as soon as they had the chance," many had worked at the post office for over five years, earning seventeen shillings a week. Even budget-conscious officials admitted that such wages were "insufficient to enable young women ["operators" was crossed out], especially such as are independent upon their own exertions for support, to maintain themselves in a suitably respectable manner."[37] A year before the situation reached Parliament, Fischer, despite his reservations about female fingers, requested that the second- and third-class female telegraph classes be amalgamated at the Central Office so that long-serving female telegraphists could finally enter the higher salary bracket. With men filling almost all new vacancies, Fischer's gender balancing act was unsuccessful, as were the parliamentary petitions. At least fifty long-serving women remained in the third class for at least another two years.

In a last-ditch change of strategy to win female telegraphists some wage concessions, Fischer commissioned a report, titled "The Social Rank of Female Telegraphists," at the Central Office. The survey listed the third-class telegraphists along with their fathers' occupations and specified whether the fathers were still alive. In a paternalist attempt to rectify some of the inequities, Fischer tried to align GPO female salaries to perceptions of independent fiscal need: women with working-class fathers who had passed away were recommended for wage increases or promotions. This gambit to implement a kind of telegraphic moral economy did not move the GPO secretary, but it does indicate unease about the relationship between post office wages and the fiscal upkeep of its "respectable" female staff. For the most part, outside commentators were sympathetic to the women and indignant that the GPO seemed to be curtailing female employment.[38]

The conflict between male and female telegraphists illustrated underlying tensions between the GPO's administrative designs and its cultivated image as a paternalist employer of women. When its exploitative practices reached a breaking point for male telegraphists, management changed tactics, restricting female employment and forcing the remaining female telegraphists to work with no prospects of promotion. This victory for male telegraphists marked the resurgence of telegraphists' organizing in London, instigating further antagonism between male agitators and the dwindling number of women operators. Meanwhile, the GPO managed the negative press by issuing public assurances of women's value to the telegraph system. Administrators found themselves scrambling to manage the consequences of telegraphy's respectability politics and the containment strategies of task delegation, volatile female fingers, and the unspoken dangers of London's nighttime commute.

FOUR

Bodied Telegraphy

Through the weakness of man females were accepted into the
service; through the weakness of man they are supported in the
service; but strength of mind is required to place the service
under an efficient and suitable staff of clerks.

"CYMRO,"
The Telegraphist, July 1887

We desire no great advantages or concessions on the plea of our
sex, nor do we want that tolerant pity with which we are sometimes regarded; we only want fair play.

"SE DEFENDENDO,"
The Telegraphist, February 1885

WOMEN TELEGRAPH OPERATORS' WORK AFFECTED conditions and
possibilities for all GPO telegraphists. The male staff, who continued to
dominate large urban offices, expressed diverse opinions as to whether their
female colleagues were a detriment or an asset to the status of their profession. Men and women telegraphists laid claim to professional respectability
in self-conscious and often fractious relation to each other. Telegraphists'
publications and Telegraphists' Association records, mostly but not all written by men, testify to the contentiousness of this gendered labor.

Men and women often had differing interpretations of the kind of social
capital that could be achieved through telegraphic work. For telegraphists
who saw their work as professional and intellectual—and deserving of much
greater compensation—women telegraphists were highly problematic. Both
male and female telegraphists attempted to harness telegraphic practices and
working cultures in their struggle to ascend the GPO's hierarchy, but telegraphic respectability cut both ways.

Many male telegraphists defended and enthusiastically supported women
operators, though usually with qualifications that ranged from encouraging
the gendering of specific tasks to reveling in their proximity to young women

captive to their tasks. The opinions of women workers are less in evidence, though thanks to a handful of women active in telegraphists' agitations and publications, we can also access their diverse perspectives on telegraphic work and workers.

The personal nature of telegraphy amplified these dynamics. Operators claimed to sense their coworkers' distinct personalities in the subtleties of transcriptions. Affective telegraphy created the possibility for relationships of all kinds to develop between operators: alliances, antagonisms, dalliances, provocations, and intimate connections. Telegraphy was also, according to its practitioners, a rigorous kind of nerve work: the brain could be exercised and worn down by the constant encoding and decoding of transmissions. Attempts to articulate to administrators the demands of this novel combination of mind and body work failed to enhance telegraphists' professional standing. In refusing to be alienated from their mediation labor but unable to extract social capital from it, telegraphists' options for improvements to their employment status were few and qualified, contained by telegraphy's bodied circuitry.

GRINDERS

The records and affiliated publications of the Post Telegraph Clerks Association (PTCA) are a rich source of telegraphists' opinions on their working lives. Founded in 1881, the PTCA was a result of the "Great Agitation," when the appointment of a new, Liberal postmaster general in 1880 raised the hopes of GPO workers for better wages and working conditions. The reform-minded political economist Henry Fawcett, the aptly named "blind Postmaster General," was known for an apparent openness to wages "as would secure really efficient service by obviating discontent." His arrival encouraged a petitioning campaign across the country, with telegraphists openly meeting for the first time since the 1871 strike to produce joint demands. Mindful of their bourgeois aspirations, the agitators contemptuously rejected the idea of forming a union and initially refused even to create any kind of formal association. Fawcett responded to the telegraphists' petitions with some modest increases to the lower-grade pay rates and instituted overtime pay in certain situations, but he also aligned telegraphists' pay grades with those of mail sorters' pay grades, "finally and irrevocably cut[ting] off" telegraphists' hopes of attaining the pay scales of GPO clerks.[1]

At the same time, Fawcett opened up entry-level GPO clerking positions in the savings banks, and other administrative branch positions, to women. In partnership with his wife, Millicent Garrett Fawcett, Henry Fawcett was a committed liberal feminist and an advocate for women's greater participation in all forms of public life. He used his position as postmaster general to further those aims, imagining the GPO as a public service whose policies and workings should generate social uplift and set an example for other government departments and private industries (with long-term profitability the harmonious result).

Fawcett's simultaneous championing of female office clerkships and his insistence that telegraphists remain classified as "manipulative" workers, albeit with some improvements to pay and status, led many male telegraphist agitators to ascribe their limited prospects to the expansion of female clerkships in other GPO departments. These suspicions were among the many underlying factors at play when leaders of the telegraphists' agitation agreed to form a national association dedicated to "defending our Civil Service and other interests." The association's official documents often began by quoting the language of the 1868 Telegraph Act, which defined the nationalized telegraph staff as civil servants.[2]

The labor historian Alan Clinton described the early PTCA as "a timid and conservative, not to say self-effacing organization" that "affected a tone of injured superiority" and whose "main activity . . . seems to have been to organize annual dinners at which toasts were drunk to Queen Victoria and the Postmaster General."[3] Performances of bourgeois civility were plentiful. The association's annual dinners were supplemented with concerts, recitals, outings, lectures, and other cultural activities. Telegraphists also joined the Victorian sports movement, setting up their own "Electric Cricket Clubs" in London and the provinces. They had scientific, dramatic, and temperance societies. In this way they were similar to other GPO employees, but with a marked aspirational bent.[4] The temperance society and dramatic clubs had mixed male and female membership, but a distinct strain of male homosociability was also evident in these activities, from the Central Office dining club to the more raucous social gatherings of young male telegraphists after hours.

The goings-on of these functions and societies in the 1880s were reported in the PTCA-affiliated monthly journal *The Telegraphist,* founded in 1883.[5] Its editor, William Lynd, was a former telegraphist turned entrepreneur. He was a popular author on electrical science, principal of the West London School of Telegraphy and Electrical Engineering, and by 1887 a practitioner of "medical electricity" in the seaside town of Bournemouth. *The Telegraphist*'s subtitle, "A Journal of Popular Electrical Science," positioned the journal as informing the public about telegraphy's technical workings and innovations. Each issue had a long article or two describing the latest developments in telecommunications, from submarine telegraphy to the workings of far-flung postal telegraph and cable offices and the development of telephone networks. *The Telegraphist* fused professional networking with the popular science journal, a highly successful publishing format in the latter half of the nineteenth century.[6]

In its articles, displays of technical erudition were balanced with reports, opinions, and complaints from telegraph staff across Britain and beyond. Telegraphists "in the field" submitted dispatches on their experiences managing imperial telegraph networks in contested regions such as Suez, the Sudan, and Ottoman Palestine. Lynd demonstrated telegraphists' intellectual acumen by juxtaposing technological articles with reviews of concert and theater performances and literature. It was a textual manifestation of telegraphists' professional objectives that also provided an outlet for debates about GPO policy, PTCA tactics, and a steady stream of workplace grievances.

This self-consciously bourgeois and erudite publication appears both full of professional pride and rife with simmering resentments. It used the jargon of the telegraphy subculture: telegraphic work was "grinding," performed by "grinders"; private cable operators working overseas were called "spot dodgers"; senior telegraphists were "old stagers"; and insider Morse-code jokes were common. The journal's column of short news items (the equivalent to the *Pall Mall Gazette*'s column *Odds and Ends*) was titled *Dots and Dashes*. A tangible pleasure in creating and expertly navigating this specialized world is discernible in its pages, alongside distinct narratives of betrayal. The GPO's original sin in denying telegraphists proper clerkships, compounded by the inadequacies of "the Fawcett Scheme," generated a history of ill-treatment and a gallery of heroes and villains.

Fawcett's sudden death in 1884 ushered in two years of short-term leadership with no new policies regarding GPO labor systems. Wistful articles began appearing in the *Telegraphist* outlining the need for "a Telegraphist General" who could run the network and "not be subservient to any postal official whatever."[7] In 1886, after a Conservative election victory, Henry Cecil Raikes was appointed postmaster general. Openly hostile to GPO workers' organizations, he was nonetheless greeted with cautious enthusiasm by the PTCA, who believed that he would approve of their rejection of union organizing and affectations of professionalism. Raikes was "highly eulogized" for his "impartial manner" at the PTCA's annual conference in 1887.[8] Attendees would find cause for both disappointment and justification for these sentiments.

A general hostility to postmen and sorters was evident throughout the *Telegraphist*'s run. A frequent contributor using the pseudonym "Edina" (another manifestation of this subculture—those who wrote to the journal usually appropriated the codings of commercial telegraphy) complained that telegraphists' ill-treatment was due to the appointment of postmasters untrained in telegraphy, who refused to acknowledge that "telegraph work is as distinctly different from postal work as is the difference between manual and intellectual labour."[9]

Spirited debates in the correspondence section carried over from month to month. The tactics that telegraphists should adopt in demanding greater remuneration for night duty, overtime pay, and holiday leave on par with the clerk grades were a contentious topic. Debates about promotion and grading systems also sparked controversy. On other issues there was a broad consensus: a consistent theme in telegraphists' correspondence was that telegraphic work was not fairly distributed. Whereas journalistic portraits of telegraph offices tended to emphasize a constant, hive-like hum of activity, the *Telegraphist* reveals them as spaces of spasmodic activity, inconsistent practices, and varying degrees of commitment. In the view of some contributors, the gifted and the responsible did most of the work while putting up with improperly trained novices and shirkers. In 1885, when the GPO implemented the "six-penny rate" Henry Fawcett had proposed, the cost of a standard telegram changed from one shilling for up to twenty words to sixpence for up to ten words (including the address). Telegraphists predicted their offices would overflow with newly hired incompetents brought in to absorb the increase in business. Their fears proved hyperbolic, but an overall sense of inequity remained a consistent feature in telegraphists' commentary.

A frequent grievance that animated the *Telegraphist* and became the focal point of PTCA agitation was the GPO's policy on Sunday labor. Male telegraphists in London were required to work on alternate Sundays and paid extra; those in the provinces did not receive additional wages for mandatory Sunday shifts. Headquartered in Liverpool, the PTCA found telegraphists eager to abolish this disparity. The view from London was mixed: "While fully sympathetic with my fellow-telegraphists," wrote a Central Telegraph Office contributor styling himself as Veritas Odium Parit, "there is, in my opinion, some difference in the duty. . . . In TS every clerk . . . is compelled to live some miles out of the City." On Sunday "he may have a couple hours' walk in order to get to the office," whereas those in the rest of the country lived "within ten or fifteen minutes' walk of the office."[10] Justifying Sunday overtime pay on these grounds fueled antipathy between those in the capital and workers the rest of the British Isles. Telegraphists were keenly sensitive to inequities within their ranks.

Women did not work on Sundays. This exemption was, like their exclusion from night shifts and racecourse work, an assertion of moral righteousness.[11] The GPO, which had briefly banned all Sunday mail delivery in the 1850s in response to effective campaigning by the evangelical Lord's Day Observance Society, maintained the policy in London and offered limited services elsewhere. Women's entrance to GPO positions coincided with the reemergence of influential evangelical reformers within the administration. The promotion of the devout preacher and temperance campaigner Stephenson Arthur Blackwood up the GPO ranks to secretary by 1880 amplified the link between Protestant zeal and postal labor policy.[12] While accepting that the telegraph network could not shut down entirely, administrators limited hours of public access and telegraph work.

"FEMALES IN THE TELEGRAPH SERVICE"

Women telegraphists, who did not work at night or on Sundays and were not often assigned the busiest circuits, became a target for frustrated men who felt women's presence increased their workload and undermined their wages. "The female sex was never suitable," opined "Cymro" in the *Telegraphist:* "Owing to the presence of the female sex, we are forced to work double the night duty we would otherwise be required to perform." He lambasted GPO officials who saw female labor as a cheap expedient and "did not consider the fact that a larger staff is necessary to cope with the inferior working power of that sex."[13] "Pons Ælii," an active PTCA member and frequent *Telegraphist* contributor, felt similarly: women were "in the enjoyment of many advantages denied the males. . . . [T]he greater number of females employed . . . the greater will be the proportion of night and Sunday duty which the male staff are called upon to perform."[14]

Pons Ælii, lamenting that "philanthropic but non-practical people concluded that females were pre-eminently fitted for what they considered the light and delicate work of telegraphy," made a further case for the inherent manliness of managing urban telegraph networks: "Those who are practically acquainted with telegraphy, well know that the strain which a heavy circuit entails is so severe that only a very small percentage of the female staff are capable of managing one." He also argued that the marriage bar was a disincentive for female telegraphists to "attain proficiency in manipulation," as "most, if not all girls on entering the service look upon their connection with it merely as a temporary means of subsistence until they have secured a permanent domestic position for themselves." He also inferred that male telegraphists were the casualties of a larger political agenda: "Undoubtedly the number of female clerks was largely increased during the late lamented Postmaster-General's term of office, and, considering the influence he was subjected to, it can scarcely be a matter of surprise that he had a generous partiality for the weaker sex." The Fawcetts' legacy still rankled. Still, Pons Ælii accepted that it "may be desirable to employ girls to attend to single needle and minor single current circuits," thus buffering men from lower-status and technologically obsolete work.[15]

Even male defenders of women in telegraphy concurred that their capacities were limited. In an essay on the spread of women's labor in general, "Saul" noted that he had "never worked with a safer or swifter clerk than a lady" and that "at commercial work at any rate, [women] are quite equal to the majority of male clerks." Also active in the PTCA, he saw men and women's labor interests as "really identical" and advocated for women to take a more assertive role in petitioning for better holidays and sick leave. However, he also asserted that female telegraphists "injured the telegraph service" and that "men and male clerks cannot be blamed if sometimes they grumble about the night duty and the unpaid Sunday labour, which falls entirely on them." Physical limitations underlay some of his reservations: "As telegraph clerks, the employment of ladies must necessarily be limited owing to their health, which . . . suffers under extra pressure, and prevents them from being reliable officers." But cultural parameters were equally relevant: "Our work is of a peculiar nature; necessary but trying night duties have to be performed, . . . [which] these ladies cannot undertake," and there were "certain classes of work which they cannot perform so well as male clerks." These included billiards, coursing, racing, cricket, yachting, shipping, money, and other descriptions of special work." He argued that "the policy of employing ladies should be followed with caution, so that there may always be a fair proportion of male clerks."[16] Formal PTCA meetings and petitions to the postmaster general regularly included demands for women to be either banned from certain offices or for their number to be limited to one-fifth of the male staff.[17]

Female telegraphists had an influential ally in the *Telegraphist's* editor. William Lynd was an enthusiastic promoter of "scientific ladies." His many projects included educating his young daughter in biology and taking her on naturalist field trips.[18] He observed that the "employment of ladies in the Telegraph Service always was, and always will be, a sore subject. The gentlemen think that they have been the cause of the low rate of wages paid by the Department."[19] Lynd was unconvinced: "if all the ladies were discharged tomorrow the male clerks would not receive an additional penny per week." He noted that the female students at his telegraphy school regularly outperformed their male colleagues and reminisced that he "had the pleasure of meeting many lady telegraphists who were quite capable of taking a news wire and holding their own against manipulators of the opposite sex." Confident that "a large percentage of ladies" were equal to current GPO tasks, he thought it "hardly fair" to deny "courageous" women who "go out into the world to earn their bread, and sometimes help to keep an aged parent, the employment offered by the Telegraph Department of the Civil Service."[20] Lynd's reliance on long-standing tropes of women workers as auxiliary family earners and caregivers effectively sanctioned their entry into telegraphic work.

Lynd's sincere conviction that "the employment of females is *not* a mistake" was doubtless partly due to the need to attract young women to his school, but he made efforts to create space for women's perspectives in the *Telegraphist*.[21] He experimented with ways to attract female readers and contributors, including the addition of a regular feature titled *Our Girls Column*, and he made sure his journal's female correspondents were given room to respond to their critics. Following Pons Ælii's attack, Lynd named the next month's "Prize Essay" a contribution from "Efel," a woman (likely a senior telegraphist working in Swansea's main office who was then one of the PTCA's few female members). Her wry defense of "clerkesses" called on "our gentlemen friends in the service ... to frankly admit that many of us can work to them on good circuits satisfactorily, and that a lot of things said about our incapacity are exaggerations." There were "no doubt, stupid and indolent girls in the department," but some performance disparities were due to reduced opportunities and expectations for women: "The men, on account of their sex, do the 'lion's share' of the work, the girls, not being so much called upon, cannot be expected to progress with equal rapidity." Women would achieve the same standards "if given to understand that an equal share of work was expected of them."[22]

Efel's women colleagues, she claimed, had "a love for their profession, and … far from merely sitting at a minor single current circuit to read or sew, as is represented, make it their aim to compete successfully with their fellow male clerks." Knowing it was "a favorable argument against us, that the work on a busy circuit is such as girls are physically incapable of," Efel responded that "no great muscular exertion is necessary for the performance of instrumental work, and that, given equal opportunities with the male element of becoming proficient, we are then quite able to bear the strain of work on a busy wire."[23] Other women offered similar views. "Se Defendendo" observed that "when, on entering the service, we are treated as male learners are— expected to take our turn honestly at hard circuits as well as easy ones … and getting practice on all kinds of instruments (not merely writing slips or working a single needle), are we so *very* far behind our male competitors? I think not."[24] Another female correspondent, who dispensed with classically inspired pseudonyms in favor of the bluntly descriptive "One of the Maligned," inverted the argument: "At our office (which is one of the largest), the 'females' take regular duty at the best circuits, working along with a male clerk, and in not a few cases the female is superior."[25] "Seaweed" called for gender-blind meritocracy in delegation and promotion: "Then those girls who can and do hold their own with most of the male clerks, would have an opportunity of proving their right to their places, and the duffers would find their places also."[26]

Women operators acknowledged the social mores that restricted their work. Se Defendendo considered women's night duty to be impossible "unless a social revolution takes place, making it right and proper for girls to go to and from business at all hours."[27] "As regards Sunday duty," she noted in a follow-up letter, "If women should ever be called upon to perform it, however unpleasant it might be on religious or other grounds, still we are not physically unsuited for it."[28] Reacting to complaints that women's lower wages were still disproportionately generous given their limited hours and tasks, Efel observed, "It is argued in our disfavour that girls only resort to telegraphy as a means of procuring pin-money, and that therefore the salaries are frittered away on us. … Very many of us have no other resources and depend *solely* upon our remuneration as a means of subsistence." She nonetheless concluded her essay with a stereotypically ladylike plea to her male coworkers: "Do give us a chance. We don't want to break down any barriers. But we must earn our daily bread. If it wasn't for that, we could not stay in our situation a day after knowing what you think of us."

Sensing underlying anxieties about not just female telegraphists but the widening sphere of women's work in general, Efel argued, "We are not Amazons, nor yet Helen Taylors, and most of us do not claim to be strong-minded, but are quite content still to be the 'weaker vessels.'" Women's entry into telegraphy was not the result of feminist campaigning but of decisions by GPO patriarchs: "When certain fields of labour are thrown open to us *by men themselves,* in which we feel we can fairly succeed, surely we have a right to enter upon them?" In claiming that women's telegraphic work was not socially radical and "grant[ing] readily that "the average masculine intellect is stronger than our own," she resorted to claiming that this was "a fact which does not unfit us for telegraphy, the actual instrument working of which is certainly not a highly intellectual employment."[29]

Perhaps the only member of the PTCA to advocate for the respectability of her profession on the grounds that it *wasn't* intellectual labor, Efel resituated telegraphy in relationship to other forms of burgeoning feminized service-oriented industries: "The mere working of a wire is not, it seems to me, a much more manly avocation than measuring out yards of tape and elastic behind the counter of a linen-draper's shop."[30] This particular tactic flew in the face of the *Telegraphist's* project and did not garner a response from male telegraphists, who maintained that the active "manipulation" of public information along the wires was skilled work at least equivalent to that performed by the Civil Service's professional clerk grades. Efel's example highlights the double-edged ramifications of arguments for telegraphic respectability and the extent to which men and women's interests did not always converge.

The dangers of implying that women telegraph operators reflected or contributed to revolutionary change were apparent when Pons Ælii, responding to Se Defendendo's comment that many women telegraphists were "not so eager to marry," observed, "This implies that girls in the Telegraph Service are not so eager to undertake the duties to which Nature has so eminently qualified them to fulfill," and alluded to unspecified forms of misconduct by female telegraphists: "This is not a pleasant subject to touch upon, so I will merely state I am acquainted with cases (rare, I am pleased to say) where young ladies have been invited to resign for the commission of little vices which are charitably supposed to be generally confined to the rougher sex."[31]

This line of attack drew the ire of a number of contributors, including an overseas cable company electrician who felt compelled to jump to the women's defense and accused Pons Ælii of lacking "every spark, I will not say of chivalrous, but manly feeling, when, in a public journal, he makes allusion . . . to the 'little vices' of his fellow lady-clerks? . . . . Its very vagueness is its worst feature." He found proof in the *Telegraphist*'s own pages contradicting the notion that female telegraphists were "losing part of their 'weiblichkeit' (womanliness is the nearest approach)." He pointed to the *Social Notes* section, which featured "a touching account of the treat provided for the poorest children of the place by the lady telegraphists of Newcastle-on-Tyne."[32] Lynd's reporting on the charitable works of female telegraphists might preserve their reputations from the more unsettling implications of choosing work over marriage, but such dynamics curtailed women's options for defending their careers and help explain Efel's more conservative approach.

Other correspondents pointed out that sexualized workplaces were not inherently socially dangerous. Edina, who wrote approvingly of women's presence in offices and their tone-raising effects, believed that "despite the carping criticism of a few old curmudgeons . . . the atmosphere is all the brighter and healthier, and that the work is done more cheerfully for the presence of the young ladies." Women operators created pleasurable telegraphic efficiencies: "The work is better performed at a wire where there is a female, as well as a male telegraphist, and in the case of a single current wire where there is a lady telegraphist at one end. It needs no profound analysis to explain or justify such a perfectly natural state of things."[33] He echoed the sentiments of Frank Scudamore, who observed in the 1870s that "male clerks are more willing to help the female clerks with their work than to help each other. . . . [P]ressure of business is met and difficulty overcome through this willingness and cordial co-operation."[34] Like other male telegraphists, Edina was happy to have women to look at and interact with in the office so long as they kept to their single currents.

Edina enjoyed the "charming attributes" of his "fair friends," regretting "that their official sojourn amongst us is generally so brief, for we have hardly got to know them thoroughly when some Romeo from the outer world comes and snatches them away. . . . A pretty girl's clerkship in a telegraph office may be roughly but not inaccurately estimated at about six years."[35] One implication of such commentary was that the unpretty girls stayed the longest. The Central Office's Dramatic Society correspondent noted snidely that "of late amateur entertainments have been spoiled by the ladies, who are generally picked from the ranks of the worn-out old stagers . . . scraggy dames from whom a dashing young lover would (in real life) run a mile rather than embrace."[36] Older female telegraphists, unalluring and occupying positions that might otherwise go to men, encapsulated the heterosexual politics of telegraphic labor.

Whether women, conversely, enjoyed being surrounded by attractive young men at work was not a subject raised by the *Telegraphist*'s female correspondents. Of course, women presenting themselves as desiring subjects would be unlikely to surface in a self-consciously respectable journal which, despite a sympathetic editor, regularly published articles expressing or insinuating that female telegraphists were in it for "pin money" while biding their time to get married. The *Social Notes* column of the *Telegraphist* indicates that romances between telegraphists did occur. Correspondents from provincial offices—Irish and Scottish ones in particular—regularly commented on telegraphists' marriages. Most of these unions were between staff members and "outsiders," but marriages between telegraphists were not infrequent.[37] They were not intercontinental affairs like the one described by Scudamore but intraoffice ones between similarly ranked telegraphists or between female operators and male supervisors. The notice of Agnes Stirling's marriage to her colleague James Livingston in the Glasgow head office described her "fors[aking] telegraphy for domestic economy, leaving behind a first-rate example and a first-class vacancy."[38] This notice depicts a woman's telegraphic work as a temporary life stage, now definitively ended and giving way to domesticity.

Stirling's departure opened up promotional opportunities for the remaining telegraphists. Se Defendendo offered a justification for those women who chose to remain: "This sounds selfish, I admit, and may be deplored from a moralist's point of view, but many prefer to remain in the service, comfortably independent, than to marry young, and live in that genteel state of semi-starvation which is so often the result of early marriages in the middle classes." Adhering to scripts of bourgeois practicality and propriety, she found ground for those women who refused to "abandon present advantages for possible ones."[39]

AFFECTIVE INTRAMEDIATIONS

If telegraphy could lead to "electric embraces," it could also reinforce workplace gender hierarchies and enable electric harassment. Telegraphists could discern individual styles of signaling, such as the timing of Morse code sounds, and draw inferences from them: "We who belong to the fraternity know how accurate an index to character is the method of manipulating a wire," wrote the ever-observant Edina. His observations in an article titled "The Ethics of Telegraphy" illuminate the multiple levels of encoded meaning inherent in telegraphy. "An experienced telegraphist," he wrote, "can determine with the greatest exactness the precise temperament of the clerk to whom he works." His first example of this phenomenon, unsurprisingly, was "a high-strung nervous lady, who, on receiving some kind of provocation from the 'man' at the other end (the young ladies always fancy it is a man at the other end), gives the key a petulant thump, pouts her pretty lips, and indulges in a feminine swear at the 'horrid thing' who is inflicting so much agony upon her."[40] His sensualized condescension highlights for twenty-first-century readers the potential for annoyance, unwanted sexual advances, gendered rivalries, and sabotage that could play out between telegraphists. Their ability to develop a coded language within coded language created opportunities for both friendships and antipathies, partnerships and exclusions. Navigating the intricacies of these exchanges was a creative, challenging experience, one which that could assert telegraphists' control over their medium but could also put certain workers at a disadvantage.

Despite his tone, Edina was sympathetic to the "delicate creatures writhing under the torture of working to an incompetent or insolent clerk." He "knew full well how very difficult it is for a sensitive clerk to restrain his or her irritability," admitting himself "not superior to this weakness on certain occasions, and that "it is nothing short of a cruelty to an experienced clerk to submit to the incompetent, and invariably insolent, method of working affected by some of these ambitious youths, who go to busy wires with the express intention of 'making it hot' for a fellow at the other end." He went on to reveal the varied personas of other coworkers. He envied "some muscular recruit from a rural district working away, under all sorts of trying conditions, with a serenity that nothing could disturb." Edina was unsure whether "stolid individuals" like this were "so tough in the fibre or so obtuse in mental capacity" that when they were "'bullied' on the wire they evince[d] not the slightest sign of discomposure." It was a "gift" to "sit out a volley of 'cheek' from an amiable clerk at the other end," a common subversive workplace maneuver "practiced ... by 'cute' operators who like to enjoy a quiet chuckle over the fiery ebullitions of the 'fellow' at the other end."[41]

Much of this telegraphic metacommunication was predicated on fantasies about the individual at the other end of the wire. Perhaps some telegraphists enjoyed this displacement and found ways to create different telegraphic personas using the subtleties of Morse code timing and other forms of hidden signaling. It is also possible that the pseudonymous contributors to the *Telegraphist* were themselves trying on different personas, perhaps sending signals to readers or commanding column space through levels of impersonation opaque to us today.

Edina's article also illuminated the varying cognitive approaches operators had toward their tasks. There was the "fellow . . . always in a state of effervescence, who can hardly sit quietly on his seat for five minutes at a stretch." This type "did his work on the mechanical principle,—that is, he never allows his mind to get so deeply absorbed in his work as to make it laboring or exhausting to him," and "on crossing the threshold of the office for home, [he] forgets that he is a telegraphist until his return to duty on the morrow." Such an approach was "but a reflex of a particular temperament" and "does not necessarily imply a want of interest by its possessor in his work." At the other end of the spectrum was the telegraphist "who loses his personality in his work so thoroughly, and merges his whole mental faculties to his duties so completely, that after a hard day's work he feels languid and exhausted." This type of telegraphist could not disengage from his work: "Even after he has left the office, he carries about with him an official atmosphere, which clings to him throughout his leisure hours. . . . "Pity and sympathize with such a clerk, be it a man or a woman," for this telegraphist "always looks jaded and dispirited, and . . . at times, conveys the impression to the sympathetic observer that he dwells in a world which is peopled with nameless shadows, and with a vague sense of unrest."[42] Haunted by ghosts from their machines, telegraphists could be subsumed by their mediations, left anxious and unmoored after being the conduits of so many others' thoughts, needs, and desires.

TELEGRAPHIC MALADIES AND NERVE WORK

There are few occupations more trying to the nervous system than telegraphy.

OUR GIRLS COLUMN,
The Telegraphist, February 1, 1888

For telegraphists, bodily and cognitive processes were uniquely inseparable. The assumptions about men's greater stamina, for example, applied to their mental as well as physical capacities to handle busy circuits. While men's durability still gave them effective leverage in their advantageous task specialzations, male telegraphists' insistence that their work was more intel-lectual than manual made the strains of telegraphy fraught topics of griev-ance. Telegraphist's cramp, a painful repetitive stress injury, came up occasionally in *The Telegraphist*'s columns. Described as " a kind of rheu-matic pain, which suddenly seizes the operator in the shoulder or muscle of the right arm," telegraphist's cramp was increasingly raised as a problem in the last decades of the nineteenth century.[43] Suggested remedies included massage and, according to William Lynd, "Mr Puvermacher's galvanic appli-ances."[44] But it was not mentioned in official PTCA petitions to GPO offi-cials in the late Victorian period as a point requiring redress or as a justifica-tion for greater compensation, better sick leave, or longer holidays.

The mental strain of telegraphy, however, inspired much commentary among telegraphists. "In many branches of the Civil Service, six hours a day and six days per week is considered long enough for work which demands very little brain activity, and in which the nervous system is seldom unduly excited," noted "Tempus Omnia Revelat." He went on to ask rhetorically, "What . . . must be the consequences that follow working for eight hours for thirteen days at a stretch in the very vortex of activities?"[45] Telegraphists' nerves and nervous systems bore the brunt of the demands on the telegraph network. Popular renderings of the telegraph system as the nerves of com-merce and the imperial order resonated with telegraphists, who imagined their own nervous systems as both foundational and susceptible to the tor-rents of information exchanged across the global network.

Telegraphists' overcharged nerves could lead to bodily deterioration, according to Tempus Omnia Revelat. They were more susceptible to phthisis and "other forms of consumption." Sound-reading—decoding and transcrib-ing telegraphed messages through the long and short signals generated by the fastest telegraph instruments—emerged as a particularly demanding aspect of nerve work that eventually manifested in physical illnesses. Tempus Omnia Revelat, based on "carefully gathered information from my brother and sister clerks who have been sound-readers for years," noted that "the sense of hearing is a more interior sense in the brain than the sense of sight, and that consequently the brain is more intensely active when the ear is conveying sound to it than when the eye is conveying the impression of objects." Sound-reading's penetration of the brain "sooner or later . . . results in weakening of this organ to act as a medium to the will, and predisposes to disease other important organs."[46] Another correspondent claimed that the knock-on effects of sound reading could harm "either the physical or mental powers of the body," leaving telegraphists dangerously susceptible to illness. These effects could be amplified by poor office ventilation and stagnant air that lacked "those virtues which act so beneficially on the entire nervous system."[47] Environmental factors compounded telegraphists' nervous and physiological stresses.

The demands of telegraphy could affect telegraphists differently, depending on temperament and "sensitivity."[48] Those with nerves particularly well refined and attuned to telegraphy could suffer the most damage. This risk implied that those best suited to the task should be used judiciously. Men and women telegraphists were both susceptible to "nervous exhaustion," but to different degrees. Women had higher sick rates and longer work absences than men (another point raised by male telegraphists seeking limit the numbers of female colleagues). Like the sensitive female finger, the female nervous system, while well suited to telegraphic channeling, was also more fragile. However, the "sensitive" telegraphist could be male or female. Such individuals were particularly gifted at the work and, as Edina observed, internalized telegraphy to the point of losing their sense of self in the wires. These were the potential victims of "brain-mischief," whose numbers, according to *The Telegraphist,* were on the rise.

In answering his rhetorical question about the potential strain of constant telegraphic duties, Tempus Omnia Revelat emphatically declared, "The answer is to be found in the lunatic asylums, where the writer's fellow clerks are confined . . . in the jaded and worn-out appearance of male and female clerks, who are unfit for exertion of any kind after sitting with their ear to a Sounder for eight hours."[49] The PTCA stalwart Saul also noted with concern in 1884 that "insanity has attacked a number of telegraph clerks," He identified the causes in "the constant change in duties, the unsatisfactory way in which we are forced to bolt our food when on duty, the length and severity of our night-work, and the way in which nervous clerks are worried by thoughtless supervising officers." Not just sound-reading but the working conditions in urban telegraph offices "perhaps account for, if not insanity, at least, for the high sick rate."[50]

For some commentators, more worrying than nagging supervisors were the potentially damaging connections between telegraphists along the wires. Affective interactions were loaded with mental dangers. Writing for the *Our Girls Column* in 1888, an anonymous female telegraphist confided it was "enough to bear" when "two amiable spirits work together the strain of eight hours' dot and dash," but "when two excitable and slightly cantankerous natures have charge of a wire, the destruction of brain tissue must be excessive." Unfortunately, such "cases . . . of telegraphists breaking down and ending their days in lunatic asylums bear witness to the fact that high pressure working in large telegraph offices is highly injurious."[51]

For Edina, "nothing strains the nerves more" than harassment by fellow telegraphists, and "if the clerk be naturally of a nervous disposition, and gives way on every little provocation to such displays of temper, the nervous system gets thoroughly worn out, and unless a check is put upon this tendency mental illness is sure to set in." Evoking Victorian medical discourses on finite bodily capacities, he asked, "Why should we waste our vital force in that useless and hurtful manner? The ordinary demands upon the nervous resources of telegraphists are sufficiently exhausting without adding to them by gratuitous outbursts of temper." He emphasized "the vital need there is for all such clerks putting, as a matter of self-preservation, a temperate restraint upon themselves."[52] Likewise, Tempus Omnia Revelat advised "all sound-readers never to lose perfect control over themselves, as many are so apt to do, when they have fast, jerky, unsteady sending to read." "A great waste of nervous energy takes place" when telegraphists became annoyed or rattled, and "day by day" they "enfeeble those organs which alone make life endurable and worth living." The best way to maintain sound mental and bodily function was to "at all times check fitful or excited working at the wire, ever keeping in mind that the steady and quiet worker is by far the most valuable public servant." Conflating efficient cognitive practices with healthy bodies and proper state functioning, he warned that "those who work at all times under a state of nervous excitement very soon become useless to the Department . . . [and] an irritant to their fellow-clerks, and add their load to the world's great mountain of misery and disease."[53] Telegraphists' best recourse was to self-regulate their nervous energies.

A woman contributor to the *Our Girls Column* had a different but equally evocative solution to "the evil effects of telegraphy on the nervous system of both male and female operators." She recommended "music of the home" as a cure for "an overwrought brain" and encouraged the playing and contemplation of "Beethoven, Mozart, Haydn, Chopin, Mendelssohn, and Wagner." The "boisterous and exciting noise of the 'Free and Easy or the common music-hall'" was to be avoided; nor should popular compositions be indulged in at home as they "degrad[ed] high art."[54] Arnoldian prescriptions like these, a reflection of the *Telegraphist's* editorial sensibilities, signaled that bourgeois refinement was a necessary component of self-care.

Telegraphic work forged an insular community with specialized knowledge, shared experiences, and particular anxieties, but the extent to which men and women could make common cause against administrators was restricted by resentments about Sunday and night duty, opportunities for promotion, and notions of respectability. Since nationalization, some women had been involved in telegraphists' agitations, but until the 1890s, the vast majority of female operators remained mostly aloof from male telegraphists' organized attempts to address grievances.

They had good reason. The downsizing of the female staff from the late 1870s left women in the London Central Office skeptical of aligning with their male colleagues. The men, in turn, expressed little solidarity with the women. In 1881, during the Great Agitation, when Fawcett queried a group of male delegates about the wide salary disparities between male and female operators, they responded that the women could "take care of themselves."[55] And women attempted to do so by submitting their own independent petition to Fawcett that year, demanding salaries and benefits matching those of the female clerks in London's Post Office Savings Bank headquarters. Almost 70 percent of the female telegraphists—476 women—signed the petition, which stated that "the peculiar nature of the work in which we are engaged demands the exercise of great tact and discretion, close and constant application, and above all special training and experience."[56] Like the men, they defined telegraphy as a responsible, skilled, confidential profession: handling the public's information deserved the same compensation as handling its money. They also incorporated the mental and physical demands of the work in making their case for the longer holidays afforded the GPO clerks: "The inventions in Telegraphy, introduced from time to time, tend, as a rule, to increase rather than lessen the severe strain upon the nervous system."[57]

By 1889 men had incorporated bodied politics into their own petitioning. On top of one month's holidays, male clerks demanded sick leave on full rather than two-thirds pay on the grounds that "the extreme irregularity of the duties and peculiar mental strain inseparable from the work" led to greater susceptibility to illness, and that "permanent clerks in other branches of the Civil Service performing regular or shorter hours" did not have their wages reduced while on sick leave.[58]

Some telegraphists, like Saul, identified longer holidays for women as an issue that both reinforced gendered divisions in telegraphy and encouraged women's membership in the growing PTCA. For others, including a number of male delegates at the PTCA annual meeting in Belfast in 1887, extended leave for women was undue "favoring" that damaged male telegraphists' prospects. These men were outvoted by others who argued that "interference with the female staff would not do themselves any good whatsoever" and that "the female staff worked for the benefit of the males."[59] Resolutions attempting to keep the number of women's appointments in large telegraph offices to one-fifth of the men's were regularly proposed at these meetings but were also increasingly voted down, indicating that opinion among male PTCA members was shifting toward accommodation with female coworkers. However, female membership in the PTCA remained low. The weekly dues of one shilling, plus payments for the illness insurance scheme—the highest contributions of all the GPO workers' organizations—and workplace hostilities discouraged women's official involvement.[60] William Lynd's attempts to solicit contributions from women to the *Telegraphist* had limited success. "The indifference of the ladies passes our comprehension altogether," he noted in 1886, and he thought it "strange . . . that our most enthusiastic lady supporters are clerks at sub-offices."[61] With no night duty, limited if any Sunday hours, and less variation in telegraph machinery, gendered divisions at suboffices were likely much less problematic.

Collaboration between male and female telegraphists to improve their status was indirectly catalyzed by the actions of a class of GPO workers they considered their inferiors. By the late 1880s postmen, having aligned with the Trades Union Congress, began advocating for shorter hours and higher salaries, using assertive collective-bargaining practices gaining prominence in other industries.[62] The current GPO executive refused to acknowledge this form of bargaining and dismissed the leading organizers. In April 1890, Blackwood, concerned about "outside influences" agitating on the postmen's behalf, enforced and modified an old rule banning GPO employees from holding free public meetings. The manipulative grades were now required to give GPO authorities advance warning of any such meeting; meetings were restricted to postal employees only; and an observer had to be present at every meeting in order to submit reports on the proceedings to the GPO executive. These conditions proved offensive to all the affected GPO grades and controversial with the public. Sympathizers, including the liberal and radical press, met the GPO's stance with ridicule. In the pages of *Punch, Reynolds's,* and the *Pall Mall Gazette,* the postmaster general was portrayed as a tyrant undermining Englishmen's right of free assembly.[63]

Male telegraphists responded with a rare showing of solidarity with other GPO workers through a unique form of electric communications protest. The year 1890 marked the fiftieth anniversary of the penny post scheme, and throughout the year GPO executives organized and hosted a number of celebratory galas. On the evening of July 2, the South Kensington Museum of Science and Art (today's Victoria and Albert Museum) hosted a jubilee "conversazione" presided over by Raikes, Prime Minister Lord Salisbury, and the Duke and Duchess of Edinburgh. Preparations for this event involved filling the museum with displays of post offices and telegraph circuits, including models of post offices from 1790, 1890, and 1990. (The 1990 example was presided over by "specially selected" female staff in evening dresses, speaking to each other through an "electrophonoscope" that linked its users by "sight and speech.")[64] Aristocratic guests and a limited invited public could purchase jubilee paraphernalia and send letters and telegrams to one another from various parts of the museum.

The highlight of this spectacle of modern communications was a grand royal procession, culminating in the presentation to the Duchess of Edinburgh of a special "telegraph wire and apparatus," which would send a simultaneous signal to telegraph offices around the country, "inviting" telegraph personnel to "unite with their colleagues . . . in giving simultaneously three cheers to Her Majesty the Queen."[65] At precisely 10 p.m. the Duchess sent out the signal. Across much of the British Isles, telegraphists remained silent. In London's Central Telegraph Office, four hundred telegraphists who had been compelled to participate in this accolade met the signal with ringing silence, followed by groans.[66] Officials at the Central Telegraph Office only exacerbated the situation when they called for three cheers for Postmaster General Raikes: the telegraphists' groans grew much louder.[67] A press report on the incident was picked up by the *Times* and other papers.[68] Raikes first heard of the event the following morning, and he acted swiftly to interrogate the telegraphists and expose the ringleaders. This investigation went nowhere, as the telegraphists refused to talk.[69]

This protest deeply unsettled administrators. Eight days later, in a much more public and proletarian spectacle of GPO defiance, London's postmen went on strike and marched throughout the city. While short-lived, the strike vividly embodied the postal network's subversive potentials: striking postmen displayed a rebellious mobility, turning their daily work circuits into currents of disruption. As with the telegraphists in 1871, however, the GPO had a well-planned containment strategy: it hired auxiliary postmen and dismissed large numbers of suspected organizers. The GPO's internal security branch coordinated with London's Metropolitan Police to limit the overall numbers of striking postmen through dismissals, arrests, and intimidation. And the executive promised concessions to telegraphists and sorters if they refrained from supporting or joining the postmen. The union-averse, class-conscious PTCA and the Fawcett Association (the sorters' organization, named in honor of the former postmaster general) agreed to remain aloof from the strike, and on July 14 male and female second-class telegraphists were rewarded with pay increases.[70] Thus bought off, telegraphists kept their distance from other postal grades and the larger union movement into the early twentieth century. As one PTCA delegate put it, "We are aiming high . . . therefore I think that to associate ourselves in any way with the Trades' Councils would be a lowering of our standards."[71] In 1891, the PTCA formalized this sentiment, announcing that it did not "consider it advisable, or indeed practicable, to affiliate our Branches to the Trades Councils of the United Kingdom."[72]

The concessions gained from the postmen's strike, particularly the decision to raise women's salaries alongside men's, had an unintended consequence: the settlement prompted London's female telegraphists to join the PTCA for the first time. The *Women's Penny Paper* announced that "it was with much trepidation" that London's female telegraphists made common cause with the men, as "it was feared it would earn for them the ill will of the supervisors." However, it also reported that women's willingness to join the association reduced long-standing tensions, going "a long way towards dispelling that feeling which the male staff had that the lady clerks were interlopers and filling situations which should be held by men." Joint association membership "has led to a better understanding between the two staffs, a mutual increase of respect, and has established a bond of friendship hitherto nonexistent."[73] That said, women's reasons for joining the union went beyond the desire to reconcile with their male counterparts: "It strengthened the association to a considerable extent. . . . Now that female labour is becoming more general at the telegraph service (there are nearly 1,000 girls in the Central Telegraph Office), and women are competing with men, they are learning to look after their own interests, and not trust to the very precarious support from the male clerks."[74]

The PTCA's support for women remained precarious and uneven for the rest of the century. Calls persisted for women's relative numbers to be reduced, as did accusations that they undermined men's aims. In 1899 many delegates still thought the PTCA should aim to ban women from telegraphy altogether.[75] It would take further telecommunications innovations and a realignment of the meaning of telegraphic work to bring women and men together as consistent partners in urban telegraph offices. Women's early emphasis on the physical harms of telegraphy in their demands for workplace improvements would bear fruit in the twentieth century, when telegraphist's cramp became the subject of a government inquiry, but the Victorian era of GPO telegraphy was notable for its effective restraints on the aspirations of telegraphists. Gendered policies and practices, including the weaponizing of respectability by GPO administrators, created challenges for telegraphists as they sought to establish their intellectual and economic worth.

They failed in this endeavor. Telegraphists never achieved civil service clerk status, and although their identification with middle-class professionalism won them minor concessions, these came at the expense of postmen in a top-down, divide-and-conquer strategy on the part of GPO officials. It was not self-evident that telegraphy should be defined as a "manipulative" occupation rather than an intellectual art performed by information "manipulators." However, its physical and mental requirements defied easy categorization. This indeterminacy further allowed the ideological and cultural power of discretion to dictate the terms of telegraphists' marginalization.

FIVE

_____

Unintended Networks

ON FEBRUARY 4, 1870, the eve of British telegraphy's nationalization, GPO executives invited major London press organs to attend a special evening ceremony at London's postal headquarters. Reporters watched as a "corps" of five hundred uniformed telegraph boys marched from Telegraph Street to St Martin's-le-Grand, accompanied by the Post Office Rifles Volunteers Regiment Band. On arrival, they were joined by a Post Office Rifle guard of honor. Together, they marched into the cavernous GPO circulation room, stood at attention for the national anthem, and performed basic drill movements in front of their new commander, Secretary Frank Ives Scudamore. Scudamore instructed his youthful army that while in

> the Queen's uniform . . . the public themselves would act as inspectors over them, and that if they were seen idling, overing posts—(laughter)—or seen playing at marbles in a sly corner or a blind alley—(renewed laughter)—those members of the public who saw them indulging in such lax practices would be very apt to report them . . . .[but] they would be actuated to work diligently by a higher motive . . . namely, a sense of duty.[1]

These spectacles reflected the GPO's awareness that public hopes for nationalization were not limited to a larger, faster, cheaper telegraph network. An editorial from the *Sunday Times* in late December 1869 expressed the hope that "when the telegraphs are placed in the hands of the post Office . . . something will be done to reform the manners of telegraph boys." The telegraph delivery staff appeared to be particularly unruly, even compared to other urban youth: "They are about the slowest class in existence," not even having the "ordinary briskness of your London street boy." Telegraph boys seemed to take "malicious pleasure" in "neutralizing the dispatch of the electric wire by their own slothfulness." London's old telegraph network had been willfully undermined by young messengers "creeping and sauntering," "cracking walnuts," and haggling for street foods. The boys gazed into print-shop windows and took up space in "the thousand and one gratuitous street exhibitions of the metropolis," failing to appreciate that London streets should be regarded as orderly conduits for delivery. When pressed for time, they resorted to cheating. This could not continue: "I do not believe that anyone can say that they ever, under any possible circumstances, saw a telegraph boy running; when a telegraph boy is in a hurry he generally takes a Hansom cab. Let us hope we shall, under the new *regime,* have some reformation in these matters."[2]

Under the new regime, London's telegraph boys may indeed have assumed a more orderly appearance. They may have looked smart in their new uniforms. A few of them may even have abstained from eating food from street vendors or looking at prints or exhibitions while on dispatch. But many continued to enjoy the city in ways similar to their nonuniformed peers, and some found other, more secret and subversive paths to pleasure and gain.

London telegraph boys represented not only the technological ordering of time, space, and information but also an expanding homoerotic landscape. Their deliveries ensured the efficient flow of information to the wealthy and predominantly male consumers of the telegraph; their concentrated presence in certain enclaves of London reinscribed financial, state, and imperial might.[3] Yet, as the Cleveland Street scandal of 1889 was to make abundantly clear, some telegraph boys worked in the underground male sex trade. GPO archival sources from the 1870s reveal that Cleveland Street was only the most public display of a long-standing problem for the London GPO administration.[4]

Just as women's presence in the telegraph service resulted in new administrative modes of labor management, the problem telegraph boys posed to administrators had productive consequences. An earlier series of events, culminating in the prosecution of one man and one telegraph boy on sodomy charges in the spring of 1877, left a trail of memoranda, letters, and reports that expose sexual misconduct in London's late Victorian communications network. These records illuminate the intimate links between sexual subcultures and the proudly touted British communications network. The young telegraph messengers who doubled as rent boys exploited the possibilities of London's sexual underworld and the mobility that went with their job. Before the rise of the telephone and wireless, the transmission of information depended on face-to-face human contact. The arrival of the telegraph was a transformative moment of modern interaction, when rapid exchanges of information still depended on ritual encounters between strangers. London telegraph messengers' duty to cross boundaries and be party to secrets, to deliver the confidences and desires of their wealthy customers, opened up possibilities for them to disrupt these overlapping networks of discretion.

London had well-established sexual markets for elite men and working-class male youths.[5] The uniformed telegraph boy added a new dimension to its pederastic traditions. The readiness and ease with which some London telegraph boys transitioned between sex work and postal work, both out on delivery and inside offices, was part of the modern communications order. This duality was hardly to the telegraph boys' advantage, however, as it rested on the inherent inequities between messengers and their clientele. Much urban scholarship conflates urban mobility with upward mobility: for example, historians have cited the expanded mobility of middle-class women in the late nineteenth century as evidence of their increased economic and political influence.[6] The unfettered movement of telegraph messengers, however, was the result of these boys' functioning as providers of others' information and pleasures. They did the dirty work of crossing urban boundaries to supply the city's important citizens with all the information and pleasures they could pay for. Their multiple roles created discordant visions of late Victorian London, amply demonstrated by the GPO's reaction to the exposure of an organized homosexual market emanating out of the telegraph service. Administrators had to grapple with an unanticipated supply-and-demand cycle created out of the gap between wires and consumers. Their response reveals the more coercive values inherent to the telegraphic metropolis.

THE LONDON TELEGRAPH BOY

Upon nationalization in 1870, the GPO took over the employment of approximately three hundred telegraph boys and quickly hired five hundred more. By 1877 over two thousand telegraph boys worked in telegraph offices and on the London streets. Usually hired at age fourteen, new telegraph boys started their careers as the lowest-paid employees at the GPO, earning five shillings a week. In most London districts, more experienced boys switched from a fixed wage to a "docket" system: the more telegrams they delivered per day, the more they earned. On turning seventeen, senior London telegraph boys could use their knowledge and experience to make twelve shillings a week on average. This put them on par with beginner male telegraphists and well ahead of female telegraphists, whose starting wages were eight shillings a week.

Aspiring telegraph boys were supposed to be nominated by respectable acquaintances, but frequent advertisements for telegraph messengers in London's newspapers suggest that authorities dispensed with the niceties of nomination as the telegraph service expanded. Of those actually nominated, many had postmen fathers.[7] Prospective messengers had to fill out application forms listing their age and address, their father's occupation, their former schools and schoolmasters, and the names and addresses of two references. They also had to get a doctor to vouch for their health. Given the demand for London messengers, and the shortage of telegraph-boy supervisors in the 1870s, it is likely that this information was rarely corroborated.

Once their applications had been accepted, the boys had to pass a short examination that involved "writing tolerably a few lines; Reading manuscript; Adding a few figures together, simple and compound."[8] In the early 1870s a test for reading difficult handwriting was added. Like other GPO employees, telegraph boys had to pass a medical inspection once they had been conditionally hired. They had to be at least 4 feet 10 inches tall, with a minimum chest diameter of twenty-eight inches. Their eyes, teeth, and feet were inspected, and they were examined for signs of previous diseases. They began training by tailing older messengers to learn methods of internal office delivery, then moved on to the mastery of outdoor routes. In the 1870s telegraph boys as young as thirteen were found throughout the metropolis, but by the 1880s, new telegraph messengers often remained inside telegraph offices or filled telegram canisters for the pneumatic tube system until they were fifteen.

Telegraph boys were not permitted to join the fledging GPO postmen's unions. As messengers they were associated with, yet not quite part of, both the postman's work of outdoor delivery and the more prestigious and insulated culture of the telegraph operators, whose organizing efforts were geared towards civil service professionalism, to the exclusion of postmen and other GPO grades. Outdoor labor performed by uniformed youths did nothing for the PTCA's image. Telegraph boys' indeterminate status in the GPO helped to ensure that they remained at the bottom of the wage ladder, though they could aspire to being hired as assistant postmen or occasionally mail sorters when they turned eighteen. A handful of the "brighter boys" were offered telegraph training, although most telegraph clerkships and other office positions were reserved for boys with more schooling and higher up the social scale.[9] Telegraph delivery was a form of apprenticeship for the GPO mail-delivery establishment.

Outdoor messengers wore tight-fitting blue serge uniforms with scarlet piping and shako caps made of the cheapest fabric and leather.[10] They were subject to morning inspections and suspended without pay if their uniforms were disheveled or torn.[11] Their visibility circumscribed their public behavior to a certain extent, as was demonstrated by an unfortunate encounter in St James's:

> Mr. Tilley met telegraph messenger No. 561 in St. James Street this morning smoking and looking dirty and untidy. Mr. Tilley told him not to smoke on duty; and he considers that if the boy passed before the Inspector before starting he was no Credit to that Officer's supervision.[12]

The fate of Messenger No. 561 and his inspector is unknown, but Mr. Tilley, soon to be Sir John Tilley, secretary to the postmaster general (the second-highest ranking member of the GPO executive), initiated a proposal to include more identifying marks on messengers' uniforms in order to identify troublemakers. The idea was eventually thrown out because the cost of embroidering was deemed too high.

Messenger 561's example highlights the disadvantages to the authorities of having low-paid boys on the front lines of the new communications order. Their youth and working-class status made them a potentially vulnerable and capricious staff. Smoking was particularly evocative of troubled urban boyhood.[13] The London press, heavy users of the telegraph, displayed a mixture of amused exasperation and patronizing enthusiasm toward the young messengers. Humorous anecdotes about telegraph boys mixing up deliveries or being distracted by street games while on duty were fairly common, and a grumpy poem in *Moonshine* bemoaned "the lazy and blundering / Telegraph boy."[14]

The *Licensed Victualler,* a gossipy, jocular London mouthpiece for publicans and the brewing industry, took the opposite view, celebrating the messengers' youthful exuberance: "Whoever yet saw a telegraph boy run off his legs or distressed in any way whatsoever? . . . Who can come forward and say he is fallen in with any specimen of the *genus* who has not been sharp, perky, full of animal spirits, and, in a general way, up to date?"[15] This representation of the telegraph boy has none of the negative associations of urban boyhood commented on by the *Sunday Times.* The combination of admiration and condescension captures telegraph boys' appeal, but in the city those animal spirits could be volatile and dangerous.

Telegraph boys also featured in children's literature. Shortly after nationalization in July 1870, the evangelical periodical *The British Juvenile* featured a glowing endorsement of the new telegraph boy. Using similar rhetoric to the *Sunday Times* editorial, the magazine piece derided the old system for producing telegraph boys who were unsuitable for the work required of the present moment, when, thanks to telegraphy, "we can fabricate artificial lightning and supply it per order at a fixed price." The piece described the nationalized service and celebrated the wonders of GPO employment. It elaborated its claim that "good boys" were "all better off under the wing of St Martins le Grand":

> Under the old arrangement . . . they were never thought about at all, and in underground kitchens or dismal attics they had to spend their days. . . . Now, when the post office authorities took up the matter, all this was changed. Large and commodious rooms were procured for the boys, well ventilated, comfortably warmed; rooms where the boys waiting for hire might feel themselves at home.[16]

This description was fantasy. From nationalization until the 1877 prostitution investigation, telegraph boys actually congregated in small kitchens, often sharing space in the basement of telegraph offices with lavatories and the machinery that generated electricity for the telegraph machines and powered the underground pneumatic-tube system. They were usually supervised by low-paid matrons or older telegraph boys who had achieved the rank of "corporal" or "lance corporal." But supervision was inconsistent: in some London offices telegraph boys were simply corralled near mail sorters and other indoor staff on the lower floors in the hope that someone would keep an eye on them. The kitchens had tables, chairs, and cubbyholes for the messengers' overcoats and waterproof gear. The number of boys sharing these spaces varied greatly depending on the size of the office and the volume of telegraph business. Telegraph boys' indoor workspaces began to resemble the article's description only after 1877, for reasons that would have horrified *The British Juvenile*.

Rosy portrayals in the press of telegraph boys' working life went hand in hand with repeated assertions that "sharp, clean, spruce, wide-awake, go-ahead, fast young lads are the boys now in the telegraph service." The *British Juvenile* article alluded to a "Master Fastboy," who "wears the Queen's buttons" and had his "head screwed on the right way." The article made clear that these new civil servants had to distinguish themselves from "those over 'sharp' lads who can talk 'slang,' read of boy bandits, and boy good-for-noth-ings of every sort." Along with just the right qualities of fastness and sharp-ness "that put a boy in a right position, and lead him to go straight on," a telegraph boy had to exhibit personal discretion: "Master Fastboy is particu-larly cautioned against divulging any official or private information. He must have his eyes and ears about him, but his tongue must be still. . . . It is very necessary to check this, especially in the case of a public officer—for so the Telegraph boy really is—and any tripping in this way is followed by severe punishment."[17] The sanctity of private communication so fundamental to the GPO's vaunted status was never far from the surface in public depictions of the telegraph, the post, or any other facet of the GPO's social role.

Administrators stridently reasserted the GPO1's commitment to privacy during the influx of youthful communications workers. Quasi-military tele-graph-boy parades around St Martin's-le-Grand and other government ven-ues, such as Somerset House, demonstrated telegraph boys' acquiescence to state discipline.[18] Rules for delivering telegrams further emphasized discre-tion and discipline. One messenger could not hand off a telegram to another; telegraph boys could not themselves convey or transcribe a spoken reply; their telegrams had to be carried in their GPO-issued pouches, along with all money received and forms documenting payment and return delivery; and they had to ensure that a telegram was placed in the intended recipient's hands (or, more often, the hands of the recipient's servant). Telegraph boys were also instructed to use the same "double knock" on front doors that postmen had adopted earlier in the nineteenth century. This communica-tions ritual signaled the special importance placed on the post and telegraph. It also relayed to those inside that the deliverer had a right to linger on private thresholds.[19]

Telegraph boys themselves took part in imagining the telegraphic city. They reportedly developed their own language to describe deliveries and customers. A "lag" was an unusually long distance to cover; a "cop" was a house or business that tipped.[20] Their uniforms may have marked them out for potential disciplinary infractions, but it also permitted them free rides on omnibuses and entry into venues normally prohibited to working-class boys, so long as they were on duty. Their ability to move across town unfettered was reinforced by the law: cab drivers could be fined by police courts if they refused to drive boys on urgent deliveries.[21] As Gregory Downey notes in his study of American telegraph boys, uniforms functioned like a modern press pass, giving the boys access to the city's venues of pleasure and power.[22]

While telegraph boys developed a subculture centering on urban mobility, London was being reshaped according the dictates of the GPO. Access to high-speed communication divided the city along familiar class lines. Telegraph delivery to homes and workplaces relieved people from interrupting their schedules to check for incoming messages at post offices. To enhance both the prestige and the efficiency of this system, GPO administrators designed telegraph dispatches to appear as personalized deliveries. Unlike postmen, who carried multiple letters and delivered the post according to laid-out routes, urban telegraph boys were, in theory, sent to deliver single telegrams immediately on arrival. In practice, telegraph boys at busy London offices were sent out with up to three messages at a time, but they were instructed to give the impression that they were carrying only one.[23] This personalized service combined old ideas of servile deference with new expectations for telegraphic efficiency.

As the telegraph service expanded, it also went underground. When the new Central Telegraph Office was built in 1874 at St Martin's-le-Grand, it was the hub of a new technological marvel: pneumatic tubes designed to transfer written messages between the main telegraph stations "in a few seconds."[24] Thirty-six miles of pipeline stretched east and west from the Tower of London to the House of Commons. Canisters containing telegrams were fired by compressed air along these tubes to their receiving stations, where the telegrams were transferred into the hands of the district telegraph boys. "A stream of telegrams . . . continually flow[ed]" under the metropolis, and contemporaries who were aware of the tubes thought them "very wonderful in their working."[25]

Along with other subterranean infrastructure projects, such as the sewer system and underground railway, the pneumatic pipeline was vaguely understood by its users as part of the natural development of the modern city.[26] With the new technology hidden underground, telegraph consumers developed new conceptions of information transfer and the city's landscapes. The telegraph boy, dressed in the blue uniform of the GPO, was the last publicly visible vestige of urban telegraphy.

Like police and soldiers, telegraph boys elicited sexual interest from upper-class men searching for "rough trade" on London's streets. In some ways, telegraph boys occupied a similar place in the city to guardsmen, the most prominent and probably best-organized sector of male prostitution.[27] Guardsmen's uniformed presence on the London streets was among both the most reified and the most troubling versions of late Victorian masculinity. As

Matt Houlbrook has compellingly argued, the guardsman's exalted status as the "ideal man" informed both heteronormative and queer productions of national manhood, and the soldier hero/rent boy, by "existing in a constant tension," produced "an instability of meaning that made the guardsman central to the imagined landscapes of British masculinities."[28] By contrast, telegraph boys were in no way exalted—at best they were soldier heroes in training. The postman symbolized benign state business devoid of romance: the days of adventurous King's Messengers were long over. The telegraph boy's cultural resonance had more to do with the promises and anxieties encompassing urban youth than with masculine prestige. Boyhood inflected the gendering of this laboring body quite differently from that of other men in uniform.

Telegraph boys' duties made them uniquely available participants in the late Victorian sex trade. Expected to traverse every corner of the city in the course of their work, they could literally arrive on a customer's doorstep; and their presence at almost any hour of the day or night, in almost any neighborhood, was unremarkable. Improvements in public transportation helped telegraph boys get around the metropolis rapidly and, as Matt Cook has pointed out, provided new opportunities for discreet, anonymous sexual encounters between men, often of different classes, and greater access to homoerotically inflected urban landscapes.[29] Telegraph messengers' furtive sexual liaisons with elite male customers mirrored their GPO pledge of discretion and confidentiality when it came to telegrams. These men would be just as compromised as the messengers if their encounters were revealed.

MALE PROSTITUTION AND THE LONDON GPO

The year 1876 was an auspicious one for the telegraph network. Though it had yet to make a profit, the system had grown exponentially, and the supposed ubiquity of telegraph offices was the GPO's chief publicity asset. Administrators now planned to reorganize the network, reducing district offices' role in transmission and routing almost all dispatches through the Central Office at St Martin's-le-Grand.[30] Centralization, they argued, would speed up service and enable better monitoring of irregularities. Frederick Baines, at this point the surveyor general of telegraphs for London, reported favorably on this transition throughout the year. He also took an interest in the welfare of telegraph boys: in his spare time he made arrangements for providing them with reading materials and other wholesome activities to occupy them between dispatches.

Baines's concern for telegraph boys began in 1875 with a memo from the postmaster general, the Tory MP Lord John Manners, who had tipped Baines off about the "disorderly conduct" of telegraph messengers at the Vere Street post office. Manners had received a letter from a clergyman reporting on vague admissions of disturbing behavior by boys preparing for confirmation.[31] In response, Manners began an informal inquiry into messenger supervision and what the boys did in their downtime. This exchange and other internal memoranda from 1876 illustrate a growing concern among officials about supervision of messengers. In July, Tilley attempted to standardize female matrons' supervision and pay, but this issue was left unresolved. A new concern over what was occurring outside GPO premises quietly took priority.

A minute from Tilley to the postmaster general dated September 5, 1876, alludes to an internal investigation of telegraph boys' activities: "I submit that the following boy messengers be at once dismissed from the service, viz.: Buck, Fovargue, Thompson, Juddick, Isaacs, Cave, Tindall; and I would suggest that copies of the report and its enclosures should be sent to the Home Office." Tilley further requested that the home secretary look into police negligence in "not having called the attention of the Department to these proceedings of which they must have been cognizant."[32]

The report that prompted this minute, produced by Thomas Jeffery, head of the Missing Letter Branch, is absent from GPO, police, and Home Office archives, but existing documents name the culprits and criticize police ineptitude. The boys came from at least three different offices: R. Isaacs worked at the West Central District Office on the Strand, and J. E. Tindall was stationed at Kensington. Later correspondence identifies the "Chief" office, at St Martin's-le-Grand, along with the West Strand office and the West Central District in general, as the center of the problem.

In response to Tilley's minute, the postmaster general confirmed the telegraph boys' dismissal and ordered that Jeffery's report be sent to the Home Office, but he cautioned the secretary "to appear not to cast blame on the police."[33] The case had already resulted in frictions between investigative bodies that the postmaster general did not want to exacerbate. Moreover, as H. G. Cocks and Charles Upchurch have noted, the Metropolitan Police had adopted a cautious approach to prosecuting sex between men. Before the Criminal Law Amendment Act of 1885, procuring enough evidence to make an arrest for sodomy between consenting partners could be difficult, and police wanted to avoid becoming implicated in extortion or libel charges.[34] Their reluctance was compounded by powerful legal and moral discourses that discouraged public discussion of the "nameless offence" except by calling it just that. Lawyers, magistrates, doctors, and politicians concurred that publicizing the "infamous crime" would encourage its spread or at least adversely affect public morals.[35] Furthermore, the police commissioner, Colonel Henderson, inclined to caution in sexual policing; he had reluctantly agreed to clear the Haymarket's night houses two years earlier. In response to numerous complaints about indiscriminate arrests, he insisted that his officers leave women sex workers and their clients alone unless they became rowdy, indecent, or impeded free movement on the streets.[36]

In any case, a squabble erupted between the Missing Letter Branch and the Metropolitan Police, and in November, the Home Office responded with another report on telegraph boy behavior (also missing from the archives) that cast aspersions on post office constables. Tilley's follow-up summary of Metropolitan and GPO policing to the postmaster general reveals how Buck, Fovargue, and the other messengers had been investigated:"On the occasion when Constable Butler [of the Missing Letter Branch] was accosted in the Haymarket by the Superintendent [of the Metropolitan Police], he had not . . . been specially employed a considerable time in watching Telegraph Boys in the Haymarket in relation to these offences." Tilley argued that "that there being some reason to suspect what was going on, it was determined to have the Boys interrogated to see what could be elicited," but "prior to doing so it was deemed expedient to send Butler to the Haymarket for a few nights just to observe their conduct without telling him the nature of the suspicions that were entertained."[37] Constable Butler may not have been told directly why he was asked to observe telegraph boys in the Haymarket—which had been notorious for prostitution throughout the mid-Victorian era and was still a haven, though less fashionable, for sexual bartering in 1876. But the Haymarket's notoriety as a center of vice strongly suggests that the GPO kitchen disturbances were also of a sexual nature.

By early January 1877, telegraph boys were explicitly linked to homosexual practices, though Victorian propriety continued to obscure exactly what transpired. Part of the secretary's minute 149, titled "The Immoral Conduct of Boy Messengers: Assessment of Mr. Jeffery's' Report" contains a blank space. Underneath, the postmaster general remarked, "These distressing disclosures conform in the belief that the kitchens have been the source of the evil. I approve of the proposal to be adopted."[38] Later that month, the postmaster general responded to another missing minute, titled "Immoral Conduct and Dismissal of Certain Boys," by ordering detectives to be stationed "about the Office concerned."[39]

This incomplete file offers tantalizing suggestions of the existence of a well-developed sexual subculture in the GPO. Workplace sexual interactions among the boy messengers may have resembled those among privileged boys at public schools, with the obvious difference that telegraph boys accepted money for sex. The kitchens and basements in telegraph offices appear to have been sites of initiation into urban rent and of homoerotic encounters between boys. The fact that the dismissed boys came from different offices suggests a network of commercial sex that crossed the boundaries of kitchen, office, and street. Telegraph boys' knowledge of city streets, offices, theaters, and residences, so essential to their work, proved a valuable asset in engaging with more liminal urban topographies.

The draft of Jeffery's final report, titled "Immorality among Boys," survives intact. Presented to the secretary on March 31, 1877, it provides an exhaustive list of the causes of and remedies for male prostitution at the GPO. He introduces the report by noting the endemic nature of homosexual misdeeds among the messenger staff:

> The vice ... as existing among the Telegraph Boys engaged on Night duty at the Chief Office, was found to exist in an equal, or greater, degree among a similar class of employés in some of the Metropolitan Districts.... [T]he facts brought to light by more recent enquiries give a clearer insight into the character and extent of the evil.[40]

Jeffery observed that the "causes no doubt are various," but he broke down his findings into three categories of evil influence: "the bad source of supply for Telegraph Messengers"; "things within the service that tend to this result"; and "things outside the Service and beyond the control of the Department."[41] These categories emphasize the divisions between inside and outside and the spatial divisions within the GPO administration. Yet movement across these imaginary boundaries inevitably destabilized them. Jeffery's report often contradicted itself on which categories represented the greatest danger.

Jeffery's first targets were the homes, neighborhoods, and class of the telegraph boys. He noted that the offices most affected by immorality were supplied with telegraph boys from Bermondsey, Whitechapel, and "the low parts of Chelsea." These boys, he wrote, "had but one parent or none at all, and almost from their birth had been thrown on the care of some relative whose guardianship was but nominal." Their living conditions, he argued, were enough to foster moral depravity: "The sad effects of bad training, or of extreme poverty, or both combined, were seen in many of the boys, in an utter absence of truthfulness, except when falsehoods would no longer screen them, in a greediness for money, and a willingness to prostitute themselves even for very small sums." Jeffery surmised that the degenerate telegraph boys "had no particular liking for the vice, as a vice, but, whatever dislike they had for it, was entirely and easily overborne by the money which was tendered to them by their seducers."[42]

Jeffery's reading of poverty and moral depravity aligned with popular middle-class discourses of the slum as producer of disease and of moral, physical, and social degeneration. Homosexuality, along with female promiscuity, incest, infanticide, rape, and other sexual sins, was an outcome of poor living conditions and the attendant collapse of "natural" human sentiment.[43] His further musings into this "bad supply" of telegraph boys underscored the class dynamics underlying telegraph boy labor: since it was impossible to get "a superior class of boy" on the five-shilling starting salary offered to telegraph messengers, the GPO was forced to hire "little more than the residuum." The department's terrible wages were essentially to blame for appealing only to the lowest, and therefore most corrupt, class of worker.[44]

Jeffery goes on to posit what others had long assumed: that the structure of the workplace also fostered homosexual practices. He noted that the "idle life" many telegraph boys led in the office was conducive to vice, for "boys when together in numbers, without useful employment or exercise, or recreation of any kind, are sure to be planning mischief or doing something they should not." Supervision was a key problem, especially when older boys supervised younger ones: "The system of Corporals and Lance Corporals is of little or no value in a matter like this, as some of the worst boys were found in those ranks, and even when they were not personally involved, they often winked at, if they did not actually encourage, the vice in other boys." Memoranda, letters, and this report repeatedly identify kitchens as the origins and focal points of a well-developed and dangerously mobile homoerotic youth subculture. These unspeakable actions spilled out of the GPO buildings: "Another cause of mischief is that of sending off duty a large number of boys together, especially when there are two or three bad ones amongst them, as in such a case the corrupt influence spreads very rapidly."[45] The seed of suggestion, the influence of older boys in charge, and the listless downtime between deliveries all coalesced to foster "immorality."

"But of all the causes within the Service that have tended to promote this vice is that of Night Duty." Jeffery's emphatic declaration preceded a long list of the evils of having boys working on the streets after 8 p.m., the magic hour when respectable London lost its hold on the city. "It was very apparent that much of the demoralization came from the Streets," Jeffery argued, and the more telegraph boys were forced to be out at night, the greater the chance of exposure to "temptations of the worst and most powerful kind." The boys' late-night commute home was equally dangerous: those whose homes were "long distances from the Offices where they are employed," and whose parents might be asleep or absent, could "if so minded, keep out to any hour of the morning." For Jeffery, the city streets themselves were a source of moral contagion. Day and night, "the naturally demoralizing influence of a Street life on juvenile character" was at work on telegraph boys, especially given that there was "no check on the conduct of the boys out of doors."[46]

Jeffery's final category of evil influence, "Things outside the Service, and beyond the control of the Department," is the most unstable, for London's streets, offices, pleasure venues, and private residences were inseparable from the telegraph network, as he had previously made clear. Among the targets of his condemnation were the large number of brothels and houses of assignation where "committing this crime with comparative impunity" was a matter of course. Then there were the public houses. Jeffery apparently found "few cases of this evil . . . in which the boys were not in the first instance, and then repeatedly afterwards, taken into Public Houses and plied with drink." He described "lewd conversations at the Bars or Counters and the exhibition of indecent pictures" and was shocked at how "openly was all this done. . . . [I]t is difficult to understand how the proprietors of such establishments, or the persons responsible for order in them, did not know what was going on."[47]

Jeffery further alluded to the challenges of policing homosexual acts: "There are again the immense obstacles in the way of the Police obtaining the necessary evidence to prosecute for a crime of this kind, and the natural objection they have against taking legal measures, unless the evidence is of the clearest character." This reluctance created a legal obstacle for the GPO:

> Considerably more than a hundred boys have been under examination in the matter. . . . [A] great many of these have been dismissed on very clear evidence of their guilt. . . . [T]he rest have been more or less involved . . . [and] the names and addresses of the men concerned have in various instances been known, and yet out of all this only one man and one boy can be prosecuted for the capital offence.[48]

Even allowing for hyperbole, telegraph-boy prostitution appears to have been fairly commonplace in the capital. The marginal status of telegraph boys in the department and the streets provided cover for after-hours work in the sex trade, and their youth, uniforms, and availability made them desirable to Jeffery's final and most troubling category of evil influences: "the number of bad men who are always lying in wait, especially near Post Offices, to beguile the boys and bribe them with money, of which such men appear to have an ample supply." He portrayed London's wealthy sodomites lurking around GPO buildings in their pursuit of telegraph boys. Jeffery went on to surmise that without the presence of "these men to seduce the boys, this form of immorality would in all probability be quite or almost unknown, so far as the Telegraph Messengers are concerned."[49] Jeffery concentrated homoerotic desire in the figure of the elite urban sodomite. The act of sex between men could be encouraged from below, but the desire for sex between men trickled down from society's upper echelons. In his description of the sodomite, Jeffery envisioned a decidedly queer communications system: telegraphy drew the sodomite out in the open; desire traveled along networks of wires and boys; the class positioning of telegraph consumer and worker was reiterated through sexual liaison; and the London underworld, like the underground system of wires and cables, was manifest in the figure of the telegraph messenger.

Notably, Jeffery's description of bad men lying in wait around post offices was the only part of the draft cut by Tilley from the final report. His editorializing is a striking example of the erasure of the carriers of homosexual desire. Across the board, government administrators embraced this tactic, using boys' "immorality" as code for the sexual market whose specifics they were forced to confront. There is also a class element underlying the omission: the GPO executive kept their concerns focused on their young working-class employees and avoided mention of seducers with ample means.

CONTAINING TELEGRAPH-BOY VICE

Jeffery's assessment confirms what other historians have suggested regarding English cultural understandings of class and homoeroticism before the rise of sexology: the city itself was a progenitor of vice, as were poverty, disease, and moral degeneration. On another level, however, the GPO's concern with "immorality" mapped out the interplay between the telegraph system and London's homoerotic landscape.

Jeffery's report, in conjunction with Home Office correspondence, also confirms the hunch of James Smith, the "one man" who was convicted of corrupting telegraph boys in 1877.[50] His conviction is unusual in that there were no corroborating witnesses to testify against him. The telegraph boy with whom Smith slept in his premises had accepted five shillings in payment, which technically made the boy an accomplice. By English law at this time, the evidence of an accomplice had to be corroborated by others. In Smith's prosecution, that requirement was ignored.[51]

Late Victorian notions of boyhood subjectivity drove the attorney general's office to adopt a cautious approach toward homoerotic containment.[52] This reading relies on the interplay between two very different sources of archival evidence: the records of the Post Office and of the Home Office, which were driven by two different forms of official logic. Smith was of concern solely to the Home Office; whereas GPO officials, whose priority was to restructure their boy labor force so as to minimize opportunities for homosexual dalliances, never mentioned his name. The Home Office sources present the series of interactions between telegraph boys and their client Smith in the context of sodomy laws and the strength of evidence required to produce a conviction. Office kitchens, poor wages, night duty, and the intersections of wired communication and sex had no place in the legal solution to the problem of male prostitution. Rather, the tricky matter of sexually complicit boys and the reliability of their evidence drove Home Office correspondence. The one point the two institutions agreed on was the need for a scapegoat outside the civil service on whom to lay the blame. Ultimately, however, it was the culpability not of James Smith but of the telegraph boys that the Home Office and the GPO found distressing.

Smith, a self-described gentleman (the press identified him as a tradesman), was arrested at 3 a.m. on February 19, 1877, near his home in Islington for sexually assaulting a messenger named Walter Bushrod. He was brought before Clerkenwell Police Court and remanded until February 27. At this point, Bushrod drops out of the proceedings, and another telegraph messenger, George Wright, enters the scene. Home Office correspondence and Smith's later appeals reveal that the switch in messengers was planned. On February 8, eleven days before Smith's arrest, the Treasury solicitor, Augustus Stephenson, sent a letter to the Home Office outlining his legal opinion on prosecutions related to telegraph boys. Three messengers had admitted to committing "the full offence" with Smith, but their uncorroborated evidence was not considered strong enough to secure a conviction.[53] Bushrod appears to have been planted as bait. According to Smith's appeal, he met Bushrod in the streets of Islington and asked Bushrod to come into his rooms while he "wrote a letter." As they walked towards Smith's lodgings, Bushrod accused Smith of importuning him for an "immoral purpose" and "guided" Smith into custody.[54] Bushrod's entrapment goes unmentioned in the proceedings that followed.

Bolstering both the legal case against Smith and its moral urgency, in Stephenson's view, "there is on the Men now in this case a matter for consideration which did not arise in the cases of Bolton [sic] and Park and men of the same character, when all those further implicated were grown men, of their own choice and free will indulging in these practices." His comparison refers to the trial of Earnest Boulton and Frederick Park (also known as Stella and Fanny), the gender-fluid couple who were ultimately acquitted of conspiring to commit sodomy in 1871. For Stephenson, Smith was

> *a man, without doubt* —whatever may be the *legal evidence* obtainable— making it his business to debauch and corrupt telegraph boys. . . . I think it is a matter for consideration whether some scandal should not be risked for the protection of children and to show that persons like Smith cannot indulge their passions with complete impunity.[55]

Whereas in previous assessments of the telegraph boys, their youth made them dangerous, untrustworthy subjects, here it is reframed as a vulnerability stemming from children's lack of free will. Paradoxically, the telegraph boys' evidence was admissible because they were not yet old enough to speak and act for themselves.[56]

The letter also makes clear that James Smith was a walking target. Shortly after his arrest, memoranda proliferated between the presiding magistrate, the police commissioner, the Treasury, and the Home Office. Stephenson was called in to conduct the prosecution, reiterating his willingness to "risk some scandal for the protection of mere boys."[57] Stephenson picked his most promising "victim." Seventeen-year-old George Wright was brought in and counseled to plead guilty, and he turned queen's evidence. This was enough for the magistrate: both Wright and Smith were convicted of buggery on April 11. Smith was sentenced to life in prison and Wright to ten years.

In late April Smith appealed to the Home Office. He had a rather different perspective on the telegraph boys' free will. Proclaiming his innocence and noting his connections to various Tory luminaries, Smith suggested that George Wright was either confused or involved in even more nefarious activities. He claimed that he had run into Wright at midnight the previous summer on a drunken meander home. He had often employed Wright to run errands and saw nothing untoward in asking Wright to walk back with him to his House at 27 Park Lane, Islington. Wright "lived on the Surrey side of the water," and, because of the late hour, Smith "unwisely told him he could remain all night if he liked." He had showed Wright a "book of Photographs of statuary (mythological subjects chiefly)," and on a later occasion showed the book to some of Wright's "friends," though he couldn't be sure, given that he was going through a period of heavy drinking. Later on, in January, Smith claimed, he had found Wright and another telegraph boy waiting for him outside his house at 2 a.m. He invited them in, and Wright had described to him how "there had been some unpleasantness at the office about the Book . . . that Scotland Yard had been consulted about it." Smith claimed Wright had begged him not to go the Post Office and sort out the misunderstanding, and the two boys had spent the night. On the night of his arrest, he had met Walter Bushrod and "entered into conversation with him in order to find out if he knew anything about the alleged unpleasantness at the office. . . . [H]e did and hence, in order to draw him out, I said more than I should otherwise have done and eventually asked him to wait at my rooms whilst I wrote a letter for him to take to Wright."[58] On the way back to his rooms, Bushrod "guided" Smith to the police.

Smith went on to argue correctly that Wright's testimony was legally inadmissible and that "the Treasury ought to have obtained some independent Testimony before pressuring for a conviction instead of relying on the unsupported testimony of lads who admitted having allowed themselves to be defiled for two shillings." Smith's telegraph boys were either too impressionable or willfully trying to ruin him; just as in Jeffery's report, their cheap virtue made them less than trustworthy citizens.[59]

Smith used his superior status as a framing device in his tale of innocence. He represented telegraph boys as all-purpose servants about town, whom a respectable gentleman could call on at will. He pleaded for clemency on the grounds of his genteel lifestyle: having "been reared amidst every indulgence and luxury . . . penal servitude would mean death in a few years." He observed that "the crime for which I am sentenced has been very prevalent amongst the Telegraph lads and that many have been found out and dismissed in consequence and that the authorities were determined to prosecute me . . . as a warning to others."[60] He was right, but the pressure exerted by the state to convict him was enough to overrule the usual English legal requirements of corroboration. In correspondence after the trial, Smith's pleas for genteel immunity were dismissed out of hand. A. C. Hepburn, one of Stephenson's clerks at the Home Office, described the case as a collaborative state effort to "put a stop to such revolting practices [in the Telegraph Department] and to bring the principal offenders to justice. Their endeavours cannot fail to be materially assisted by the Conviction of Smith and Wright and the exemplary punishment inflicted on them."[61] In Smith's case the state creatively manipulated the law in its zeal to shut down the sexual networks proliferating from the GPO.

As it turned out, Stephenson's fears of publicity were unfounded. Other than short mentions in a few London newspapers, including the *Times,* Wright's occupation went unmentioned. The popular euphemism "unfit for publication" took the place of specifics of the sodomy charges, and the trial generated no widespread media attention.[62] The crime was presented as a singular occurrence, and the GPO's reputation remained intact for another twelve years.

George Wright was quietly released two years later; Smith, after three appeals to the Home Office, was released in 1896 for health reasons. More immediate aftereffects of the investigation were discernible in revised GPO labor policy. The GPO executive's reading of homosexual practices among its youthful staff led to new forms of spatial, sexual, and class discipline. Jeffery's recommendations for eliminating prostitution among telegraph messengers were followed almost to the letter, and the usually tight-fisted Treasury approved the additional expenditures (which Jeffrey estimated at £500 a year for the Chief Office alone) without complaint.[63]

There was one direct benefit for London telegraph messengers: a pay raise. The GPO estimated that a wage of seven shillings a week would suffice to stamp out homosexual licentiousness and entice the "better sort" of boy. To provide the telegraph boys with morally improving diversions, efforts were made to allow them access to postmen's libraries (often blocked by affronted postmen), and kitchens were nominally improved, or at least finally all provided with wholesome reading material. New regulations were also introduced. Boys no longer supervised other boys in London: new classes of inspector and matron were hired to monitor the messengers. Even thirty years later, when the next generation of officials suggested reinstating corporals among the senior telegraph boys in London, members of the old guard strenuously resisted, reiterating the damage that self-regulating boys could do to the capital's telegraph service.[64]

The postmaster general approved the establishment of a new class of inspectors devoted to investigating prospective telegraph boys' homes and references. This penetration of working-class homes by GPO officials coincided with the growth of state and philanthropic investigation into the homes and lives of the London poor.[65] These practices heralded the beginning of more direct interactions among government, philanthropists, and those whose neighborhoods were deemed deserving of elite attention. The Treasury absorbed most of the costs of the inspections, but disciplinary infractions now came at a price. Shortly after the new policies took effect, telegraph boys in London and across Britain could expect to be fined between twopence and sixpence for bad behavior. In Ireland, a telegraph boy's penalty "stamp" was displayed on his weekly wage chart, a visible marker of the disciplinary culture applied to even the youngest members of the British civil service.

Pubs and night duty were off limits for central London telegraph boys for the rest of the century. They faced the same sorts of restrictions on their behavior as those applied to respectable urban women, including the GPO's women telegraphists. Undoubtedly many telegraph boys (and women) ignored these missives, but in this instance fears of prostitution transcended gender divisions, and GPO policy left young men as suspect as women when it came to sexual danger and (mis)adventure.

Initially these policies affected only telegraph boys; however, they ushered in policies of internal and external surveillance that eventually extended throughout the GPO. Up to the 1876–77 investigation, the GPO had four constables who conducted investigations into post office irregularities. Other crimes committed by employees were left to the Metropolitan Police. In the wake of the Immorality report, the GPO police force expanded its personnel and its mandate. Two new constables were added to the payroll, and the force took up all manner of crimes involving GPO staff and miscreant postal consumers. As for Thomas Jeffery, he found the telegraph boy case so distressing that after submitting his report, he took four months' sick leave. On his return to work he was rewarded for his vigilance by being promoted to controller of the London Postal Service, with his assistant, John Philips, replacing him as head of the Missing Letter Branch.

Two different facets of the Victorian state, the GPO and the Home Office, collaborated to act quickly and decisively in containing immorality by throwing cash, inspectors, and a very loose interpretation of sodomy laws at the problem. The result was more comfortable working conditions but stricter discipline for telegraph boys, an increasingly draconian supervisory culture throughout the London GPO, and nineteen years' prison time for the scapegoat in the affair. The telegraph/rent boy was a liminal figure, positioned between public utility and state regulation, between market discipline and sexual subterfuge, between accessibility and discretion, and between high and low society. The forms of sexual bartering in which he was found to engage, the techno-moral regulation resulting from that discovery, and the legal system's reaction to it illuminate clandestine aspects of the telegraphic order of London life.

SIX

Tapped Wires

IN THE SUMMER OF 1889, the GPO's Confidential Enquiry Branch discovered that telegraph boys from London's Central Telegraph Office were selling sexual favors to elite men in a house of assignation at 19 Cleveland Street, a townhouse in Fitzrovia, just off Tottenham Court Road. The brothel's owner, Charles Hammond, had procured a supply of teenage messengers through various contacts at the GPO to service gentlemen who arrived at his house without an escort. Chief among Hammond's suppliers was Henry Newlove, a former telegraph boy who had recently been promoted to third-class clerk and "tracer" in the telegraph secretary's office. According to unpublished statements taken by GPO constables, at least four telegraph boys had admitted to sexual encounters with Newlove in the basement lavatories of the Central Telegraph Office. After a series of these clandestine hookups, Newlove had suggested to each of the boys that they could make money "going to bed with gentlemen" at 19 Cleveland Street. They took up his offer.

When GPO officials learned of the prostitution ring in July, Newlove was arrested. When questioned, he implicated some illustrious clients, including Lord Arthur Somerset, the son of the Duke of Beaufort and equerry to the Prince of Wales. The revelation set off a chain of events that led to the public exposure of one of London's most secretive cross-class social networks.

As details of the confidential investigation leaked out, scandalized commentators in the liberal press interpreted these sexual acts as vestiges of ancien régime debauchery forced upon respectable civil servants (the youths' lavatory encounters went unmentioned in the coverage). The Cleveland Street or "West End" scandal generated three trials and countless headlines in the fall and winter of 1889, finally winding down in the spring of 1890. The scandal resulted in Somerset's permanent exile and jail time for one of his lawyers, Newlove, an additional Cleveland Street procurer, and the radical journalist Ernest Parke, who publicly accused the Earl of Euston of being another Cleveland Street client and lost the ensuing libel trial. The telegraph boys were dismissed but weathered the storm relatively well, depicted as innocent victims sacrificed to rich men's vices.

The cast of characters in the Cleveland Street scandal—aristocrats, radicals, MPs, and telegraph boys—were actors in a showdown between the radical liberal press and the Conservative government.[1] Media accusations based on leaked police reports became the subject of parliamentary debate when the radical Liberal MP Henry Labouchère accused the Tory administration of covering up for Somerset. No more leaked information was published, and gross indecency committed by debauched aristocrats became news again only in 1895, when Oscar Wilde's own disastrous libel trial led to his incarceration.

This chapter explores two crucial aspects of the scandal that much excellent scholarship has nonetheless largely overlooked: the manner in which the Cleveland Street brothel was discovered, and the telegraph boys' contribution to both the narrative contours of the scandal and to subsequent public depictions of sex between men. The scandal resulted from an extensive network of information monitoring in the capital. The exposure of 19 Cleveland Street testifies to the emergence of new forms of communications policing and their consequences for the balance of power between competing authorities. On a broader level, it represents a shift in the state's vision of public and private realms, and the extent to which the latter could be intruded upon for the public good.

Existing literature tends to suggest a unified state response, obscuring the fact that it was GPO constables, not the Metropolitan Police, who discovered the house of assignation at 19 Cleveland Street. Distinguishing the GPO police from the Met and other security forces reveals a sophisticated network of postal administrators, constables, and agents who exposed the brothel and its patrons.

The Confidential Enquiry Branch of the GPO was a recent innovation. The GPO had been steadily expanding its internal police force since 1877, when the discovery of widespread prostitution among telegraph boys and attendant conflicts with the Metropolitan Police had prompted substantial administrative attention and more rigorous monitoring of both postal employees and the information transferred through postal networks. The GPO's concerns about telegraph boys grew to encompass other London insurgencies, namely militant Irish anti-imperialism and union activity among post office workers. Its increased vigilance came full circle with the discovery of the activities at Cleveland Street, and its revelations amplified inherent tensions between Victorian doctrines of freedom and discretion, and state-controlled information services.

When the details of the Cleveland Street investigation were published in the *North London Press,* a radical liberal newspaper, they reaffirmed powerful narrative tropes about the degenerative effects of aristocratic power and corruption. They also dramatized the role of a mushrooming communications infrastructure in the surveillance of Victorian London's political and sexual cultures. The telegraph boys involved—and their clients—were the targets of a more watchful GPO. Furthermore, the Cleveland Street scandal's most compelling narrative, that of innocents corrupted by depraved aristocrats, located "vice" in select social actors, thus reaffirming the telegraph boys' normative masculinity and aspirations to respectability, and their employers' positive associations with the modern city. London itself was a character in this drama. The label "West End scandal" neatly alluded to a part of the city where such illicit activities were widely believed to occur.[2]

In the many twists and turns of the narrative, the telegraph boys tended to drift to the background. But this is largely the result of how the press, the legal system, and the general public chose to see them.[3] As Morris Kaplan observes, the radical and liberal papers railed against the Conservative government's putting debauched aristocrats and peers above the law. A recurring theme in the chorus of condemnation was that these privileged individuals had corrupted respectable innocents.[4] The judges and lawyers presiding over the numerous hearings, depositions, and court cases related to Cleveland Street also tended to vindicate the telegraph boys, granting them amnesty from the Criminal Law Amendment Act. Even in the House of Commons, the telegraph boys remained "more sinned against than sinning."[5] The telegraph boys were never called "beasts" or "wretches." Accusations of homoerotic vice were directed toward the brothel agents—including Jack Saul, the flamboyant professional "Maryanne" who testified at one of the trials—and "My Lord Gomorrah" Arthur Somerset, whose decision to flee England amounted to an admission of guilt in the eyes of the public.[6]

The Cleveland Street scandal occurred at the end of a decade punctuated by media events linking disreputable sexual markets to class politics. The *Pall Mall Gazette*'s 1885 series of articles titled *Maiden Tribute of Modern Babylon,* which portrayed innocent working-class girls as victims of a morally bankrupt, sexually insatiable aristocracy, anticipated some of the features of the Cleveland Street press coverage. Kaplan has highlighted these dynamics, arguing that "respectable" working-class telegraph boys were caught up in middle-class attacks on "both upper-class decadence and lower-class brutish-ness." Aristocrats were "portrayed as preying on the sons of working-class families eager to improve their lot." The cultural potency of young, uni-formed state employees as victims resulted in insinuations that "their cor-rupters posed a threat to the nation itself."[7]

Since 1877 the GPO had worked hard to cultivate the image of the respect-able telegraph boy, one whose sexual corruption could pose a threat to the nation.[8] By 1889, the idea of telegraph boys as willful sexual agents had become incompatible with their public role as symbols of efficient modern technology and state-sponsored "improvement." When journalists and poli-ticians used the West End scandal to attack the Conservative government (and the monarchy; Somerset was also a member of the royal household), they mobilized a narrative that positioned the telegraph boys as unknowing, passive working-class victims.

Although the telegraph boys involved in the scandal escaped censure for sexual depravity, they nonetheless served as "corrupting" agents in their own right, by undermining assumptions about the security of information trans-mission between consumer and worker. Their public betrayal of aristocratic indiscretions challenged one of the basic tenets of GPO practices: the per-formance of privacy. By conflating different forms of service, informational and sexual, they broke down carefully constructed Victorian boundaries between displays of free intercourse and private discretion. They destabilized relationships between elites and personal service providers, with momentous consequences. By tearing down the veils of secrecy surrounding Cleveland Street, telegraph boys' revelations made manifest London's sexual under-ground. They united both high and low society in disreputable acts and revealed processes counter to the civilizing goals of orderly urban communi-cations. The force of this betrayal resulted in both a public spectacle that unraveled some individuals' lives and a reconfiguration of GPO policy that spurred increasingly authoritarian approaches to the management of these young, unruly communications workers.

THE RISE OF GPO POLICING IN LONDON

The Cleveland Street revelations emerged during a decade of renegotiations of the role of government in the monitoring of public and private spaces and communications. Histories of the post office tend to mark the 1880s as a golden age when telegram delivery costs decreased, GPO services expanded, and labor relations improved, mostly thanks to the progressive leadership of Henry Fawcett.[9] But these developments were accompanied by the exponential growth of clandestine monitoring operations. The post office, that seemingly benign juggernaut, had a crucial role to play in quietly renegotiating tradeoffs between the public interest and the privacy of communications.

After fractious interactions with the Metropolitan Police over the 1876–1877 telegraph boy immorality investigation, the staff of the Missing Letter Branch was increased from fifteen to twenty. In 1883 it was renamed the Confidential Enquiry Branch (CEB), reorganized, and placed under the leadership of an upper-class civil servant. By 1889, the CEB had over eighty staff members, including fifteen plainclothes policemen.[10]

The unit's executive clout and new name reflected its greater importance and broader remit. On one level, these changes mirrored the expanded role and services of the GPO, which was now responsible for many things other than letters and telegrams, including money orders and savings bank deposits. In 1883 the GPO took over the parcel post and became responsible for the delivery of all kinds of goods.[11]

The GPO acquired the parcel post at a moment when dynamite, invented in the 1860s by the Swedish chemist Alfred Nobel, was becoming an attractive weapon for Irish American Fenians plotting to defy British imperialism by force. Blowing up state infrastructure, symbolic monuments, and key citizens in the name of emancipation was hardly a new concept in London, but dynamite was much easier and safer to transport than gunpowder, and small quantities could do significant damage.

The Fenian "dynamite war" from 1882 to January 1885 had flare-ups in Glasgow, Birmingham, and Liverpool, but most of the action occurred in London. The "dynamitards" caused explosions in Whitehall, Scotland Yard, St James's Square, the Palace of Westminster, and the Tower of London, and they almost destroyed the *Times* head office in 1883. In 1884 three men were killed attempting to blow up London Bridge. Authorities discovered bombs in many other locations, including the base of Nelson's Column in Trafalgar Square. The bombers also attacked London transportation hubs. They threw explosives off moving trains near Charing Cross and Praed Street (now Paddington) Stations on October 30, 1883. The explosions injured many passengers and severely damaged trains, tunnels, and underground telegraph wires. On February 26, 1884, a time bomb detonated in the Victoria Station luggage room. Frantic searches at metropolitan railway termini revealed three more bombs at Charing Cross, Praed Street, and Ludgate Hill. Almost a year later, one of the last Fenian bombs exploded on an Underground train heading into Gower Street Station.[12]

Anxious GPO administrators perceived that communications infrastructure was a likely Fenian target. Just as the subway system embodied London's mastery of urban mobility, the movement of information and goods was central to London's position and function as imperial capital. The city's ubiquitous letterboxes and telegraph lines were often damaged in the bomb campaigns, but officials mainly worried about a direct hit on one of the post offices, especially the GPO's headquarters at St Martin's-le-Grand, by now a complex of imposing buildings with a massive new office under construction. A bomb there would have wreaked havoc on the flow and perceived security of British communications.

To defend against such an attack, GPO administrators took steps to militarize the service. They increased the number of guards at post offices and expanded the Confidential Enquiry Branch. The Post Office Rifles, a volunteer London regiment created in response to an earlier Irish bomb in 1867, also grew substantially, and another unit, the Field Telegraph Corps, was established. These volunteer units drilled together in London, and their members were stationed around St Martin's-le-Grand and the chief district offices. In one instance they mustered inside the original post office headquarters itself, determined, as Frederick Baines later put it, "to defend the old building, if need were, to the bitter end."[13] They provided support for the Metropolitan Police constables and members of the armed forces who were sent to patrol areas of London deemed likely Fenian targets, such as Buckingham Palace and the Albert Memorial. (Many members of the Post Office Rifles who entered the service to protect London soon found themselves defending British interests in Egypt and the Sudan, as African insurgents joined the attack on the imperial order in the 1880s.)

The nascent British secret police forces and the Special Branch of the London Metropolitan Police came into existence largely in response to the Fenian threat.[14] During the 1880s the post office ramped up its efforts to intercept and censor potentially dangerous information and collaborated with these undercover agencies. The GPO obliquely acknowledged this role as early as 1881, when Irish Nationalist MPs questioned Fawcett over suspicions that their private mail and telegrams were being intercepted and sent to "designated offices" for inspection. Fawcett replied that no such offices existed, and that only a warrant from a secretary of state permitted the opening of correspondence. In such a case the secretary of state "makes such arrangements as he may think that best to give effect to the warrant."[15] This was a technically accurate statement. The GPO did not have designated offices for spying on communications, but the law allowed flexibility when the state deemed private communication a public threat, and opening mail and telegrams was within the mandate of the Confidential Enquiry Branch. Various sources indicate that some Irish nationalists, Home Rule supporters, and Fenian sympathizers, including MPs, had their correspondence inspected during the 1880s and later. The remaining evidence of letter monitoring for other seditious activity (and for obscenity) indicates that GPO controllers flagged certain senders and recipients, whose mail was passed on to members of the executive for inspection. If intercepted communication was deemed prosecutable, GPO officials contacted a secretary of state (usually but not always the home secretary), who signed a backdated warrant for the inspection.[16]

The suggestion in Parliament that the GPO was violating the core liberal value of privacy did not raise widespread indignation, as it had done in 1844 when the home secretary eventually admitted to intercepting Italian nationalists' letters.[17] Many residents of cities throughout Britain were willing to mollify their hatred of "Continental" policing in order to stamp out the Fenian dynamite threat.[18] Then again, most people were unaware that the underground organs of state security were growing fast or that the GPO's policing department had more than tripled in size during the 1880s.[19] As the post office's services expanded, its role in censorship and monitoring communications went largely unnoticed.

TELEGRAPH BOY SPECTACLES

Like the GPO's security services, its telegraph system expanded significantly in the 1880s. Thirty-three million messages were sent in 1885.[20] When sixpenny telegram rates were introduced that same year, the number of dispatches increased, and in 1892 seventy million telegrams were sent to, from, and within Great Britain.[21] In 1895, London messengers carried up to twenty thousand telegrams a day.[22] Until usage declined with the advent of telephones, the telegraph was a top administrative priority. Contemporary accounts of receiving telegrams reveal a dash of nostalgia: "In the early days of the electric telegraph the receipt of a message by wire was an important event. . . . Now messages of this kind are familiar to most persons, and the excitement of bygone times has ceased to show itself when a telegraph messenger is seen to approach the door."[23] Even so, receiving a telegram was a rare occurrence for those below the ranks of bourgeois information consumers.

By 1889 approximately 2,500 telegraph boys traversed the London streets, providing the vital link between the technology and its users.[24] Their wages and working conditions had improved since 1877, and official correspondence indicates that administrators were pleased with the influx of a "better class" of boy. In the 1880s officials instituted musical bands, sports teams, and after-work classes for the telegraph boys. In the spring of 1889, the Telegraph Messenger Institute was established in London to provide them with after-hours schooling and a social club. This was the brainchild of Sir Stevenson Arthur Blackwood, secretary for the GPO from 1880 to 1893, whose devout evangelicalism was increasingly brought to bear on the leisure activities of the telegraph boys.[25] Messengers received rudimentary schooling and attended lectures on cleanliness, morality, and good living, along with dictates praising the latest GPO policies.[26] The London press reported favorably on the institute and other improving programs for the telegraph boys, which bolstered the boys' image as worthwhile investments for the continued expansion and improvement of information services.

Some administrators still viewed London telegraph boys with unease. In 1880 Thomas Jeffery, controller of the London Post Office and former head of the Missing Letter Branch, remarked in a memo to Blackwood that the current London sorters and postmen, who for the most part were former telegraph boys, had "deteriorated very much from the type of men brought into the service twenty-five or even twenty years ago." Jeffery saw London's social environment as largely responsible for this change, as most of the old "type of men . . . came up from the Country, with a fine physical constitution, somewhat blunt in manners, though sound in morals." The newer recruits were "London boys," whose dwellings, family supervision, and leisure pursuits were often "far from satisfactory."[27] Jeffery's old concerns about insufficient supervision of telegraph boys and unhealthy environments had not quite dissipated. And he voiced a new anxiety about their physical degeneration, which went hand in hand with the lax morals of "puny-looking" city boys.[28]

Jeffery and Blackwood's investment in the recruitment and moral education of telegraph boys was partly prompted by watching many former telegraph boys become postmen eager to unionize. The 1880s had begun with some improvements for postal workers. Before his death in 1884, Fawcett had listened to delegations from workers and enacted wage increases and other concessions for postmen, sorters, and telegraphists. Many postal workers posthumously hailed Fawcett as a hero of their cause: London sorters named their workers' association after him, mainly because of a popular myth that Fawcett had intended to promote them to the same grade as telegraphists. (Male telegraphists responded to this myth by forming the PTCA, whose main goal was to maintain telegraphists' superiority over sorters.) Worker optimism quickly waned under Fawcett's successors, especially the Tory appointee Henry Cecil Raikes, whose indifference to workers' grievances, overt hostility to trade unions, and authoritarian style of administration pushed postmen to look for outside assistance in their attempt to organize. Management, often using Confidential Enquiry Branch agents, kept a watchful eye on these efforts, and key organizers occasionally found themselves demoted or dismissed.[29]

As the GPO became more interventionist in the name of security, as fears about the physical and moral soundness of its urban workforce crept into official memoranda, and as sorters, postmen, and telegraphists created associations, its administrators increasingly drew on military terminology. One senior GPO official declared: "The army of the 130,000 Post-Office servants, established and auxiliary, scattered over the face of the land must be as exact and well ordered as would be an army in the field in fine condition and perfect discipline."[30] In a speech to his senior administrators, Raikes perceived himself as a field marshal: "Talk of armies. . . . The number of officers of whom I may say I am for the time being Commander-in-Chief are more numerous than any regular forces which the Secretary of State for War can show within the compass of Her Majesty's dominions."[31] Frederick Baines's vivid recollections of the GPO instrument galleries also evoked images of warfare: "The noisy hum of a thousand telegraphs in full operation salutes the ear. Busy clerks fill the vast saloons. Swift messengers flit to and fro; house-tubes at work from one part to another sustain a continual popping, as of the distant fire of some line of skirmishes."[32] The GPO's devotion to military metaphors and discipline was both a strategy and an effect of an increasingly self-conscious imperialist posture in the metropole.

What employees made of this language is unclear. Doubtless many telegraph boys found aspects of these descriptions appealing. Indeed, throughout the 1880s military-style bands for telegraph boys expanded, and some offices even organized enthusiastic telegraph boys into volunteer drilling and marching corps—the youth cadet wing of the Post Office Rifles. But even a cursory overview of literature for boys reveals distinct tensions between this ideal of state-sanctioned youthful masculinity and other modes of boyish identifications. An anonymous contributor to the *Boy's Own Paper*, "reminiscing about his days "in her Majesty's Service" as a telegraph boy, identified mostly with the uniform:

> I had often sighed for the uniform of a midshipman or a drummer, and when I found that the first was too expensive for my parents to provide, and that I was ignorant of the modus operandi of gaining the second, I turned my thoughts to the less ambitious garb of the telegraph boy. To wear that I should neither have to face either the storms of the deep or the "chaff" of the barracks; and it must be confessed that neither of these was specially attractive. It was only the uniform I vainly wished to don.[33]

While proudly conscious of his service to queen and country, this narrator identifies a dissonance between uniform and representation. His "sighing" over uniforms and the status they conveyed did not extend to the duties associated with military service or the rough "chaff" of the barracks.

In another story, published in *Young England*, "My Last Scrape," the uniform has different significations. The narrator remembers a schoolyard argument that was interrupted by the disconcerting sight of a telegraph boy:

> That was the first time that one of the new telegraph boys had appeared within our boundaries, and we all hurried off to inspect him, presently crowding round him, hooting at and hustling him, snatching off his cap, and even going so far as to lay hands on the pouch in which he carried those important dispatches of his. Vainly endeavouring to maintain his official dignity amid our turbulence, the Ganymede of the post office pushed on through the mob.[34]

Here the uniform is a subject of derision and fear, a target of "mob" violence when it intrudes on the boys' play space.

The reference to a "Ganymede of the post office" reminds us of telegraph boys' more subversive associations. The messenger uniform continued to hold an attraction for middle- and upper-class men in London's homoerotic subcultures. The Uranian poets of the fin-de-siècle, who "worshipped youth, spoke of the transience of boyhood, and delighted in breaking class barriers," praised the physical virtues of telegraph boys.[35] John Gambril Nicholson admired "the lad that's lettered G.P.O.," and Philebus (John Barford) complained that "these young modern Mercuries never wait[ed] long enough at the house where they are delivering a message."[36] Contrary to GPO administrators' intentions, public displays, parades, and drilling likely enhanced telegraph boys' image among London's queer subcultures.

The telegraph boy's status as a militarized yet youthful object of elite homoerotic desire put him at a crossroads between the modern metropolis and the old city of decadence and corruption. The broad thoroughfares of 1880s London, under whose foundations lay networks of pneumatic tubes (not to mention the new underground railways) were also paths leading into the city's labyrinth of mystery, vice, and secret pleasures.[37] Telegraph boys also stood at the intersection of different authoritative regimes: the GPO project of orderly state communications was at odds with the sexual desires of aristocrats, and these two groups vied for control over telegraph boys, both in and out of their uniforms. The journey from St Martin's-le-Grand to Cleveland Street crossed imaginary landscapes that created an unbridgeable divide between the telegraph boys' actions and their public image.

To maintain public trust, in the 1880s GPO officials strove to present its workers as soldiers: hard-working and completely subject to the discipline of the state. Writers and journalists reproduced this GPO image, particularly in the fictions and documentary articles in boys' magazines, but also in press coverage. In their portrayals, telegraph boys personified the speed, noise, and interactions of city life.

As icons of progress and urban celebration, telegraph boys were incompatible with labyrinthine sexual underworlds; their military-style uniforms of blue with scarlet piping made them a highly visible part of the landscape. Public exposure of the messengers' sexual dalliances in the basement lavatories at telegraph headquarters and in a Cleveland Street brothel posed a quandary to those who invested telegraph boys with symbolic meaning, the more so because in 1889 the GPO was engaged in the delicate balancing act of ensuring citizens' privacy while opening mail and tapping wires in the name of state security. The GPO was highly motivated to distance itself from the boys' acts; luckily, almost everyone else also resisted the association of male prostitution with the GPO workforce. To see telegraph boys as both physical manifestations of progress and degenerate sodomites proved too contradictory. Radical journalists, the courts, and politicians responded to this narrative incompatibility by suppressing and modifying the evidence of the telegraph boys' indiscretions. The differences between police reports and press, legal, and political representations of the scandal make clear the cultural investments in London's telegraph boys, homoerotic subcultures, aristocratic power, and state regulation in the modern city.

CLEVELAND STREET: FROM GPO
INVESTIGATION TO MEDIA SCANDAL

The police documentation held in the Cleveland Street dossier at the National Archives highlights the discrepancies between the admissions made by telegraph boys involved in the scandal and the media reports. Settings and dialogue shift between the two versions; costumes change significance; and practices are manipulated and erased. At stake in these differing accounts is the moral of the story.

The investigation began on Thursday, July 4, 1889. One of the Confidential Enquiry Branch's numerous constables had closed in on a prime suspect: according to an internal investigation, small amounts of money had gone missing from an office in the receiver general's department on the second floor of the Central Telegraph Station. The regular spot-checks and inspections of telegraph staff were increased. When Charles Swinscow, a fifteen-year-old indoor telegraph messenger, was frisked and discovered with eighteen shillings—three times his weekly salary—in his pocket, GPO authorities assumed they had an open-and-shut case.[38] Swinscow's movements would have been carefully tracked as he ran a constant stream of messages from one part of the building to another. His breaks would have been short and time spent with other telegraph boys limited.

GPO Constable Luke Hanks interrogated Swinscow, who insisted he had earned the money by "doing some private work away from the office." The notes on the interrogation then read as follows:

HANKS: For whom?

SWINSCOW: For a gentleman named Hammond.

HANKS: Where does he live?

SWINSCOW: At 19 Cleveland Street near Middlesex Hospital.

HANKS: What kind of work did you do for him?

SWINSCOW: Will I get into any trouble if I tell you?

HANKS: I cannot say.

SWINSCOW: Must I tell you?

HANKS: Certainly.

SWINSCOW: I will tell you the truth. I got the money for Mr. Hammond for going to bed with gentlemen at his house.[39]

Hanks immediately left Swinscow and reported this information to his supervisor, John Philips, no stranger to telegraph boy rent.[40] Evidently Philips told Hanks to get as much information as possible out of Swinscow in a written statement. In Hanks's presence Swinscow wrote that he had "made the acquaintance" of another former telegraph messenger, Henry Newlove, a few months previously. They had gone "into the lavatory at the basement of the Post Office building . . . went into one water closet and shut the door and . . . behaved indecently together."[41] The basement of the Central Telegraph Office is worth describing: according to Frederick Baines, it was filled with "powerful steam-engines and boilers, vacuum chambers and cylinders of compressed air, all used in working the . . . pneumatic tubes." These machines were "constantly at work compressing air into one chamber and exhausting it from another, so driving or sucking . . . messages through the leaden pipes which . . . are laid from the Post-Office."[42] Aside from providing a spectacular sensory backdrop for all the "indecent behaviour" going on, this passage reveals that Swinscow and Newlove's sexual interactions literally took place next to the beating heart of London's telegraph network.

After a week of clandestine rendezvous, Swinscow recounted, he and Newlove were once again together in the basement lavatories when Newlove suggested that Swinscow come with him to 19 Cleveland Street, where "you'll go to bed with gentlemen, you'll get four shillings each time." Swinscow then described meeting Charles Hammond, the proprietor of the house, going "into the bed" with a gentleman in the back parlor of 19 Cleveland Street, and receiving a sovereign for his services. He passed this on to Hammond, who paid him four shillings.[43]

Pressed by Hanks, Swinscow dropped more names: fellow telegraph messengers George Alma Wright (no apparent relation to the George Wright convicted of similar offenses twelve years earlier) and Charles Earnest Thickbroom, who were both seventeen. They were immediately brought before Hanks in the Central Telegraph Office's interrogation room and ordered to produce statements. Wright confessed to his own lavatory encounters with Newlove, which had also culminated in Newlove's suggestion to go to Cleveland Street. Wright described going to the house once and having sex with a "rather foreign looking chap" and getting four shillings from Hammond. Later Newlove had asked Wright to find another "nice little boy" who was "younger and shorter" and would go to Cleveland Street, and Wright introduced him to Thickbroom.[44] Thickbroom denied being interested until the four shillings were mentioned. From that point his statement reads like the others: he and a gentleman "got into bed and played with each other," and Hammond paid him four shillings out of the half-sovereign he had received.[45] Thickbroom returned to the house on another occasion, with the same result.

Next Henry Newlove was brought before Constable Hanks. The nineteen-year-old third-class clerk and "tracer" was a rarity, as almost all London telegraph boys became either postmen or sorters.[46] Newlove must have had unique appeal, which made his role as Cleveland Street procurer especially troubling for administrators. Hanks read the other boys' statements to Newlove, who confirmed their accuracy. All four were then suspended, told to hand in their uniforms, and sent home.

Describing an individual's dress was standard police procedure at this time, but in his report, Hanks was particularly attentive to the question of uniforms. He had demanded that the boys write down their state of dress at Cleveland Street: Swinscow had changed out of his uniform before going to Cleveland Street; Wright was not in uniform "except for the trousers";[47] Thickbroom had been in full uniform on both occasions. The GPO's recent increase in both its fiscal and social investment in telegraph boy uniforms was evident, if implicit, in Hanks's officiousness.

All this information about uniforms, assignations, and networks of commercial sex was duly collected by the Confidential Enquiry Branch, which reported it directly to the postmaster general. Raikes immediately contacted the Metropolitan Police commissioner, and the case was given as a priority assignment to Inspector Frederick G. Abberline (well-known thanks to his supervision of the Jack the Ripper case and also technically still in charge of the Whitechapel murders), who quickly granted arrest warrants for Newlove and Hammond.[48] Abberline went to arrest Hammond at 19 Cleveland Street on Sunday morning (July 7), but Hammond had been tipped off two days earlier by Newlove and was lying low at a relative's house in Gravesend. (He left the country shortly thereafter, and spent his time on the Continent shadowed by John Philips, who received special funding for the assignment through the Confidential Enquiry Branch.)[49] Meanwhile, Hanks headed to Camden Town and arrested Newlove at his mother's house on Bayham Street.

Hanks reported that when he walked Newlove to the police station, Newlove vented his frustration that another post office employee, "Hewett," had gotten away while he hadn't. Hanks's report then notes, "He said to me, 'I think it very hard that I should get into trouble while men in high position are allowed to walk around free.' I said 'What do you mean?' and he replied 'Why, Lord Arthur Somerset goes regularly to the house at Cleveland Street, so does the Earl of Euston and Colonel Jervois.'"[50]

GPO authorities responded to Newlove's statement by rounding up the other telegraph boys and taking them to Lord Somerset's various London haunts in order to get positive identifications from them. The telegraph boys were then called on to give information to both Met and Confidential Enquiry Branch detectives. They were also visited by Arthur Somerset's lawyers, who offered each of them £50 and new clothes if they immediately left for Australia. Some of the telegraph boys tipped off GPO constables about this offer, and Arthur Newton, Somerset's solicitor, was duly charged with conspiracy and obstruction of justice.

Back at the GPO, there was concern that Newlove, Swinscow, and the others were part of a much larger GPO sex market centered on Cleveland Street. On July 18, Inspector Abberline submitted a report based on information from his subordinates at Scotland Yard: "Although at the present stage of the case (until Hammond is arrested) I have not deemed it prudent to interrogate other boys at the Post Office, I have every reason to believe that a large number have been defiled at this house."[51] The report further noted that the boys were "very deficient in knowledge of simple things that surprised me. . . . I came to the conclusion that they were ignorant of the crimes they committed with other persons."[52] Although Swinscow, Wright, Thickbroom, and another telegraph boy, George Perkins, likely tried to convince the police of their innocence, they may also have had a very different understanding of homoerotic practices than did their middle-class interrogators. In the 1876–77 investigation, Thomas Jeffery had surmised that the boys "had no liking for the vice, as a vice." But in this instance, the telegraph boys' "deficiency" of sexual knowledge—their inability or refusal to acknowledge they had committed vice at all, according to the standards of their interrogators— suggests that homoerotic behavior was not a particularly reviled activity among telegraph boys. Statements such as "He put his person between my legs and an emission took place," "We got into bed quite naked. He told me to suck him," "I put my person into his hindparts. I could not get it in, though I tried and emitted" provided vivid evidence for the prosecution of Cleveland

Street's patrons, but police were shocked by the boys' nonchalance when describing these sexual encounters.[53] Regardless, these interviews stand as proof of the telegraph boys' sexual relationships and of their rebelliousness against both GPO control and officials' standards of sexual behavior.

MY LORD GOMORRAH'S DEN OF VICE

Exposure of the moral failings of telegraph boys represented a breakdown in the GPO's system of indoctrination and provoked anxieties about the entire enterprise of civic improvement. Equally serious for authorities, by naming names, telegraph boys had disclosed secret information and undermined networks of elite respectability. Fortunately for the GPO, a number of factors intervened to protect its faulty system from exposure. The progression of the Cleveland Street affair from an internal GPO investigation into a protracted newspaper scandal targeting aristocratic vice was mainly due to the narrative conventions available to commentators and the manner in which the crimes of Cleveland Street were prosecuted.

Once the Metropolitan Police informed the Department of Special Prosecutions at Whitehall that Lord Alfred Somerset and Henry Fitzroy, Earl of Euston, had been named as clients of the Cleveland Street brothel, Tory officials engaged in a flurry of communications, coded reports, and avoidance of responsibility. By late September, the consequent bureaucratic delays, combined with growing rumors and gossip in London's elite clubs regarding 19 Cleveland Street's patrons, generated accusations of government corruption in the liberal and radical press. By late November, thanks to Ernest Parke, the "West End Scandals" had become news across the country and the world. Parke had received insider information concerning the investigation from either GPO constables or the Metropolitan Police, who had been frustrated that the Department of Public Prosecutions and the Treasury had effectively stalled the case against Somerset.[54] Parke fumed that " it was a scandal and disgrace that these things should be ... [that] the poor and the humble should have the barest measure of mercy meted out to them, whilst if only a man be a peer ... if he does not evade punishment altogether, it is made as light for him as it is possible to make it."[55] The perpetrators of these "horrible" and "repulsive" crimes were rich and powerful men; the victims were innocent telegraph boys.

This narrative meshed with accounts that championed telegraph boys as paragons of working-class virtue and "fleet-footed, sharp-eyed" Mercuries of modern London. At worst, their youth and class status might make them careless or inefficient, but they were never portrayed as corrupt.[56] Cast as heroes in stories of technological innovation and state power, they became figures of pathos when radical and liberal pundits accused Conservative policies of favoring the aristocracy over telegraph boys.

The journalists who pursued the scandal were selective about disclosing the details of how the Cleveland Street brothel and its patrons were discovered, as they were intent on placing the blame for sexual misdeeds and unfair treatment squarely on a morally retrograde aristocracy undeserving of its privilege. W. T. Stead, the *Pall Mall Gazette*'s famous editor, was the first journalist to reference confidential information from the investigation: the day after Newlove's final hearing at Marlborough Street Police Court—a week before his sentencing at the Old Bailey—Stead mused, "The question Sir Augustus Stephenson [now Treasury solicitor and director of public prosecutions] will have to answer is whether the two noble lords and other notable persons in society who were accused by witnesses . . . are to be allowed to escape scot free."[57] Later on, in an article titled "A Little Child Shall Lead Them," Stead portrayed telegraph boys as vulnerable wards of the state:

> Here is our own Government . . . what have they done to protect their own telegraph boys? Mr. Raikes is Postmaster General. But not even his position could secure the prompt exposure of the criminals. The protection of the telegraph boys did not count beside the necessity of casting a shield over personages high in society.[58]

Stead portrayed the GPO (presided over by a Tory) as subordinate to forces of old corruption. To make this narrative culturally legible, he suppressed knowledge of the telegraph boys' sexual practices. This manipulation of police evidence was paradigmatic of other published accounts of the scandal.[59] Journalists reduced the boys' testimony to accusations against their aristocratic defilers. The presence—or partial absence— of uniforms during sex in a brothel represented an attack on modern order instead of a willful rejection (or reinterpretation) of the uniforms by their wearers. Perhaps most strikingly, the sites of "gross indecency" were reduced to one London vicinity. The press referred to "the Cleveland Street Scandal" and the "West End Scandal" interchangeably. Not once did headlines proclaim the "Post Office," "St Martin's-le-Grand," or "Telegraph Office Basement Lavatory" scandal. Cleveland Street was technically adjacent to the West End, but it was close enough to allude to the neighborhood's reputation for illicit sexual pleasures

"The West End Scandals, some further sketches," *Illustrated Police News*, December 4, 1889. With thanks to the British Newspaper Archive.

and buffer the GPO from further association.[60] Sex between men was not supposed to happen in the City; it was confined to the West, protecting St Martin's-le-Grand, and its employees, from disgrace.[61]

These narrative manipulations, which effectively vindicated the telegraph boys, were not limited to the media; although they were all over fourteen, the age of consent, Swinscow, Thickbroom, Wright, and Perkins were also innocent in the eyes of the law. They were eventually dismissed from the post office but never charged with gross indecency.

Thanks to the Criminal Law Amendment Act, Crown prosecutors had more powerful means to bring charges against the telegraph boys and their clients in 1889 than ever before, but in the boys' case they chose not to. It was the social status of some of the boys' sexual clients, rather than tricky issues of compromised witnesses, that obstructed the legal proceedings. Stephenson, the director of public prosecutions, attempted to convince the attorney general to approve a warrant for Somerset's arrest. His frustrated memorandum echoed his earlier concerns and outlined the necessity for proceeding against Somerset on the grounds of the moral corruption of youth:

> The circumstances of this case demand the intervention of those whose duty it is to enforce the law and protect the children of respectable parents taken into the service of the public, as these unfortunate boys have been, from being made the victims of the unnatural lusts of full-grown men—and no consideration of public scandal—owing to the position in society or sympathy with the family of the offender—should militate against this *paramount duty*.[62]

For Stephenson, Somerset's actions were as much an affront to "respectable" working-class parents as they were to the "unfortunate" boys—an emphasis missing from his 1877 opinion on telegraph boys' sexual antics. The GPO's cultivation of a "better class" of boy had proved effective, but these boys had been exposed to "unnatural" adult lust and may have been permanently tainted while in the GPO's employment.

Henry Labouchère demonstrated similar reasoning in the House of Commons on February 28, 1890: "Is there any man who will not feel indignant that boys employed in one of our public offices should be tempted into indecencies more gross than were ever committed under Louis XV?"[63] If the Cleveland Street Scandal's revelations were even more sordid than the worst excesses of absolutist *France,* then Britain surely must act to protect its public servants. In addition, Labouchère lauded the GPO's quick response to the charges: "Newlove would never have been prosecuted had it not been for the action of the Postmaster General and the Secretary of the Post Office. The matter occurred in the Post Office, and they . . . insisted that action should be taken in the matter."[64] Here Labouchère demonstrated access to more police information than the public had, but by not elaborating on the "matter" that occurred in the Post Office, he cast 19 Cleveland Street as the sole locus of vice. In his telling, the GPO remained a progressive institution above reproach, and Newlove's younger accomplices were left unblemished by the sex scandal. The boys' voluntary journeys from the City to Fitzrovia to have sex for pay were ignored.

Both prosecutors and defense lawyers in the subsequent hearings and trials likewise protected the telegraph boys' reputation. In the hearings for the trial of Somerset's lawyer, Arthur Newton, and in Ernest Parke's libel trial in January 1890, Newlove was the scapegoat for the other boys. The hearings for Newton's trial featured testimony from Thickbroom and Perkins, but as they were brought in only to describe the clandestine attempts of Newton's assistant to purchase their silence, prosecutors had no need to go into the details of their activities at Cleveland Street.[65]

The defense's decision not to use telegraph boys' testimony during Parke's trial was a stranger, more telling feature of the legal fallout from the scandal. Parke's lawyers relied almost exclusively on the testimony of Jack Saul, an aging prostitute whose "theatrical" behavior and defiance of convention led a defensive article in *Reynolds's Weekly* to call him a "filthy, loathsome, detestable beast."[66] Saul proved a disastrous witness. Even the most radical papers treated his testimony as unreliable, and Euston's reputation remained intact. Saul's description of picking up Euston and having sex with him at Cleveland Street did not sway the jury from believing Euston's account: he had gone to the house after receiving a card that advertised *"poses plastiques,"* and after realizing the true nature of the place had stormed out. *Poses plastiques* were erotic displays of women posing in revealing costumes, and Euston's story was plausible given Cleveland Street's location in a raffish district. It was not difficult to imagine that Euston had received erroneous information and been accidentally led to a den of even greater vice than he had sought.[67] In fact, Euston's story seemed to confirm ardent heteronormative desires, which fit nicely with his reputation as a sportsman and womanizer.[68] The jury was certainly convinced, and Parke ended up serving a year in prison.

It is unclear why Parke's lawyers relied on Jack Saul as their main witness. Parke's accusations were based on police statements collected from the telegraph boys, who could have been compelled to testify. Newlove had named Euston along with Somerset back in July, and if his word had been enough to convict Somerset, it might just as well have been used to implicate Euston. Scholars have noted the absence of credible testimony at Parke's trial and found it "a mystery." The explanation may lie in the cultural logic at work in protecting the telegraph boy.[69] By not calling on the boys to testify in the case, the court ensured that homosexual vice was contained in the figure of Saul.

Euston's victory against Parke finally allowed conservative commentators to respond to the scandal directly and in force. Previously, conservative-leaning papers had tended to stay away from the scandal or allude to it in code. The *Licensed Victualler,* for example, commented on Cleveland Street in fleeting references interspersed with other gossip: "I suppose the language of the eccentric swells is Telegraphese. An appropriate punishment would be to *boycott* them. . . . When the police visited Cleveland Street they got in by the back door."[70] The day after Euston's victory, however, the *Daily Telegraph* published a diatribe: "The condemnation of Parke to imprisonment for twelve calendar months prevents for that time, and perhaps for all future time, a foul-mouthed slanderer from inflicting any further injury on society and poisoning the very air we breathe."[71] The *Saturday Review* claimed that Parke "deserves as much mercy as a polecat. Nay, he deserves much less."[72] In the view of conservative commentators, it was Parke and his fellow radicals, not the aristocracy, who had plunged into the depths of London's depravity and associated with male brothels and Maryannes. Yet like their opponents, conservatives held telegraph boys above reproach. Only one paper ever cast direct aspersions on telegraph boys—by linking them to another scandal concerning an Irish aristocrat. In July 1890, the *Scots Observer*'s Tory journalist

Charles Whibley commented that Oscar Wilde's *Picture of Dorian Gray* was appropriate only for "outlawed noblemen and perverted telegraph boys."[73]

While radical liberal ideology certainly informed the narratives of the *North London Press, Reynolds's Weekly,* and the *Pall Mall Gazette,* even conservative papers and lawmakers were loath to point out that the telegraph boys of Cleveland Street were neither "innocents" nor repelled by the prospect of having sex with one another or with gentlemen while carrying out their duties. From what we can tell, the boys survived the scandal relatively unscathed. According to 1901 census records, Charles Swinscow, by then twenty-seven and a wine dealer, was living in Islington with his mother, siblings, new wife, and infant child.[74] Thickbroom also managed to thrive after Cleveland Street, and according to Colin Simpson, Lewis Chester, and David Leitch, his middle-class descendants "remember[ed] [him] with affection."[75] Newlove's fate is unknown.

In various narratives aimed at London readers, the telegraph boy represented late Victorian progressivism. This explains the almost universal decision of officialdom and the press to shield the telegraph boys from censure in the Cleveland Street scandal. They were the chosen sons of the aspiring working class and highly visible examples of the GPO's attempt to create obedient workers and citizens through quasi-military discipline and activities. Their ubiquitous presence signaled London's technological, economic, and imperial strength. That these same boys could also be social actors in an urban sexual underworld was a possibility untenable to all but those who participated in that underworld.

Attitudes toward telegraph boys demonstrate the extent to which class dynamics, state policy and politics, notions of urban landscapes, and experiences of communication systems combined to produce social meanings out of sexual acts. The telegraph boys functioned as buffers between normative and degenerative masculinity. Members of the press, the bench, Parliament, and officialdom mobilized powerful narratives of respectable manhood to protect telegraph boys from the stain of sexual deviancy, and this reaction stabilized and perpetuated the boys' iconic status within the GPO and beyond. The press narratives had a lasting influence on British notions of sexual norms and subversions, and the legal outcome of Cleveland Street set an important precedent for cases of gross indecency, including Oscar Wilde's famous trial. The scandal perpetuated the notion that homosexual vice was restricted to degenerate members of the aristocracy and an equally degenerate caste of Maryannes.

THE LEGACY OF CLEVELAND STREET
AT ST MARTIN'S-LE-GRAND

The Cleveland Street scandal demonstrated that in spite of all its efforts over the previous twelve years, the GPO had not purged male prostitution from its ranks. After some telegraph boys, supposedly of the "better sort," were once again caught servicing well-heeled men, not to mention having sex with each other on GPO premises, the executive resorted to two different tactics. To help ensure the moral rectitude of currently employed telegraph boys, the GPO increased the number of libraries, raised funds for the recently established Telegraph Messenger Institutes, and organized more music bands and sports leagues for the boys. However, entrance requirements for telegraph messengers were also enhanced and their apprenticeship status suspended. In November 1890, Raikes ended medical examinations for telegraph boys in anticipation of making them temporary rather than permanent employees. A year later, the policy became official. Telegraph boys were dismissed when they turned eighteen and could be hired back at the GPO only after four years' military service. Given what other scholarship has revealed to us about homoerotic cultures and the British military, the GPO's turn to enlistment as a solution to male prostitution was probably futile. But it demonstrates how seriously the GPO took the sexual infractions of its young workers.

Telegraph boys out on the job encountered a London more heavily policed than ever before. The telegrams they delivered were subject to increased censoring as part of the GPO's clandestine arrangements with the Special Branch and the Home Office. As for 19 Cleveland Street, its sexual notoriety was soon eclipsed by that of a house in Brighton. The house had been occupied by Katherine O'Shea and, as the public learned in November 1890, by her longtime lover, Charles Stuart Parnell, the parliamentary leader of the Irish Nationalists. O'Shea was married to another Irish MP, William O'Shea, and when their divorce case hit the press, Charles Parnell was disgraced. The Liberal Party leader William Gladstone, responding to (and probably agreeing with) outrage from liberal moralists, ended his association with Parnell, who was forced to resign as leader of the Irish Nationalist Party. His departure from the House of Commons allowed the divided Liberal Party to sidestep the issue of Irish home rule. The cause was shelved for another twenty-four years.

Parnell's disgrace and the Cleveland Street Scandal bear out Morris Kaplan's observation that "accusations of any kind of sexual irregularity could be political dynamite during the final decades of the nineteenth century in England."[76] The very real dynamite in Fenian bombs, along with urban sexual culture, high political intrigue, and information security all coalesced to produce a martial city. London's imperial power was tested, and various representatives of state power, not least the GPO, competed to stabilize urban rule. In the process, liberal principles begat authoritarian practices. The Cleveland Street scandal was a clash of liberal values: it was a victory of state-sponsored "public good" over a corrupting elite privilege resting on privacy, silence, and discretion. In this shifting legal, social, and moral landscape, young communications workers forged other kinds of service networks, uniting power, pleasure, work, and city spaces in dangerous ways.

SEVEN

Martial Mercuries

WHILE THE CLEVELAND STREET SCANDAL generated headlines, another alarming manifestation of telegraph boy misrule garnered administrative attention. In December 1889 Robert Tombs, the London postal service controller, sent a memorandum to the GPO secretary, Arthur Blackwood, bemoaning "common practice among the Boy Messengers to bend the peak of the uniform cap into such shapes as suited their fancy, and to wear the cap at the back of the head so as to show 'fringes' or 'curls.'" For Tombs, this gave "the boys a very unbecoming and in my mind disgraceful appearance in the Streets as indicating fastness."[1] The GPO had long struggled with double-edged adolescent "fastness." While Tombs's request for a less malleable messenger cap was denied, telegraph boys were subject to increasing administrative scrutiny through the fin-de-siècle and up to World War I. By 1914, London's telegraph boys were the GPO's most heavily subsidized and closely managed employees.

Tombs's heightened concern with appearances may have been exacerbated by the Cleveland Street scandal, but telegraph messengers' fast hairstyles were one of many problems facing Post Office administrators in the 1890s. London postmen had been organizing to assert their demands for better pay and working conditions, participating in clandestine meetings and taking advantage of developing trade union networks.[2] Administrators responded by targeting what they perceived to be the source of all their ills: London's unruly telegraph boys. They resorted to intensive discipline, even blurring the line between messenger service and military service, in order to both stamp out telegraph boys' promiscuity and prevent them from maturing into unionized postmen.

When this tactic proved unpopular for recruiting the "better sort" of telegraph boy, the GPO dispensed with forced military enlistment but maintained the trappings and practices of military discipline and experimented with a variety of extracurricular activities in its attempts to shape telegraph boys into a healthy, efficient, politically docile workforce. The volume of reports, committee hearings, testimonials, and internal memoranda concerning the GPO's boy messenger staff stood in inverse relation to their actual numbers, which peaked in London in 1897 at 3,200 and then declined to approximately 2,800 by 1914. Archival sources bear witness to a sea change in GPO policies governing telegraph boys, who became targets of educational and fitness schemes orchestrated by an increasingly interventionist state bureaucracy. This culminated in telegraph messengers' major role in the "boy labor crisis," which generated moral outrage and state investigation from 1905 to the onset of the Great War.

The increased attention paid to decreasing numbers of telegraph boys reflected the GPO's attempts to mold young male minds and bodies into a healthy, efficient, politically docile workforce. Their fortunes in the Edwardian period revealed larger shifts in British governance. As in the Cleveland Street Scandal, London's telegraph boys became test subjects for progressive and reactionary forces. However, these young workers' cultural significance extended in new directions. They were emblematic of a strident culture of military spectacle extending throughout urban Britain. Their increased presence in parades and barracks, wearing refurbished uniforms on bodies more carefully chiseled than ever before, was a manifestation of the extent to which telegraph boys had become a gauge of the health of the imperial nation. As the state increasingly assumed welfare responsibilities previously delegated to private philanthropy, telegraph boys were prominent emblems of this shift of power between reforming agents. By the beginning of the Great War, telegraph boys had fully transformed into symbolically resonant government wards, subject to compulsory schooling and fitness regimes throughout their messenger careers, then carefully absorbed into the GPO establishment on reaching adulthood. Mounting public pressure further galvanized officials to make their telegraph boys into successful long-term state employees. The right of guaranteed lifetime employment ultimately awarded to telegraph boys meant that during World War I they had to be replaced by telegraph girls, reversing fifty years of urban spatial policies of respectability and discretion the GPO had cultivated.

Just over a year after Charles Swinscow's fateful run-in with the GPO's Confidential Enquiry Branch detective triggered the Cleveland Street Scandal, London's postmen staged a walkout. Their strike on July 10, 1890, appeared self-defeating.[3] It lasted just a day, only a small proportion of the capital's postmen participated, those who did so were dismissed, and the rest of the letter-carrier staff saw no immediate concessions. Historians have stressed that while the strike itself was a bust, it was nonetheless part of a series of pressures exerted by GPO employees that eventually resulted in better pay and working conditions.[4] These improvements, however, were far from straightforward results of worker agitation, and they had contradictory effects for the telegraph boys who, on reaching adulthood, were London's main source of postmen.

For the postmen, higher wages and better conditions were arguably secondary to their demands for free assembly and recognition of their union.[5] In defiance of executive orders, London postmen and union delegates had been meeting in secret during late 1889 and the spring of 1890. Radical newspapers, including the *North London Press,* predicted that, inspired by the dockers' and match girls' strikes, the postmen would foment the next round of urban collective action.[6] The Postmen's Union (PU), formed that fall, rose to prominence. Although it never received official recognition, the PU did manage to secure an informal meeting with the GPO's third secretary, Herbert Joyce, who was concurrently acting as Henry Raikes's liaison with the Home Office concerning the Cleveland Street affair.[7]

When Joyce offered no concessions, the agitators resorted to more confrontational methods of negotiation. PU leaders organized a number of highly visible gatherings, inviting the public to both witness and participate in their grievances. In one instance PU union members announced an illegal meeting and its location by marching through the city streets to the beat of a postmen's band. Eight hundred postmen participated in London's first May Day celebration in Hyde Park. The PU also planned a march through the City on March 16 in an attempt to disrupt another Post Office Jubilee "conversazione" taking place at the Guildhall that evening.[8] The Metropolitan Police, the city commissioner, and the postmaster general responded by issuing a direct ban on the postmen's actions. In defiance, postmen formed smaller parades near district branch offices, all heading to an outdoor meeting at Clerkenwell Green. The uniformed participants were hounded most of the way by the Metropolitan Police.[9] The marches were disrupted several times, but 1,500 postmen eventually assembled.[10]

This action resulted in the suspension and demotion of eighty-nine postmen and marked the escalation of postmen's labor agitation and administrative repression. As outdoor meetings increased in frequency through May and June, so did violent scuffles, suspensions, and dismissals. The tension finally culminated on July 8: in preparation for strike action, GPO administrators called in auxiliary postal workers. Postmen violently clashed with the "blacklegs" at St Martin's-le-Grand and the Mount Pleasant office in Clerkenwell that morning and again on July 9 at Mount Pleasant, resulting in some injuries. That evening administrators offered concessions to the telegraphists and sorters if they refrained from joining the postmen. They also began proceedings for mass firings of postmen at the Mount Pleasant office, and they arranged for a large police contingent to surround St Martin's-le-Grand, Mount Pleasant, and other large post offices the following morning to quell unrest and prevent a walkout.

At around 4 a.m. on July 10, Blackwood ordered the dismissal of nearly one hundred postmen from Mount Pleasant. According to some newspaper accounts, those dismissed rallied outside the building until 8:30 a.m.; according to others, they promptly left en masse and began a march to St Martin's-le-Grand.[11] Their route to GPO headquarters, less than a mile away, wound around the Western Central and Eastern Central postal districts. Marchers called on postmen at other branches and those out on early delivery in the streets to join them; another hundred reportedly did so.[12] On reaching GPO headquarters they were dispersed by a mass of city police. According to journalists, the postmen continued to parade throughout the day, marching from Waterloo to London Bridge to call out more postmen. Meanwhile, news of the Mount Pleasant dismissals had spread rapidly, doubtless influencing the decision of the vast majority of postmen not to participate.

The conflicting news coverage is perhaps indicative of the postmen's success in appearing to occupy multiple city spaces at once: their disruption of the normal flows of the metropolitan streets reaffirmed their centrality to the maintenance of urban order. A few news articles mention that at some point that day the parading men were joined by another organized march consisting of around one hundred telegraph boys.[13] The messengers' participation in the strike is not remarked in administrative documentation, postal workers' association publications, or correspondence, but eyewitness accounts report telegraph messengers at Mark Lane in the City holding their own protest meeting the morning of the postmen's strike.[14] According to *the Daily News,* "A hundred telegraph messengers had expressed a wish to join the demonstration." Strike organizers advised them "only to strike in case they were ordered to perform the work of letter-carriers." But some defied both the postmen's wishes and GPO authority, flanking the postmen's parades for the rest of the day.[15]

Most of the London telegraph boys remarked on by the *Daily News* and others acquiesced in the GPO's strike-containment measures. In the Eastern District, telegraph messengers acted as temporary postmen. A journalist noticed this practice because it broke from a telegraph boy's usual solitary routine: "They were walking about in the district in batches of two and three, and carrying ordinary postmen's bags."[16] Telegraph boys, whether striking or obeying GPO orders, remained visual markers of urban information flows and disruptions.

The postmen's strike resulted in the dismissal of over four hundred postmen and "a number" of seditious telegraph boys.[17] Telegraphists indirectly benefited from the spectacle, and their aloofness from the strike reaffirmed the hierarchies of GPO work, with office work and proximity to private communication valued above outdoor work. By July 1891, however, the postmen themselves experienced some improvements, including the relaxation of rules regulating workers' assemblies.

These innovations were based on recommendations from a confidential internal GPO report whose findings were circulated to GPO and Treasury officials in November 1890 and published in 1891. The report, titled "Postmen: Their Duties and Pay," was also known as the report of the Joyce Committee, named after its busy chairman, Herbert Joyce, the GPO third secretary and the postmaster general's chosen deputy for managing discomfiting encounters. The Joyce Committee had accepted petitions from postmen across Britain advocating for higher pay, overtime rates, superannuation terms, shorter hours, improved promotion prospects, better-quality uniforms, and a separation of letter and parcel delivery. The report sanctioned higher pay for suburban London postmen, a boot allowance, the elimination of postmen's ranked wage levels, and higher overtime rates that applied to Sunday deliveries.

The report's second major set of findings, addressed in a section titled "The Recruiting Ground, or Source of Supply," identified telegraph boys as a major source of GPO demoralization. Although this issue had "not been referred" to the committee by postmen, the "question" of postmen's recruitment was "so intimately connected with the matter on which we have been called upon to report, and so seriously concerns the well-being of the Post Office, that we should have been wanting in our duty if we had omitted it from our consideration."[18]

Alan Clinton has argued that the Joyce Committee findings were a favorable response to the postmen's strike, but the report for administrators it represented a long-term approach to building a compliant workforce.[19] While it recommended some concessions to the postmen, one of its main goals was replacing the pool of metropolitan telegraph boys from which London's troublemaking postmen were hired. After the Cleveland Street scandal, Joyce had intimated Raikes's desire of "stamping out as far as lies with the Department the vicious practices which it has feared have widely spread among the boy staff."[20] The Joyce Committee report was the first official attempt to do so. Its preoccupation with telegraph boys is evident in the official summary: "The postmen's force is recruited from the force of telegraph messengers . . . and, appointed as the telegraph messengers now are, we have no hesitation in recording our opinion that this is not a satisfactory recruiting ground." The expanded telegraph-messenger inspector force and Confidential Enquiry Branch had not quelled concerns about inadequate supervision and the need to "weed out" unsuitable boys. Even though 50 percent of telegraph-boy candidates were barred from the service following inspections of their homes, a "rougher class" of boys grew up to be London postmen.[21]

Old concerns about urban poverty and physical, social, and moral depravity were resurrected in testimony. According to James Lawrence, head of the London GPO Appointments Branch, "The city boys are recruited from the Eastern District, Poplar and so forth, and that is where we are at a disadvantage." These boys, coming out of "wretched courts," produced a "poor lot" of postmen compared to those recruited before the nationalization of the telegraph.[22] This older generation of postmen had come from the country, where one would find "a better man than you would from a city slum." Urban telegraph boys turned postmen were "a poor physical class," they were "more troublesome," and their "conversation bad." They were also accused of shirking, and their intelligence, while not necessarily inferior to that of country boys, was channeled in dangerous ways. London's assistant controller, in a leading question to London's East Central District chief inspector, expressed concerns that the telegraph boy cum postman was "too intelligent." The Inspector responded that "vulgarly speaking, they know too much." City boys were wanting in self-regulation compared to their country cousins, who "had already learned to restrain themselves in their private life."[23] A lapse in reforming GPO policy had further contributed to the deterioration of postmen's behavior: the quiet reinstatement of night service for boys over sixteen, as a financial expedient, had led to negative resonances throughout the GPO.[24] Current London postmen had "very frequently been on night duty in the telegraph service," resulting in "the worst class of men [the GPO] has ever had."[25]

The Joyce Committee reiterated many of the findings of Thomas Jeffery, the old Missing Letter Branch head, who fourteen years previously had located the city telegraph boys' propensity for immorality and physical depravity in their interactions with urban environments. It concluded that "life on the streets, such as the telegraph messengers lead, is calculated to impair rather than promote the habits to be desired in a postman."[26] Their knowledge of London's pathways, especially its nighttime thoroughfares, once again singled the telegraph boys out for special treatment. Both their movements throughout the city and their domestic environments compromised their transformation into respectable, obedient postal workers.

A minority of administrators testified that, given telegraph boys' superlative ability to deliver messages rapidly across London, they made the best kind of postmen.[27] But witnesses were influenced by prompts and leading questions from Herbert Joyce and other committee members. These included "I certainly have observed that the present younger men are distinctly inferior in type to the older men," and "In fact it comes to this, does it not, that the whole postal service has been largely used to provide places for the inferior telegraph staff?"[28]

This line of questioning reflected political anxieties. In concluding one of his interrogations, Joyce referred to the postmen's strike as the "lamentable occurrences which took place July last," and inquired whether there were "many boy messengers among the postmen who gave such trouble then?" The respondent replied that they were "very prominent" in it and that a "great proportion" of the postmen dismissed during the strike were former telegraph boys.[29] The reference to "July last" also evoked the events of July 1889 that led to the Cleveland Street scandal. Telegraph boys' direct involvement in male prostitution was never explicitly mentioned, but it tacitly informed the proceedings: when some committee members suggested reinstating the rank of corporal among the telegraph boys to improve discipline, the idea was quickly thrown out on the advice of Tombs, who, along with Herbert Joyce, had been party to the 1877 investigation and the previous year's scandalous occurrences.

One pacifying tactic adopted by the GPO executive was borrowed from the London Metropolitan Police.[30] Breaking a twenty-year policy that treated telegraph boys as GPO apprentices, the committee recommended that London's postmen be once again recruited from the country, that metropolitan telegraph messengers be subject to a "vigorous weeding out" on turning sixteen, and that those old enough for advancement to the job of postman be sent to the country on two-year probationary assignments.[31]

For the postmaster general, this proposal did not go far enough. In one of the handful of dissents from the report's conclusions, Raikes recommended to the Treasury that "a preferable course . . . will be to alter not so much the force from which the London postmen are recruited as the manner in which that force is trained." To promote "habits of obedience and smartness of appearance," Raikes's proposed that on turning eighteen, telegraph messengers would be "encouraged" to enlist, and "after five years' military service, they [would] be appointed postmen if they bring back with them good characters."[32] Raikes had already made arrangements for this scheme to take effect before the Joyce Committee findings were released. The official circular went out to London GPO offices on November 10, 1891.

TELEGRAPH BOYS ON PARADE

Raikes did not live to see his scheme take full effect. He died suddenly on August 24, 1891, and was succeeded by Sir James Fergusson, who approved of telegraph messengers' de facto conscription, arranged for ex-soldiers to be given preference for postmen's vacancies regardless of any GPO experience, and decided that telegraph boys' military training should begin even before they left the GPO. Fergusson was inspired by the policies of the London Postal Service and Central Telegraph Office (CTO) controllers. Tombs had recently hired former army sergeants to inspect and supervise telegraph boys at central offices. The CTO's controller, Henry Fischer, had filled telegraph boys' time between dispatches with military drills, performed in hallways, kitchens, and basements. Telegraph boys had marched in military formation for public events previously, but regular drill was an innovation.[33] Fergusson decided to introduce the practice nationwide to improve the discipline and the appearance of telegraph messengers, who, as far as Fergusson was concerned, had "yet to learn that they [were] not street urchins but H.M. servants."[34]

Tombs reported on the first interdepartmental training drills, which took place in the middle of December. At 8 p.m., 240 telegraph messengers from the City District and branch offices finished their shifts and converged on the Mount Pleasant sorting office. They were lined up in a shed that, as Tombs pointed out, had been the treadmill house during the building's previous incarnation as Coldbath Prison. Three GPO clerks who were also officers in the Post Office Rifles drilled them. Four additional sergeant commissioners, newly hired as London telegraph messenger inspectors, joined their ranks. The Telegraph Messenger Institute's drum and fife band accompanied the proceedings, contributing "in no small degree to inspire the Messengers." According to Tombs, the boys "appeared to enter into it with great spirit," although a handful of them fainted due to "want of food." Buns and milk were subsequently provided, and Tombs requested that in future the department subsidize the costs of telegraph boy drill rations.[35]

At the same time as telegraph boys became temporary, disposable employees, drilling developed its own administrative momentum. From the Central Telegraph Office and Mount Pleasant, weekly drilling spread throughout London and the rest of the urban British GPO. Whether they were enthusiastic or reluctant, starving participants, telegraph boys in London and other cities found their leisure hours squeezed, as they either had to show up early or leave work late once or twice a week. Senior GPO executives eagerly pitched ideas to one another about drill prizes, battalion and company formations, and branch flags for the telegraph boys to display during drill. Fergusson and the newly hired sergeant inspectors advocated for reinstating corporals, but the older generation of administrators once again firmly rejected the proposal for reasons that were literally erased from department memoranda.[36]

The GPO endowed its enhanced disciplinary procedures with a pronounced martial aesthetic. Telegraph boys, "wearing as they do the uniform of the Queen, are under an obligation to conduct themselves in a manner which shall never bring that uniform into disrepute."[37] Their fast hairstyles were checked, their uniforms were more rigorously inspected, and their bodies became increasingly subject to strict aesthetic standards. Army tailors were brought in to design better-fitting uniforms and accouterments for the boys. Starting in 1892, telegraph boys were required to salute their "commanding officers" and senior GPO officials.[38] As in 1877, the intensification of telegraph-boy monitoring brought side benefits. So as not to sully their uniforms while lunching off pieces of paper with their fingers, London telegraph boys were now issued knives, forks, and plates in their kitchens. Tombs also suggested that providing them with towels would be a further "step in the right direction."[39]

By the summer of 1892, the GPO began negotiations with London volunteer regiments to borrow drill halls. The Eastern Central District and Central Telegraph Office messengers once again led the way, drilling at Charterhouse twice a week. In August, the *Daily Telegraph* printed an article by the GPO secretary, Arthur Blackwood, on these drilling spectacles. Writing in the third person, Blackwood "expressed the pleasure it had given him to see the zest with which the boys had performed" and "felt sure that such of them as might elect to enroll themselves in the regular army on the conclusion of their messenger service would not regret the preliminary training they now received."[40] He did not mention that "electing to enroll" in the army was a requirement for advancement, or that the boys were carrying broom handles as substitutes for rifles.[41]

On the day this commentary was published, a new postmaster general took office. Arnold Morley was a cabinet minister appointed by Gladstone to head the post office after the Liberals' election victory in 1892. While Morley acclimatized to his new position, GPO bureaucrats continued to expand the drill scheme. By September, it was up and running across the country at borrowed military barracks and halls. From Kensington Barracks to Clapham's Recreation Grounds, to militia barracks near Kings Cross and skirting Victoria Park, telegraph boy drill extended across central and suburban London.[42] Metropolitan telegraph boys had also dispensed with broomsticks; the GPO acquired disabled carbines from the Horse Guards for drill practice. Administrators reported that the boys enthusiastically embraced this new regimen.

Drilling not only cut into the telegraph boys' leisure time but also intruded into their neighborhoods, which led some of London's residents to complain. Others questioned Raikes's enlistment scheme. Objections came from within the GPO as well: supervisors who had defended the telegraph messengers before the Joyce Committee now approached Morley with evidence that in spite of the "zest" for drilling, the enlistment scheme had already resulted in the "messengers as a class deteriorating" because "the better sort of boy . . . would not accept employment . . . under the new conditions."[43] Those who did accept the GPO's terms displayed "a reckless feeling," as the prospect of mandatory enlistment made them feel "they had little to lose by being dismissed, making it very difficult to maintain discipline."[44] The newly appointed boys, "finding there is nothing to look forward to, assume a 'don't care' spirit." Provincial postmasters, already skeptical of the Joyce Commission's London-focused innovations, argued against enlistment.[45]

Telegraph messengers' families also opposed the measure: "Parents take alarm at the very name of enlistment and refuse to let their sons enter the Post Office."[46] Parents' concerns received official voice in November 1892, when the radical pacifist MP William Randal Cremer organized a deputation to the postmaster general on behalf of the International Arbitration League.[47] Cremer's delegation attacked the enlistment scheme as contrary to families' wishes, class relations, and English freedom: "For it is impossible to restrain the outcry that would be raised by the parents of those lads, and by the lads themselves, as they grow older, that their particular class should be almost driven into the Army, while the sons of the middle and upper classes escape altogether the burden."[48] Their official resolution objected "that our class should be made the channel by which the country should be brought into a similar position with continental powers." According to one delegate, telegraph boys' army service was a step on the road toward the tyranny of universal conscription, which deserved comparison with that most provocative trope of the curtailment of English rights, "the process of enclosing a common." He reported that a telegraph boy's widowed mother had asked "whether it was a fact that an order had emanated from your authorities that the lads at the age of 18 should be drafted into the Army." He had responded that he "could not believe that anything so un-English could be instituted." This mother had threatened to remove her son promptly from the telegraph service if the enlistment scheme was allowed to stand.[49]

The International Arbitration League argued that it was "a great injustice" to "confuse with Civil Service military service." While the enlistment scheme was the most contentious issue, telegraph boys' drill also rankled with many of the pacifist committee members, who were trying to end military drilling at London board schools and the increasingly popular youth brigades. While they approved of discipline, they believed drilling gave the boys "some confused notion that the slaughter of their fellow creatures is very much the same as the slaughter of their own evil passions."[50] Some members of the deputation supported a less militarized form of drill, believing "that the body should be developed physically," but all were opposed to using actual weapons. As one member put it, "Why should it be thought necessary, when you enjoin discipline, or when you want to practice physical development, to place in the hands of the little lad a musket, a sword, or some other military weapon?"[51] Speaking both on behalf of the Arbitration League and as a newly elected member of the London County Council, Charles Freake condemned the connection between drilling and militarism: "We object as working men that these lads should have that imbued in their young minds which may make them take a certain course before they are old enough to judge for themselves."[52]

Telegraph boys became prime targets of competing forms of social engineering. While the GPO attempted to subdue both troublesome sexuality and labor unrest by limiting their leisure time and honing their fitness and obedience, pacifists sought to attack "the jingo spirit, which was so prevalent a few years ago," at its root. For the Arbitration League, London's telegraph boys' disciplinary practices had political implications: " How can we, who may be in some senses leaders in the labour movement, endeavor to point out to our own men that arbitration, conciliation, reason, must take precedence over force and violence if our rulers . . . are fostering this abominable war spirit?"[53]

This deputation impressed Morley. Facing both outside pressure and internal reviews, he abolished the telegraph messenger enlistment scheme. This concession drew the ire of the War Department and powerful bureaucrats like Herbert Joyce.[54] The GPO's links with the army were further challenged in the spring of 1893, when reports were submitted to the postmaster general by the Confidential Enquiry Branch showing that the ex-servicemen hired as postmen had higher rates of inebriation and thievery than the general force, leading to high numbers of dismissals.[55] In July 1893, Morley reinstated hiring policies that favored telegraph messengers above other candidates for urban postmen's vacancies.

Telegraph boys were still subject to "weeding out" and medical examinations on turning sixteen. They were also still subject to regular drill, which had developed a complex bureaucracy of its own. Before meeting with the Arbitration League, Morley had ordered another four hundred disused carbines from the War Office for use in telegraph boy drills, and drilling was extended to larger numbers of suburban telegraph boys.[56] The boys continued to drill with guns, with one notable regional exception: in Dublin, Belfast, Cork, and Londonderry, telegraph messengers still had to make do with broomsticks.[57]

As descriptions of late Victorian youth church brigades and cadet corps attest, the GPO's embrace of military discipline for telegraph boys reflected a widespread middle-class consensus on the proper cultivation of masculinity and a means of combating fears of degeneration and imperial decline.[58] These practices had wide appeal for many influential adults but elicited mixed reactions among telegraph boys' own communities. As for the boys, many appear to have enjoyed drilling for various reasons, not least the GPO's decision to pay them overtime on drill days.

Quotidian practices of messenger boys demonstrate how they accommodated and coopted these rituals. In 1893 two indoor messengers from St Martin's-le-Grand submitted "letters of explanation" concerning why they had substituted their own buttons for GPO ones on their official overcoats. Both M. E. Brown and H. W. Saunders stated that they had another coat with proper buttons for drill and that they used their personalized clothing on their commutes between their homes and the post office. They saw "no harm" in wearing clothing without insignia while off duty.[59] It was a small act of youthful sartorial rebellion, and probably one of many ways in which telegraph boys subtly refigured their urban personas when crossing boundaries between their private lives and public image.

In the decade following Cleveland Street, media reports approved of the messengers' appearance and discipline, associating their military training with better delivery service.[60] The elite boys' periodical *Chums* published an approving article on the growth of London drilling in 1894, accompanied by a drawing of Lieutenant Colonel J. P. MacGregor, chief commanding officer of the London drilling scheme. He provided a summary of the drill scheme: "There are no fewer than 3,500 of these lads between fourteen and eighteen years of age in London alone, who are disciplined and trained in exercises exactly similar to those which young soldiers have to undergo." MacGregor noted that "drill would not only improve the physique of the boys but brighten them up in other respects." This "brightening up" included "the replacement of the shoulder strap by a belt with a buckle. The brightness of the buckle and of the metal buttons which are now worn on the uniform is a good test of the tidiness of the boys." He also outlined the intangible benefits of drilling, belt polishing, and other manifestations of the GPO's constant supervision:

> Giving them something to do in their leisure time . . . keeping them out of mischief. They have the advantage of discipline and training during a critical and very important period of a lad's life—that is to say, between the time of his leaving school and when he is verging on early manhood.[61]

This period of transition was garnering increasing attention in the 1890s, and MacGregor, like many of his contemporaries engaged in youth work, believed that respectable masculinity was developed through fitness, duty, and military parading. He noted that his telegraph boys were "much superior to other boys of their own class" on account of the GPO's interventions.[62] Drill gave fin-de-siècle GPO administrators a tangible sense of progress. They felt confident enough in the telegraph boy corps to include them in the celebrations marking Queen Victoria's Diamond Jubilee in 1897. One hundred hand-picked messengers marched in the Horse Guards Parade. Executives and the press were pleased with the outcome, noting that only one boy fainted.[63]

The GPO's grooming of telegraph boys contributed to their perceived utility by a public who at times engaged them for other purposes: walking their dogs, escorting children across town, and waiting in line for West End theater and music hall tickets. While employing telegraph boys to wait in queues was officially banned in 1904, it apparently continued under the radar. It was ultimately suppressed thanks to the monitoring of the District Messenger and Theatre Company, who employed their own boys to stand in line for theatergoers.[64]

By the end of the century, drill veered back towards explicit preparation for military service: in 1897, at the behest of the new Tory postmaster general, Henry Fitzalan-Howard, Duke of Norfolk, telegraph boys were once again stripped of their apprenticeship status and the promise of future employment. The War Office and the GPO collaborated on an alternative scheme that would offer half of all postmen's vacancies to returning veterans.[65] Many administrators disagreed with this arrangement, pointing to ex-soldiers' higher rates of dismissal from the postal service. At first, limited numbers of ex-servicemen applied for positions, and their relatively low impact on the GPO mollified the dissenters. However, the Boer War produced a large number of veterans in need of employment, and in the first decade of the twentieth century, telegraph boys' prospects for advancement in the GPO effectively dried up.

Drilling remained unaffected by these changes. In 1906, an attempt to allow the London boys smartest at drill to wear chevrons on their regular uniforms generated a brief controversy. Long-standing administrators instantly raised an objection, noting:

> We had so severe a lesson many years ago (West Strand Irregularities) as to the dangers of the corporal system that I should be very reluctant to see it reintroduced, and I fear that if boys were allowed to wear chevrons at all times there would certainly be a tendency to place them in charge of other boys.[66]

A younger generation of provincial administrators eventually overruled them. After a year's successful trial (during which time no London boys with chevrons were disciplined), the chevrons remained on boys' everyday uniform. London officials were still reluctant to let the "half company commanders," "section commanders," and "squad leaders" monitor other boys' behavior when not drilling.

Uniformed and ranked telegraph boys marching with guns on their shoulders became a common sight in the fin-de-siècle metropolis. For those already expressing pederastic longings for "the lad that's lettered G.P.O.," such spectacles undermined administrators' intentions by drawing attention to the fit, martial, sexually desirable adolescent.[67] Any sexual transgressions that occurred after Cleveland Street between telegraph boys and amorous telegraph consumers remained hidden from authorities, but the telegraph boy remained a figure in the homoerotic pantheon.

The visibility of telegraph boys in parades and at drill may have piqued all kinds of interests in observers, but it belied the boys' dwindling numbers. In the early twentieth century, even as London continued to expand, the number of telegraph boys decreased as the telephone rapidly became a staple of business, finance, and state communication. Telegrams remained an important information conduit, but a less prestigious one. With fewer telegrams to deliver, messenger vacancies decreased. The bicycle, another technological innovation that had recently undergone improvements, also reduced the need for messengers by cutting delivery times. Both postmen and messengers in rural communities had used bicycles since the 1880s. By the early twentieth century they were staples of GPO transport in "town and country."[68] But despite their declining numbers, bureaucratic interest in telegraph messengers, which had grown throughout the late Victorian period as GPO executives played out their boy-soldier drill schemes, exploded in the first years of the new century.

BLIND ALLEYS

The educational campaigns and martial exercises to which telegraph boys were subjected closely resembled those of working-class boys' clubs and brigades. The GPO's Telegraph Messenger Institute provided the first secular, state-run version of organized extracurricular activities for working-class male youth.[69] Both in the public schools and among evangelical reformers engaging with urban working-class "rough lads," the rationalization of adolescent leisure time served both authoritarian and progressive interests.[70] In the 1880s and early 1890s, such endeavors had been motivated by concerns about telegraph boys' potential to disrupt communications and tarnish the GPO's image, but from the end of the century to the Great War, telegraph boys' physical and psychological welfare emerged as a serious concern in its own right, encompassing the boys' public image, future work performance, deference, and respectability in wider discourses about adolescent bodies and minds.

Historians of the late Victorian and Edwardian era have identified medical, psychological, and sociological discourses that regarded the "adolescent" as key to Britain's welfare. The GPO was forced to reconfigure its policies in response to the growing professional interest in adolescence. Doctors, social scientists, and political activists formed the nucleus of a broad campaign for youth employment reform. Socialist campaigners argued that the systemic devaluation of workers began with boy labor, while educational reformers advocated for compulsory schooling beyond the elementary level. Conservative luminaries and commanders frequently complained about the unruliness of military recruits from the working classes. For all of these observers, adolescence emerged as the locus of both social problems and their solutions.

An early example of the political significance of telegraph boys' welfare played out in Parliament in 1903, when those approving of boys' fitness but skeptical of military training attempted to revise the GPO's drill program. The previous year, during a parliamentary debate over the London board schools' drill practice, doctors had testified that physical training "should be carefully graduated and designed so as to be fitted to the physique of juveniles."[71] The postmaster general, who had been present during the debates, ordered an inquiry into current drill practices. One exercise was singled out as being "unsuitable even for the messengers."[72] It had been described in Parliament as "Pressing from the Ground," where "the child was to lie prone, face downwards, resting on the palms of the hands and the tips of the toes only, the body to be moved up and down by straightening the elbows."[73] As a result of this report, telegraph boys, besides getting out of doing push-ups, were subject to fewer rigorous arm, chest, and leg exercises. Younger boys were encouraged to supplement drill practice with exercise at local gymnasiums.

Telegraph boys became crucial test subjects for a nationwide youth reform movement motivated by apprehensions about racial and imperial decline.

Evocations of Anglo-Saxon decay were a mainstay of social commentary, and concerns about working-class bodily hygiene, and more explicitly eugenic concepts, appeared across the political spectrum. The Boer War's equivocal outcome, blamed by many in Britain on the poor health and performance of working-class soldiers, heightened concerns about the well-being of the future guardians of Empire. In this period, the post office insisted on an explicitly racialized workforce: telegraph boys and any other potential GPO hires had to be "British born."[74]

Concurrently, prewar England was grappling with the "boy labor crisis." The historian Harry Hendrick sees this concern as stemming from a consensus of middle-class and respectable working-class opinion that male adolescents were "dangerous" because their development was crucial to the maintenance of the nation.[75] Reformers worried about too short a period of schooling before boys entered the labor market; improper supervision during "a critical epoch in the development of the lad"; and the decline of apprenticeship in the wake of industrialization.[76] These factors accounted for adult male unemployment, fecklessness, "immorality," and physical degradation. They affected young working-class women as well, but women's employment prospects were a lower cultural priority than their role as mothers and household managers. Moreover, job prospects for respectable working-class girls were increasing with the growth of clerical work, along with jobs in modern factories, shops, and leisure industries.[77]

Within the GPO, the preference given to ex-servicemen limited the long-term opportunities for telegraph boys; and changes in communication technologies, particularly the rise of the telephone, instituted a slow but steady decline in the need for telegraph messengers. By 1911, public pressure forced the post office to end its reliance on temporary boy labor. The GPO had to concern itself with the lifelong employment of its young recruits.

The boy labor crisis was an urban phenomenon. The temporary, dead-end jobs that most concerned reformers—errand runners, delivery boys, newspaper sellers, hotel and club pages, van boys, and messengers—were fundamental to urban mobility.[78] Reformers' preferred metaphor for this kind of work was the "blind alley"—a site of dead ends, corruption, and disorder. In spite all of its street improvements and modern transportation networks, London was full of blind alleys, real and metaphorical.

This evocative spatial metaphor held particularly strong resonances for the post office. By 1909, only 19 percent of telegraph messengers found further employment in the post office.[79] That year, in its supplementary report on urban boy labor, the Royal Commission on the Poor Laws singled out the job of GPO messenger as "one of the least promising occupations into which a boy can enter."[80] The GPO was even accused of fostering downward mobility: messengers "came from very good homes . . . and [brought] characters," yet many were "leaving the Service year by year badly equipped for the necessity of making their way through life, and too large a proportion of these lads [were] finding employment in casual labour and unskilled work."[81] It was cold comfort to the GPO that over thirty years' effort of cultivating the "better sort" of telegraph messenger had succeeded. For reformers, the GPO's policies were all the more egregious given that it was a government department that should be setting an example: "If the public service is thus guilty, we must not be surprised that private employers are not conscious of wrongdoing in their use of boys."[82]

The reports' findings prompted a massive investment in the welfare of telegraph boys, including a hastily appointed internal Standing Committee on Boy Labour charged with bringing about "the complete absorption" of telegraph boys into the GPO establishment. The new postmaster general, Herbert Samuel, was an influential progressive MP whose writings helped define new liberalism, and an enthusiastic supporter of boy labor reform. He observed: "It was wrong that the State should use up two of the most important years of a boy's life and then let him drift away, unprepared for any occupation offering permanence of employment."[83]

Even before the royal commission, GPO administrators had expressed concerns about telegraph boys' poor prospects. In 1905, London administrators had attempted to make contacts between soon-to-be ex-telegraph boys and local employers; in 1907 telegraph boys were encouraged to sign up for GPO-initiated employment measures. Continuation classes at Telegraph Messenger Institutes expanded, and boys were heavily encouraged to participate. After the standing committee issued a report in 1911, London messengers were required to attend classes for four hours a week between September and April, with optional lessons provided in the summer.[84] On reaching sixteen and a half (the age of "weeding out"), messengers sat special civil service exams. Initially, administrators dictated that the results of these scores would determine messengers' futures in the post office, the Royal Engineers, or the Wireless Telegraph Branch of the Royal Navy. The military choices proved unpopular and were discontinued in early 1914. Instead, administrators experimented with providing technical training to prepare boys to sit examinations for the GPO's engineering department. More telegraphists' training positions and junior sorters' positions were offered to telegraph boys. Messengers' uniforms, still subjected to rigorous inspections, received an upgrade. The quality of the blue serge improved, and a shoulder strap supplemented the belt. The next targets of reform were the bodies beneath the uniforms.

GPO PHYSIQUES

By 1912 military-style drills were considered to assure adolescent boys' well-being. The Standing Committee on Boy Labour collected statistics on telegraph boys' weight, height, and chest measurements for comparison with regional and national averages and to measure the success of future initiatives to improve messenger boys' health. On a visit to Edinburgh in late January 1912, Samuel was "much interested" in a performance of "'physical culture' exercises given by the Edinburgh and Leith Telegraph Messengers."[85] These messengers had been trained and supervised by Henry Rippon-Seymour, an enthusiastic proponent of "Swedish exercises" and the cultivation of physique.[86] Rippon-Seymour had picked his top twelve telegraph boys to perform for Samuel as "the exception that proves the rule": to demonstrate both the overall physical underperformance of telegraph messengers and what some focused, regular training could do to improve their general health.[87]

This spectacle was the preamble to Rippon-Seymour's proposal to the GPO executive for compulsory physical fitness exercises for the entire telegraph-boy force. The proposal was based on a conceptual framework currently gaining scientific traction: "To the student of Eugenics or hereditary influences," he wrote, the physical deficiencies of working-class youth presented "a very serious outlook as to the future condition of a class which forms a very large and important portion of our race." But this state of affairs in fact provided the government with "an unprecedented and inimitable opportunity for good." Messengers entered the GPO at a "vitally important age," remaining under its supervision "during a particularly crucial period" that determined their "physical, mental, and moral" prospects.[88]

Reformulating an old concern that the urban environment compromised telegraph boys' training, Rippon-Seymour complained that "the very nature of his work almost encourages him to "slouch. Military drill was not enough to rectify physiological defects: "While it certainly inculcates a sense of obedience and discipline, it does not aid the development of the body in

structure and function. It produces merely a superficial smartness of movement, a veneer, on what may possibly be a weak foundation." The solution was
compulsory physical training, which, combined with drill, formed "a
Hygienic and Educative ideal." Noting that such a regimen would be "merely
an extension of the trend of modern educational legislation," he argued that
it was "almost a duty on the part of the State" to leave boys better physically
prepared for either postal work or prospects on the open market.[89]

Agreeing "entirely with the writer," Samuel began proceedings for the
implementation of mandatory physical fitness regimes beyond drill. He also
appeared to be swayed by some of the ideological implications of Rippon-
Seymour's argument, musing that the telegraph boys who regularly used the
London Messenger Institute gymnasium had undergone a "conspicuous
improvement effected in their physique and (probably) in their intelligence
also."[90] The GPO's Boy Labour Committee, along with the London Board of
Education, commissioned a study into the expansion of compulsory physical
exercises for telegraph boys. Initial memoranda delved into the history of
telegraph boy drilling and the Telegraph Messenger institutes across Britain,
many of which already supplied exercise equipment and gymnasium space.[91]

In addition to working fifty hours a week, telegraph boys were now
required to attend two exercise classes a week during the fall and spring, as
well as drill and institute classes. In London, the Central Telegraph Office
was fitted out with horizontal and parallel bars, a vaulting horse, rings, rope,
ladder, "single sticks," and boxing gloves. Other telegraph boys trained at
local gymnasiums provided gratis by the London County Council Northern
District. Boys trained for an annual "Swedish Exercise" competition at
Alexandra Palace. The Telegraph Messenger Institute on Throgmorton
Avenue in the City continued to offer classes and equipment. The Messenger
Institute also oversaw the existing voluntary sports teams and drum and fife
bands for telegraph boys. Every postal district in London fielded its own
telegraph-boy cricket team. Most had football and swimming teams as well.
The GPO's provisions for London's telegraph boys by the eve of the Great
War dwarfed those of contemporary boys' organizations, including the
Edwardian period's best-known, most prolific, and enduring youth initiative,
the Boy Scout movement.[92] Lord Robert Baden-Powell's imperialist junior
cadet force shared certain features with the GPO's messenger programs.
Both were the product of mingled progressive and conservative impulses, a
combination of aspirations for social cohesion and uplift, and reactionary
solutions to both urban and imperial threats.

By World War I, telegraph boys were arguably the capital's most carefully managed workforce. Their well-being and future prospects occupied the energies of senior GPO executives, Liberal and Tory postmasters general encouraged expansive welfare schemes, and the Treasury covered the growing expenses of the telegraph boy workforce.

GENDER REVERSALS AND THE GREAT WAR

Born in 1900, Edith Grenfell was sixteen when the Penzance Post Office issued her with a badge numbered T1, denoting her status as the first female telegraph messenger in Cornwall. By the end of the World War I she was one of seven young women delivering telegrams all over the western tip of the Cornish peninsula. Her daughter noted Edith's memories of "lonely and unlit roads," evening shifts, and bicycling the rugged Cornish terrain in "whatever the weather conditions." Edith and her coworkers of course "too often knew they carried the dreaded information to next of kin that a loved one had been wounded, was missing or killed in action." These messengers' "great dread" was "a recipient, either unable to read or too frightened to do so, asking them to read the telegram."[93] This became such a frequent occurrence for girl messengers across the United Kingdom that in 1916, despite the practice being explicitly banned by GPO administrators in London, it was unofficially sanctioned by local supervisors, provided that a neighbor also witness the interlocution. Telegraph girls seemed to have both facilitated and mediated collective grief.[94]

This emotional work was at first glance part of larger wartime trends in women's labor. As telegraph business more than tripled during the conflict, it increasingly fell to telegraph girls to deliver the grievous news that accounted for much of the service's expansion.[95] For the GPO, this was a particularly discomfiting trend. It undermined long-standing boundaries to women's work and notions of respectability. Telegraph messenger girls had made occasional appearances in rural communities and smaller towns prior to World War I. Blackpool's post office, for example, had hired telegraph girls since 1901 out of desperation—boys could make more money as caddies at the local golf courses.[96] In 1911, in order to meet the Standing Committee's "complete absorption" goals for telegraph boys' overall numbers, fourteen- to sixteen-year old girls began replacing boys as indoor messengers at the Central Telegraph Office.[97]

Girl messengers during World War I paradoxically represented the high value placed on boy messengers and their long-term prospects in the GPO. Thanks to years of increasing attention paid to telegraph boys, going back to the fallout from the Cleveland Street scandal in 1889 and vastly accelerated by the boy labor crisis in the first decade of the twentieth century, telegraph boys had gone from unruly urchin afterthoughts to the most cultivated and carefully managed workforce in the GPO, arguably heralding a new pact between the British state and the working-class subjects it deemed most valuable. By 1914, it was unconscionable for administrators to hire more telegraph boys than they could expect to employ later as adults. As a substantial proportion of postmen's positions were still reserved for military veterans, telegraph boy numbers had to be even more tightly controlled.

Grenfell's experiences of navigating rural roads alone in the dark and the rain represent a notable departure from the general GPO rule against female workers doing outdoor work. Large urban centers had long been considered out of bounds for female messengers. The arrival of telegraph girls in major cities represented a further disintegration of an urban order based on rigid and gendered distinctions between "inside" and "outside" information work.[98] Producing and maintaining respectability among women workers required keeping them inside offices. When they had to interact directly with the public, there was always supposed to be a counter or, as Henry James imagined it, a "cage" between them and their customers.[99] In addition, women's counter work, mail sorting duties, telegraphic transcriptions, and telephone mediations were subject to varying forms of controls to ensure public trust.

When telegraph messenger girls joined the GPO en masse starting in 1915, they were also incorporated into its practices of discretion. The blue uniforms of telegraph messengers symbolized a quasi-militarized system that guaranteed the protection of private information.[100] The messenger's pouch was a crucial accessory, minimizing direct contact between message and messenger. Telegraph girls were never fitted out as elaborately as telegraph boys, but they received a "Special Belt and Pouch," along with GPO armbands and waterproof coats. Like their male counterparts, they had to swear before a magistrate that they would "not wittingly, or willingly open or delay, or cause, or suffer to be opened or delayed, contrary to my duty, any Letter or any thing sent by the Post." By 1916, when Edith Grenfell was hired, GPO administrators had added serge coats, skirts, straw hats with waterproof covers, and boots to telegraph girls' uniforms in a tacit acknowledgment that they were not short-term hires.[101] It is unclear whether they had to attend classes, but they were exempt from drill and the ten minutes' daily exercise required of telegraph boys before starting their shifts.[102] In practice, telegraph girls were not monitored as closely as their male counterparts had been before the war. Even as wartime postal censorship increased, communications regulators paid less attention to the human mediators of war messages.

In London, girls began replacing boy messengers. They had to be of "of good physique," at least 5′4″ tall, and "fairly well-educated." Initially, as a result of administrators' concerns about telegraph girls in Central London, they worked only in the suburbs. Henry Badcock, London's telegraph controller, delayed hiring young women as long as possible. Having been a senior executive at the Central Telegraph Office during the Cleveland Street scandal in the summer and fall of 1889, Badcock was concerned that telegraph girls—like their male counterparts—could be drawn to dangerous urban spaces, situations, and people. The first London female outdoor messengers were the younger sisters of telephone operators, as managers were concerned that urban girl messengers recruited from other sources, such as juvenile labor exchanges, might "lower the tone and status" of the operating staff.[103] London, much to the concern of wary administrators, temporarily became a site where teenage girl messengers freely navigated urban terrain. Both on foot and on bicycles, they learned how to cross boundaries and navigate urban thoroughfares.

The girls' movements were, in theory at least, strictly regulated: they had to complete their duties by 8:00 p.m. sharp, on no account exposing themselves to the dangers of the nighttime metropolis. Messenger inspectors were instructed that "any cases of interference with the Girl Messengers in the discharge of their duty should be brought under notice immediately," and, "under no circumstances should a Girl Messenger employed on Telegraph duties enter a private house, or go beyond the public portion of a shop or set of business premises, when delivering the telegrams."[104] This nationwide policy reflected deeply held concerns about visible female respectability and clandestine sexual improprieties and violence (although perhaps supervisors in Penzance were less concerned about their telegraph girls' interactions with western Cornish telegraph consumers). But it was also a key symbolic practice of discretion in communications work. Edith Grenfell's frequent interactions with traumatized War Office telegram recipients inside their homes went against ingrained practices of the performance of communications privacy. Opening and reading people's telegrams was a direct flouting of her

GPO telegraph girl in London, December 1917. © Imperial War Museum.

legal obligations and of the deep-seated social codes that reified privacy. Either Grenfell either never conveyed more about her feelings on performing these acts, or her daughter did not consider it necessary or appropriate to write them down; but the combined effect of conveying news of injury and death, witnessing and managing recipients' reactions in their homes, and doing so while knowingly defying laws and social conventions upholding the sanctity of personal privacy must have been an excruciating emotional experience.

For many people, a War Office telegram conveying the news of injury or the loss of a loved one was likely the first telegram they had ever received.

Throughout the later Victorian and Edwardian period, telegraph administrators had tried to encourage greater telegraph use among the "lower orders," even creating friendly standardized Christmas telegrams, but the vast majority of British subjects did not switch over to sending telegrams. At sixpence for ten words, they were still too expensive. Fear, rather than excitement or indifference, had been most people's reaction on receiving telegrams. World War I cemented this association.

Although the telegraph boy is an iconic figure in narratives about soldiers' families in World War I, little is known about the recipients' reaction when the messenger was a young woman. The telegram officially informing the writer Vera Brittain of the death of her fiancé was delivered by a telegraph boy. Describing her reaction on hearing the "sudden loud clattering" at the door "that always meant a telegram," she juxtaposes the "tearing anguish of suspense" and the fear that her "legs would not carry" her to the door with her outward calm. Brittain, of a class long accustomed to telegrams, knew how to behave. She responded "mechanically" to the boy, who did not linger on or cross her threshold. Her reaction to the messenger was part of an act of extraordinary outward bodily control.[105] Were telegraph girls received differently in these circumstances? Was there something about an adolescent girl delivering such news that led to the intimacies Grenfell and her fellow telegraph girls were drawn into?

The GPO gave women both new opportunities to exploit their officially sanctioned mobility and intense burdens as the public handmaidens of loss. It finally relinquished its vision of gender, labor, and public space in order to meet enhanced responsibilities for boyhood welfare. To protect telegraph boys' rights to be future postmen, telegraph girls hit the streets, roads, alleys, lanes, and byways of Britain, by foot and bicycle, often delivering the worst kind of news.

EIGHT

Voices on the Wires

Voices! Voices! The voices of a mighty multitude, year in and year
out, holyday and holiday, noon and night, flow over our heads,
around us, and under our feet in a ceaseless, silent chorus. No
whisper of them ever reaches the myriad passers-by, for hermeti-
cally sealed in their subterranean tubes of lead or high over the
roof-tops in weather-resisting cables of the stoutest insulating
mediums, they pass on the electric waves to those for whom they
are intended.

HENRY THOMSON,
"Telephone London," 1903

IN 1904 MEMBERS OF THE MANCHESTER BRANCH of the Postal
Telegraph Clerks Association (PTCA) admitted a new class of GPO employee
to their organization: telephone operators, all of them women. Three years
later the national organization followed suit. Telephone operators embodied
a shift in information work and telegraphists' perspectives on it. Telegraphists'
previous aspirations for clerk status had given way to demands for skilled
workers' wages, which they pursued through closer alignments with other
GPO grades and with the wider trade union movement.

Eight years previously, PTCA delegates had attempted to ban women
altogether. Now, in a complete reversal, the PTCA became an organization
closely attuned to the demands and grievances of female staff. Underlying
this shift was the rapid adoption of the telephone for trade, governance, and
other prestigious, time-sensitive exchanges. The importance of telegraphy
began to recede, as did telegraphists' leverage over their working conditions
and status.

Now the cheaper, more accessible high-speed communications technology, telegraphy existed alongside the telephone and played an increasingly
niche role in British communications until its final demise in the 1980s.
Telephones were not the only new communications technology making eco-

nomic and cultural inroads: in the first decade of the twentieth century, the emergence of radio telegraphy led to speculation in transcontinental transmitters, competition between maritime systems that enabled interconnectivity at sea, and stories of daring telegraph men and their escapades. One of these concerned the RMS *Titanic*'s junior wireless officer, Harold Bride. He and his supervisor had remained at their posts signaling for help until the ship's power had mostly given out. Bride was one of a handful of men who survived the sinking by climbing onto an upturned lifeboat after being washed overboard. His heroics were magnified globally by the *New York Times*'s exclusive coverage of his experience.[1]

Telegraphy remained useful for exchanges that required a paper trail and information that required discretion. As an official noted in the GPO's official employee magazine, *St-Martins-le-Grand,* "We send by telegraph most important and private messages with absolute confidence that nothing will be divulged."[2] The telephone did not offer such security, and women operators were generally held responsible. The telephone operators—nicknamed "hello girls" by the 1880s, as the North American neologism began spreading in the British Isles—embodied the cultural possibilities and concerns evoked by female telecommunications mediators who spoke and listened. The telephone's steady rise among elites exacerbated gender-inflected anxieties about information dissemination and discretion.

The female telephone operator was a much-discussed figure who, for many, encapsulated the technology's vulnerabilities. More than telegraphists and in a more quotidian sense than telegraph boys, unreliable or indiscreet telephone operators posed tangible threats to users of the service. However, for both administrators and consumers, the smooth working of the telephone depended not only on female operators' unobtrusive practices and technical capabilities but also on personal characteristics: timing, tone, and inflection.[3]

Operators prized their voices, along with their demeanor, tact, and discretion, as a valuable personal commodity in their demands for professional status within the telephone industry. Through staff magazines, telephone operators described how they monitored and mediated exchanges between mostly male telephone subscribers, attempting to train callers in the use of the new technology. Even as they vented certain frustrations in print, women advocated for their skills as professional interlocutors. But as with other telecommunications workers, their claims for more agency and responsibility fell on deaf ears.

The telephone made its British debut in 1876, and by 1879 London had competing commercial telephone companies.[4] The GPO had direct interests in the telephone from the outset: because it held the right to lay wires along public rights-of-way, it entered into licensing and line-rental agreements with the first telephone companies.[5] The complex negotiations that resulted were resolved in the state's favor in 1880, when the courts declared that telephony was in essence the same as telegraphy, as defined in the acts nationalizing the telegraph network ("any apparatus for transmitting messages by electric signals").[6] In contrast to the arrangements governing the earlier nationalization of the telegraph, the GPO allowed private companies to continue operating under a thirty-one-year license, with the GPO retaining the option to purchase the companies in the future. The post office also regulated the expansion of telephone networks, nationalizing trunk lines in 1892 and expanding regional telephone exchanges. Starting in 1881, the GPO set up interdepartmental government telephone networks in the capital.[7] Private companies focused on setting up local exchanges in lucrative urban markets.

By 1889 the GPO's main "competitor" was the National Telephone Company (NTC), a product of the amalgamation of three previously existing telephone companies. In the early twentieth century the GPO restricted NTC operations to provincial exchanges. While public reaction was mixed, major factors in the curtailment of private telephone networks included expensive, inefficient service and the proliferation of visible NTC wires over the capital and other urban areas.[8] In 1901 the GPO and NTC agreed to link the two networks in London, leading to a substantial increase in the number of GPO telephone operators who dealt directly with the public, and a close but fractious relationship between GPO and NTC employees. As with the telegraph, the GPO took over the expansion of London's telephone network and channeled most lines under city streets: public ownership once again resulted in more orderly urban environments. In 1911 the GPO completely nationalized the British telephone network, at a cost of £12.5 million.

During the public-private partnership phase, the GPO focused on linking regional centers through the expansion of trunk lines, justifying this priority on the basis of demands from large business firms and prospects for greater revenue. As Jeremy Stein observes, "The exchange of commercial intelligence and the extension of the price system were privileged over other social objectives."[9] The GPO's forays into local connectivity were limited until 1901.

Meanwhile the NTC, stymied by battles over rights-of-way with private landowners and municipal authorities, was unable to keep up with the concentrated and growing demand on its urban systems, particularly in London. Public commentary on the telephone system in late Victorian and Edwardian Britain was punctuated with frustration at missed connections, dropped calls, long waits, and busy lines.

Telephone operators bore the brunt of customers' frustration, along with the challenges of connecting the state and private networks, as NTC employee publications attest.[10] An "A" operator (at the NTC) and a "B" operator (who worked for the post office) often had to coordinate trunk connections to channel a call. Since the B operators had no direct contact with the public, it was the A operators who were criticized by users when the B operators lost connections. As the GPO consolidated its control of the entire telephone network, however, its operators increasingly interacted with subscribers, creating the perception of another type of specialized public servant: a voice conveyed along troublesome wires.

For Postmaster General Arnold Morley, the telephone "was a luxury of the commercial and wealthy classes; the system could never be made an ordinary medium of communication for the great mass of the public."[11] Expensive wire installations combined with constantly evolving technologies meant that telephony came at a high price: £20 for an annual individual subscription (the equivalent of almost an entire year's wages for a beginning telephone operator), and additional costs for calls lasting more than three minutes or to locations more than twenty miles distant. While the high cost generated criticism, some subscribers welcomed the resulting exclusivity, arguing that lower costs would "crowd" the lines and lead to poor service.[12] Telephone directories from this period are indicative of its commercial appeal and limited public reception.

Expansion of telephone service depended on appealing to affluent subscribers.[13] Some of the earliest advertising for Bell telephones in Britain described them as devices with "purposes other than the hitherto recognized field for telegraphy." These included speedy communication "between the manufacturer's office and his factory; between all large commercial houses and their branches; between central and branch banks . . . in fact wherever conversation is required between the principal and his agents or employees."[14] The power dynamics were clear. However, accompanying this text was an image not of a master of industry calling his factory-floor supervisor but of a young couple. Reading the image left to right, the well-groomed man is doing

THE TELEPHONE.

Image from circular advertisement for Bell's telephones, 1877. BT Archives, EHA 5608.

the talking, and his female recipient is apparently listening (though it's unclear how, since the illustration shows no earpiece) and perhaps contemplating her response, a receiver suggestively held to her lips. Separating them is a "half full size" image of a telephone receiver and transmitter, with their receptors facing the man and the wire attachments pointing toward the woman. (Perhaps, given the hole shown in the receiver and the placement of the instruments, the artist also wished to make a penetrative allusion.) Victorian telephone marketing, for all its corporate focus, understood and exploited the erotic opportunities afforded by the telephone.

TELEPHONE OPERATORS

The (hetero)sexualized image of telephone networking in the Bell telephone advertisement gives no hint of human mediation. Yet the illustration anticipates the centrality of female labor to the telephone system.[15] Liverpool exchanges first experimented with women switchboard operators in 1880. As with telegraphy, learning proficiency and low wages quickly made young female operators a mainstay of British telephone networks. Histories of the telephone written in the first decade of the twentieth century also mention that women were preferable to unruly boy operators.[16] Administrators preferred girls aged between sixteen and eighteen, who were "more easily moulded" than older applicants.[17] Operators' wages started at ten shillings a week, rising in increments to twenty shillings for senior operators and up to thirty shillings for supervisory grades. According to an NTC telephone supervisor in the early twentieth century, operators were "drawn from all classes," but the most successful applicants were products of urban commercial colleges, which trained middle- and lower-middle-class girls in clerical labor. Eighty percent of working-class applicants from board schools were deemed "unacceptable," and many prospective operators were dismissed after being interviewed as "not being of class required."[18] Selectors also noted applicants' dress, handwriting style, and general deportment.

Most important, applicants' voices had to pass muster. According to Florence Minter, the NTC's examining matron for London, "Foreign accents, failure to correctly sound the letter r, or a lisp are of course inadmissible." Pronunciation was tested both in conversation and in a reading test, which was effective in exposing flaws in the performance of what would shortly be dubbed "public school pronunciation" (what is known as heightened received pronunciation in Britain today) among London prospects: "Many girls who apparently speak correctly fail signally here." Provincial offices tested the "clearness and quality" of applicants' voices by having them read numbers and exchange names over a telephone. Improper pronunciation was one of many obstacles to working for the telephone service.

Competition for positions was fierce. Between 1902 and 1906, thirty-four thousand women had reportedly applied to work for the NTC in London alone. On average, only 11 percent of applicants succeeded to telephone learnerships. Even so, examiners (themselves former operators) insisted that it was becoming "increasingly difficult to find a suitable number of girls of the right type and of even the very moderate degree of education required." Young women from the upper middle classes were often unsuitable candidates: "The worst failures are girls from convent or small private schools. . . . [A]lthough they speak and look well and would doubtless meet the general idea of the class of girl we require, the examinations invariably prove them educationally unfitted for a business career."[19]

To meet the new demand for telephone operators in the late 1890s, GPO administrators first looked to young female telegraph learners, "selected from those not under 17 or 18 years of age who display general intelligence, patience, etc. and were the quietest in manner and least cockney in pronunciation."[20] GPO telegraphy and telephone networks began sharing a common labor pool, eventually organized as "girl probationers." The relative value of telegraph and telephone operation and the various tasks associated with the system became the subject of heated debate.

For Treasury officials, concerned with the expenses of the GPO's ever-growing mandates, telephone wages "should be framed with strict regards to economy." Austen Chamberlain, then financial secretary to the Treasury (who would briefly serve as postmaster general before becoming chancellor of the exchequer in 1903) handled negotiations with the GPO over telephone operators in 1901. He envisioned that most of the duties were "within the competence of an inexperienced girl of 14 or fifteen" and should be governed by the same policies and paid on the same scales as telegraph boys.[21] Both were mere conduits of information: girl operators were telecommunications skivvies who simply transmitted messages through the physical labor of making connections at switchboards. Like telegraph boys, they should be weeded out before they had to be absorbed into the pension-earning, permanent classes of GPO employees.

For GPO officials, the Treasury's proposals were "strikingly opposed to facts," as there "were no such duties which girls of the kind described . . . could do satisfactorily."[22] Given the complexities of telephone switchboard work, the GPO had to recruit operators either from the NTC or from their pool of telegraph learners. The fin-de-siècle GPO secretary, George Murray, distinguished telephone and telegraph labor in terms of both physicality and affect. Female telegraphists were recruited as young as fourteen "because they must acquire manual dexterity, and the earlier they begin the better." A telephone operator, by contrast, required "little to no manual dexterity, but she does require a clear and cool head; a good temper; and decent manners and address. Her qualifications are in short rather of the head and heart than of the hands." Such skills "could not commonly be formed in girls of 14 and 15, and certainly not in girls of that age starting at 8/ a week."[23] He acknowledged that telephone operation called for both cognitive engagement and emotional intelligence, and operators had to actualize in their voices an effective, respectable telephone network for subscribers.

Murray augmented his case with arguments about efficiency and morality. High turnover and the "poor material" drawn into the service on such low wages would undermine the performance of the network and thus profitability. The growing crisis over the automatic dismissal of telegraph boys at age eighteen further compounded the issues of managing a teenage workforce: the GPO secretary felt "that public opinion would never tolerate our doing this in the case of girls." Paying telephone operators the same low rates as telegraph boy rates was "neither morally nor economically justifiable." The post office's ideal telephone operator was "a girl drawn from a fairly good class, paid fairly good wages ready to stay with us until she marries or is otherwise disposed of."[24]

Murray's argument was largely successful. The Treasury agreed that new GPO telephone operators in London would be recruited at seventeen to nineteen years of age; their pay would start at eleven shillings a week and rise to fourteen shillings by their second year. If they were found "in every way fit for permanent employment" after two years' service, they would join the established employee classes, which received annual increments and whose pay maxed out at twenty shillings (£1) a week after five years' service.[25] Wages for those employed longer than five years, however, were still an open question. The wrangling between the Treasury and the GPO executive led to a series of reports attempting to adjudicate "superior" and "inferior" telephone work, with concomitant salary levels. GPO operators' duties were varied and difficult to parse, with women both facilitating calls between local exchanges and trunk lines (superior work) and filing the correct call "tickets" to keep track of costs (inferior work). Any attempt to reorganize these tasks to allow different pay classifications would lead to redundancies and inefficiencies. The Treasury and the GPO finally settled on a "strict efficiency test" in 1903. Well-graded operators could, after five years' service, eventually attain to a weekly wage of twenty-six shillings. Such positions were "strictly limited" and effectively reflected the pay of female telephone supervisors in London's trunk exchanges.[26]

Telephone operators' pay scales became a matter of urgency because administrators wanted to downgrade telephone work, separating it from telegraph work and its wage levels as quickly as possible, while the two systems shared a common pool of recruits. This was not lost on the Postal Telegraph Clerks Association, one of whose 1903 reports noted that "the work in the Trunk Telephone Service is performed largely by telegraph people."[27] The establishment of lower pay grades for telephone operators than for female telegraphists reflected more than just concerns about network expenses. Despite the requisite "head and heart skills" good operators possessed, and however "superior" the complexities of telephone work were in many exchanges, telephone operators were among the least valued forms of telecommunications labor. The respectable voice on the wires was of little fiscal value.

One of the unintended consequences of this ordering was the Postal Telegraph Clerks Association's admission of telephone operators to its ranks.

Telephone operators augmented the association's numbers and posed no threat to telegraphists' wages. Telegraphists saw opportunities in expressing their grievances to administrators through telephone operators' concerns. In addition, since operators were drawn from and often absorbed back into the telegraphic labor pool (operators who wished to advance up the GPO ranks could sit for telegraphists' civil service exams after two years' service), their recruitment and retention also affected telegraphists. Although telegram numbers were starting to fall, for most telegraphists the idea that telephones would supplant telegraphy was nonsensical.[28] The systems were seen as complementary rather than successional, catering to different needs and to distinct clienteles. Telegraphists continued to use all available resources in their quest for better pay, but they backed away from insisting on their superiority to other GPO grades. The PTCA's new leadership felt affinity for the upper grades of industrial labor that were increasingly promoting a broad trade union movement and, with the birth of the Labour Party in 1900, were now explicitly represented in national politics.[29]

While one of the PTCA's most fervent union advocates in the early twentieth century was the senior telegraphist Mabel Hope, many of London's female telegraph staff opposed the Women's Trade Union League's overtures for affiliation.[30] Within the PTCA, however, female telegraphists and telephone operators became an influential constituency, making up 30 percent of its members by 1908.[31] In 1910, its male and female leaders voted overwhelmingly that "where other conditions of employment are equal, wages should also be equal, irrespective of sex; and this demand be an essential to the PTCA programme."[32] This was a tempered, perhaps even cynical response to continuing gendered divisions of telegraphic labor. Male telegraphists were still generally assigned to the latest machines and the most prestigious circuits, even though female operators were assigned to these wires more frequently. Night duty remained a male preserve, and the PTCA frequently evoked this arrangement as justification for different pay grades for men and women. However, "equal pay for equal work" became a regular demand in association petitions and would later be a feature of postal workers' union negotiations with administrators.

Ironically, night duty also brought GPO telegraphists and telephone operators together—quite literally. Although the GPO did not assign women operators to night shifts,, the NTC began to do so in London in 1885, when the last of their male operating staff had either moved up to supervisory positions or left the company. The NTC insisted that women on night shifts remain in the offices until eight in the morning, when they could commute home at a respectable and safe hour. In contrast, the Post Office incorporated night telephone service into its existing gender-segregated shift system. Administrators decided that female operators should work no later than 8:15 p.m.[33] The GPO's male telegraph staff took on night telephone duties, with some positions offered to senior telegraph boys as the boy labor crisis began influencing GPO policy. Occasional petitions to extend women's working hours were shot down, except under "quite exceptional" circumstances.[34] If employing women for night shifts could not be avoided, the GPO secretary insisted that those selected be "physically strong" and with homes within "easy reach" of the exchanges.[35] This policy persisted until the onset of the Great War. In August 1914, the GPO executive reluctantly permitted women operators to work at London offices until 9:15 p.m. During the war, women eventually pushed men out of telephone operation altogether.

The PTCA, the NTC, the GPO executive, and the Treasury had different stakes in the employment of telephone operators and exerted different pressures in the creation of this new role. Competing administrative logics produced an operator calibrated to imbue the wires with respectable competency yet barely capable of supporting herself financially. Her voice was meant to manifest the telephone's possibilities and deflect criticism of its deficiencies. However, quiet manners and public school pronunciation did not insulate the telephone operator from subscribers, many of whom saw her as the root cause of the system's ills.

HELLO GIRLS

There was broad public skepticism about the value of women switchboard operators. Along with projecting their confusion and frustration with a troublesome new technology onto the operators, telephone subscribers, who were overwhelmingly men involved with trade and commerce, accused young women at exchanges of interfering with and listening in on conversations. Public expectations regarding the sanctity of private information and widely held perceptions of girls' susceptibility to distracting intrigue proved difficult for both the private telephone companies and the GPO to manage. Many commentators positively relished the idea of an inquisitive girl listening in on the wires, a reaffirmation that many bourgeois Victorians and Edwardians were certain that their private discourse was inherently worth overhearing.[36]

The popular press generated the trope of the "wicked telephone girl," whose petty jealousies led to her to deliberately misdirect or drop calls. In a 1895 story in *Every Week,* such a figure, having "lost her temper, and set her heart on being avenged upon somebody," disrupted a call between a doctor and the father of a sick child in need of a house visit.[37] In 1896 she orchestrated a well-timed line switch that caused a wife to collapse in a fainting fit on hearing her husband apparently confessing to an affair.[38] She was still at it in the *New London Journal* in 1907, when, "disappointed and angry" at her beau, she tricked another husband into thinking the local blacksmith had assaulted his wife.[39] The wicked telephone girl was a figure of comedy, but her popularity rested on her power as an omniscient mediator, eavesdropping with malicious intent and knowing just when to cross wires, drop calls, and interrupt conversations to produce the most damaging effects.

GPO publications articulated internal concerns about overly inquisitive telephone operators. *St-Martins-le-Grand* magazine, reflecting on the telephone system in 1899, noted that it was "well known that in the great majority of communications by telephone, the switch operators can readily come into circuit and overhear what is said," and that the Newcastle telephone exchange had taken extra precautions against operators tapping calls: the connection would apparently short-circuit automatically if such behavior was detected.[40] The author believed these security measures were overly "sentimental," as "the busy switch operator has rarely time if she had any inclination for tapping conversations." Observant supervisors were the public's best line of defense against inquisitive operators, as they "would quickly detect any habitual tendency to this gratification of female curiosity."

Some of the country's most powerful institutions refused to take any risks. Telephone connections between government departments were established in 1891, and the Treasury relied on specially appointed male operators. In 1909 attempts to institute a female staff were rebuffed, due to the "exacting nature" of Treasury telephone business. When pressed as to what precisely this entailed (and after refutation of the Treasury's initial objection that there were no "accommodations" for women in the building—lavatories had been installed for the female typing staff), a Treasury official responded that the cabinet ministers who used the lines were not "bound to ordinary operating rules" and "require messages of a confidential nature to be transmitted for them." Further, parliamentary business would be "very trying for female operators," and "the very important nature of the general communications passing through the Treasury switch and the amount of responsibility devolving on the operators" made women unsuitable.[41] The female operator was ignorant of government procedure, and the fiscal affairs of state had to be protected from untrustworthy female ears.

Telephone operators could also be accused of paying too little rather than too much attention to subscribers' conversations, their carelessness evident in mistaken or dropped connections. The trope of a young woman telegraphist distracted by a novel or other feminine pursuit evolved into that of the flighty telephone operator, and this new incarnation was subject to much more animosity. *Pall Mall Magazine* published a derogatory poem in 1911 titled "To Any Telephone Girl":

> Of course you heard me well enough and knew
> I asked for Gerrard 2166;
> The trouble is you never seem to fix
> Your mind on what you undertake to do.
> I cannot tell what system you pursue,
> Nor how, within the space of twenty ticks
> Those simple numbers you contrived to mix
> And put me on to 6122.[42]

When the *London Journal* was not chronicling the deliberate misconnections of wicked telephone girls, it dwelled on the mistakes of careless ones: "When Mr. Meddlar tried to use his telephone . . . the 'hello girl,' probably dreaming of her social triumphs, instead of giving the number called for, connected him with a line over which a conversation already raged." The aptly named Mr. Meddlar went on to cause his own mischief, aided and abetted by the operator's mistake.[43] *Judy,* the conservative satirical magazine, was particularly vindictive toward telephone operators. In 1904 it mocked the "Hello! Girls of Holborn" for staging a small walkout, and in 1906 it published a piece tabulating their inadequacies, concluding that "if you are very patient the Telephone Girl will condescend to stop reading her penny novelette and put you on to the right number." Improving her performance was futile, however, because "the wedding ring is the only ring in which the Telephone Girl takes any interest."[44] Generalized hostilities to women's entry into new labor markets fused with what we might call telemisogyny, the association of problematic telecommunications with women interlocutors.

Many telephone users looked to technological progress as a solution to the myriad problems women operators posed. Press commentators eagerly anticipated the coming of automatic exchanges, as "there were few subscribers who cannot recite a tale of delays, interruptions, and inattention due to the 'girl at the exchange.'[45] "The advantages of the [automatic] system are obvious," opined another editorial, as it "precludes the intervention of the 'Hello girl' in the midst of an important conversation."[46] Operators were also held responsible for other insidious and troubling aspects of modern communication. The *London Daily News* "doubted whether, taking one phase of telephony with another, any other modern boon is responsible for the employment of as much regrettable language." The automated exchange was "thus... interesting from a moral standpoint as well as in its scientific commercial aspects."[47]

London's Science Museum has models of Almon Strowger's innovative dials and selector switches, which helped pave the way for automatic exchanges in the UK (the first public automatic exchange was set up at Epsom in 1912). In 2014, the plaque that introduced Strowger and his devices bore the legend "The girl-less, cuss-less telephone," evocative of the late fin-de-siècle frustrations generated by women running switchboards. The verbal violence unleashed by telephones exposed cracks in the veneer of masculine comportment and rattled self-disciplining subjects, for whom technical innovation was associated with social progress.

"ELEMENTS OF A GOOD SERVICE"

Not all press coverage of telephone operators was negative. "Whenever I hear a businessman bullying and blustering over the wires," opined a journalist in the *Manchester Courier*, "I wish he could just be transported to the Telephone Exchange, and watch for three minutes those girls at their work during the 'rush' hours."[48] Articles describing visits to telephone exchanges were encouraged by administrators, who believed that some of the hostility directed at their employees and exchanges could be mitigated with inside knowledge: "As telephone officials all over the world recognize, it is most desirable that frequently-complaining subscribers should be shown over a busy exchange. To know all is to forgive all."[49]

As with telegraphists, sympathetic press portrayals of telephone exchanges juxtaposed public imaginings of distracted or inquisitive operators with firsthand descriptions of exchanges where "calls come fast and furiously, deft fingers fly over the switchboard; if one girl breaks down another one takes her place immediately."[50] Another description noted that "The operators are all as busy as can be.... [A]ll this constant activity goes on quietly, deftly, we might say elegantly and in comparative silence; for the low tones of the girls' voices in making the necessary inquiries are in general soft and pleasing."[51]

Deft fingers and pleasing, discreet voices were mere accessories to the larger communications machine: in 1889 *Chambers's* assured its readers that the "young lady operators have nothing to do" with the technical aspects of switchboard design or maintenance, as "it would puzzle their minds worse than a raveled skein of thread or an equation in mathematics." Rather, the work these women performed demanded "tact, quickness, and a certain endurance; for the constant strain on the attention and the everlasting movement is such as children, boys, or young women can support, but men may suffer from."[52] In 1913 the *Courier* confirmed that "the brain of the little Hello Girl" was fully occupied in connecting subscribers. This article deflected telephone user anxieties, noting that "the girl who is busy at a switchboard that is constantly in use has very little time to concern herself with the news that is passing over her wires," and quoted an operator stating that "we soon learn to be blanks as far as memory goes."[53] Such press accounts concurred that young female telephone operators were secure vehicles of mediation. In these constructions of telephone labor, operators appeared as diminutive "human machines," unobtrusive, "elegant" extensions of switchboards and wires.

Again, as with telegraphists, tropes of bourgeois respectability emerged in positive media coverage of telephone operators: they came from "a very good class of society . . . mostly daughters of professional men or well-educated members of the middle class."[54] In 1902 an approving *Living London* categorized operators as "bright, well-educated girls, who are, in many cases, the daughters of professional men, doctors, barristers, clergymen, and others." Well brought up and trustworthy, such telephone operators implicitly manifested the discreet professionalism of their fathers in their interactions with telephone subscribers.

Some telephone consumers singled out particular individuals for special praise. In contrast to the Treasury's attitude, the Foreign Office expressed dismay when their in-house telephone operator, Miss Adams, left the office in 1907. The Foreign Office's chief clerk, William Chauncy Cartwright, sent an unprompted, glowing testimonial to the postmaster general, stating that "great credit is due" to Adams "for the rapidity with which she organized and executed the telephone service, as well as for the tact and civility which she showed on all occasions."[55] Adams was no passive automaton: her value emanated from her intelligent, personalized interactions with officials. Tact and civility were the affective signifiers of effective telephone operation.

If telephone subscribers were quick to judge switchboard operators, the operators also formed opinions about their customers' conduct.

> In no other business does general efficiency depend so much on the combined effort of customer and operative. . . . If telephone users would cast the idea of machine out of their minds, and use the same courteous and common-sense practices in talking by telephone as they observe when talking to a fellow human being face to face, they would appreciably raise the efficiency of the telephone service.[56]

These lines were written by a former telephone operator in an article titled "Telephone Etiquette" in 1908. She was writing for the *National Telephone Journal,* the NTC's employee magazine. Staff magazines began appearing in the late 1870s and 1880s, exemplifying the expansion, specialization, and institutionalization of late Victorian periodical literature, and became a staple of corporate culture in the interwar period. These early magazines usually catered to the upper echelons of employees and managers and were designed to imbue a sense of corporate identity and esprit de corps. Alongside articles from management describing company policy, staff magazines offered news and commentary on softer forms of work discipline, including corporate sports teams and clubs, and provided an outlet for employees' creative writing.[57] The GPO's magazine, *St-Martins-le-Grand,* established in 1890, published articles by senior clerical staff and GPO executives on a wide variety of topics, along with descriptions of postal affairs.[58]

The National Telephone Company began issuing a monthly employee magazine in 1902. It was a collaborative exercise between management and staff, designed to instruct workers in company policies and provide an outlet for staff reflections on their work. Highly technical articles appeared alongside poems, personal reminiscences, international telephone news, illustrations, and operators' descriptions of daily life in the exchanges.[59] Within five years of its inception, The *National Telephone Journal* began widening its target audience, and by 1907 it was cultivating female telephone operators, the NTC's largest contingent of workers, as both readers and contributors.

The launch of the *National Telephone Journal* coincided with the expansion of mass media aimed at young middle- and working-class women.[60] Their increased income and consumption of popular periodical literature drove publishing houses to cater specifically to their interests.[61] At the same time, printing innovations and publisher amalgamations had greatly increased publishers' ability to reach a mass audience. The *National Telephone Journal* appealed to female employees by celebrating women's successful telephone careers through articles written by the operators themselves. These articles endowed senior telephone operators and supervisors with a qualified corporate agency. Women appeared as individuated contributors to company success, instructed workers in best practices, and created a forum, albeit heavily mediated, for employees to share experiences of their working lives. These writings—with all of the insights and opacity inherent to the genre out of which they emerged—vividly encapsulate the micropolitics of telephone labor.

From 1907 until the *National Telephone Journal* folded in the wake of nationalization, the magazine ran a regular feature titled *Telephone Women,* whose stated objective was to "increase the personal element" of the publication and laud women who had "earned distinction in the field of telephony" alongside the engineers and inventors featured in its preexisting *Telephone Men* series.[62] The first employee to be featured, in the July 1907 issue, was Ellen Marian Ralph. She had graduated from the private Blackheath girls' school in 1878 and began work as an operator at the United Telephone Company's Avenue Exchange in the City of London. She moved locations frequently, working at three different exchanges in her first two years. In 1884 she became clerk-in-charge at the United's Deptford exchange, then went on to supervise operators at another five exchanges in the City, which by 1889 had all been acquired by the NTC. She was appointed head of London's first telephone operating school in 1899. The narrative was punctuated with reflections on technical developments in the early years of telephony, with the author describing much of the now-antiquated circuitry she had operated. At the time her short biography was published, she had reportedly trained over three thousand operators in multiple environments and systems. In May 1907, the company threw a party in her honor to mark her twenty-five years of service to the telephone industry. It was widely attended, and her popularity was attributed to "her conscientious work, her ability to impart to others her knowledge of telephone technicalities, and her extreme good nature and cheery disposition."[63]

Ralph's profile set the format of those to follow. A brief description of the subject's place of birth and schooling was followed by a description of the offices she had worked in. Giving details of past switchboard layouts, technological innovations, and the exponential growth of telephone usage, the women's biographies offered technical histories of the telephone that engineers, managers, and operators could all appreciate. These articles always concluded with an appreciation of the operators' superlative characters, often accompanied by a list of their hobbies.

The formulaic approach of *Telephone Women* threw certain life patterns into high relief. Successful London telephone operators tended to have a secondary education and to have experienced a high degree of workplace mobility, consistent with wider trends in London's expanding clerical female workforce.[64] The women featured in the *National Telephone Journal* had all begun their telephone careers in the 1880s and 1890s. Most London operators had gone to private girls' vocational schools before entering the telephone service in their late teens and early twenties. Women often worked at several different locations. In a career spanning twenty-eight years, Minnie Francis Butler worked at eight different exchanges as an operator and seven as a supervisor.[65] Some of the women profiled moved out of telephone exchange work altogether. Fanny Louisa Holmes worked as an operator from 1888 to 1896 before being transferred to a clerkship in the traffic superintendent's office. From there she was promoted to oversee the NTC's interactions with the GPO, acting as a liaison between the private and public telephone services.[66]

Holmes, the writer tells, us "confesses to no particular hobby," admitting that "her chief interest has always been in her work."[67] Other women, although professing equal enthusiasm for their work, described interests such as church work, walking, and reading.[68] Consistent with the burgeoning sporting culture of the early twentieth century, some women participated in cycling, tennis, rowing, and cricket. Streatham's clerk-in-charge, Constance Marion Gregory, "confesses to a weakness for football," albeit "watching the game, not playing it."[69] Other women's hobbies reflected interests in urban philanthropy, culture, and politics. Constance A. Forge, who joined the telephone company in 1886 and was featured in the *National Telephone Journal*'s February 1909 edition, had interests that included "'feeds' and entertainments for slum children," and "the management of highly successful dances." Her profile concluded: "She is also, it may be added, a strong advocate for women's suffrage."[70]

Suffrage affiliations occasionally emerged outside the capital: Newcastle's chief operator, Ada Ellis, was rumored to hold "advanced views as to the rights of women, though it is difficult to get her to express any strong opinion on the subject."[71] Many of the profiles highlighted the women's interests in "the promotion of juniors." Fanny Holmes did "all in her power to train the clerks under her charge to fill better positions."[72] In 1911 many London "telephone women" were reported to be members of a new Operators Telephone Society, which had already attracted over five hundred members.[73] Glimpses of women's sociability and associational life outside the NTC were framed by the suggestion that women's lives ultimately revolved around helping junior telephone operators better themselves.

The *Telephone Women* articles were peppered with positive emotive descriptors. The subjects professed to a "fondness" for their work and exhibited "a sunny disposition," "kindness," "tact," and a "helpful and always sympathetic" manner.[74] Female operators' characters were a key component of their success as mediators. Holmes, for example, reportedly spent "some of her happiest years" arranging the problematic connections between London's NTC and the GPO telephone networks.[75] The senior operators reportedly all enjoyed their work, and they were held up as role models for the younger women under their supervision.

While plenty of operators criticized subscribers, none ever complained about their wage scales. Nor did they mention the NTC's requirement that its female staff remain unmarried. Descriptions of operators' winning personalities and job satisfaction were coded work disciplines that have proved durable in all kinds of industries, particularly service-oriented ones: to this day "employees of the month" and their positive attitudes are singled out for emulation. In the early twentieth century, this strategy was an especially important training mechanism for the labor of mediation. Telephone women had to be "sympathetic" role models, never succumbing to inappropriate thoughts or impulses in their interactions with telephone customers or trainees. They were early examples and harbingers of the affective demands posed by telecommunications services and corporate culture.

Operators' sunny dispositions and cheerful demeanors were necessary components to an emotionally demanding occupation. The *National Telephone Journal* devoted much space to women's observations about their encounters with telephone subscribers. Operators repeatedly bemoaned the fact that their subscribers knew nothing of their work. Dublin's chief operator, Miss A. Duggan, observed that abusive subscribers were "frequently under the impression that the operator has little to do. . . . [A]n inspection of the exchange would show them that the operators are unceasingly occupied from morning till night."[76] The operator is very different from the general outside conception of her," wrote the London operator Winnifred Etheredge.

"She has quite other things to do than pass her time with crochet work, novelettes, or even a sly cigarette."[77] For Duggan, "a little consideration for the operator and defense of her from unjust attacks like the following: 'I suppose she had her fingers in the pages of a novel and would not answer me' will go a long way towards getting better results."[78] In another article, Etheredge noted that "it was an indisputable fact—strange, but none the less true—that men who in their ordinary business relations are models of common sense, politeness, and good temper, when they come to the telephone are unreasonable, impatient, and sometimes even abusive."[79] For Duggan, "constant faultfinding" was detrimental to the service as a whole, as "an operator who finds, when she is doing her best, that her statements are doubted, will cease to take an interest in her work and will not volunteer information which may be of use in preventing trouble."[80] Here the "wicked telephone girl" is seen as the product of ill-treatment by subscribers, worn down by continual abuse into a negligent and thus faulty conduit.

Contributors framed rude encounters as obstacles to efficiency, and they offered different management strategies for angry and abusive male clients. Etheredge suggested that, above all, good female operators required tact in dealing with men's expectations of telephone service. She acknowledged, however, that it was "not by any means an easy task when dealing with hundreds of calls to greet each caller with a bright cheerful response as if he were the only one to be considered." Furthermore, "if a subscriber was out of temper—not a very rare occurrence among city men—a cold mechanical civility only irritates him the more." And "if the operator keeps a smooth unruffled temper before all his heckling, and still answers him as politely as if he were the most considerate of subscribers it makes him feel a bit of a cad, or else he thinks she is laughing at him." Either way, such blanket politeness "does not improve his temper as no man likes to be made to feel that he has been behaving caddishly."[81]

Some calls, wrote Etheredge, were simply beyond the pale: "When an irascible caller tells one in a very forcible tone to go to a certain place, notorious for its hot climate, a polite reply seems somewhat inappropriate." Such a psychological balancing act, to be polite and courteous but not too much so, made for delicate—and draining—affective work.[82] But Etheredge felt that progress was slowly being made in training male users to be more "efficient": "Five or six years education by smart operators has managed to instill some sense into the most erratic" telephone users.[83]

Of course, some subscribers could not be schooled. Etheredge paraphrased a conversation with a "well-known" telephone "offender" who placed calls at slack periods on evenings and weekends:

Number, please.
- I say, How's your little dog?
What number, please
- I asked you how your little dog was.
Do you want a number, please.
- No, I want to know about your little dog.
I haven't got a little dog. If you don't want a number, don't keep ringing up.
- Yes, you have got a little dog. You told me he was a bigger dog than mine.

Nuisance calls were "not very numerous," but they were difficult for even "the best operators." There was an element of flirtation in such infuriating exchanges. Information had to be mediated with a smile; some telephone customers also wanted to imagine a wink. But often sexual language featured in explicitly abusive scenarios. Some men reportedly thought "that incessant fault-finding and grumbling are quite atoned for by an occasional lapse into familiarity—often far more offensive to the operator than any abuse."[84] Overt harassment was an occasional hazard of telephone operation, but frequent exposure to insults and gender-inflected complaints was a feature of telephone work that, despite optimism about change, emerged in virtually all women operators' observations about their daily lives.

Although affluent women also used the telephone, they were in the minority, and operators' complaints were overwhelmingly about men.[85] "City men" could be problematic, but office boys "were the worst nuisances of the telephone," having, among other deficiencies, "a mania for turning the magneto handle unnecessarily" and ruining connections.[86] As there was "no accounting for the vagaries of the office boy," female operators like Duggan and Etheredge used the *National Telephone Journal* as a training manual in accommodating male intemperance. Women operators' self-discipline was crucial to the smooth workings of the telephone service. Underlying much of these women's commentary was the implication that female operators were ultimately responsible for male telephone subscribers' behavior, a self-blaming trope common in other forms of women's popular didactic literature.[87]

Much commentary was devoted to the skill of injecting a cheerful and agreeable demeanor into the standard short phrases that operators used with subscribers—particularly the "Number, please?" greeting. The concentrated personal touch had to be tweaked and refined for the consumer, and vocal competence was meant to assure fast connections. One article was titled "Do Subscribers Appreciate a Cheerful Voice?" Responding with an enthusiastic affirmative, its author, Marion Bailey, reflected on the damage noncheerful or unpleasant voices could do.[88] Another writer mused, "Perhaps it would be well for us if we could speak into a gramophone, and then hear our voices reproduced," adding, "I am afraid that many of us would blush with shame."[89] She reported that her own work was impeded by the disagreeable pitch, tone, and emotional quality of her fellow operators' voices. Such pointed criticism of coworkers was rare, but her admonitions amplified the didactic undertones of the genre.

Women contributors to the *National Telephone Journal* portrayed telephone operation as a cognitively and emotionally challenging but satisfying occupation. The best operators drew pleasure from balancing company and subscribers' interests. Emily Richards, one of the first night operators in London, was "justly proud" of being clerk-in-charge of Gerrard, one of London's busiest exchanges, after a long career in the capital. Starting in February 1885, she had controlled the switchboards at the Heldon Street exchange in Westminster, one of the first two twenty-four-hour telephone networks.[90] Karolina Laing, another night operator, described night service in the early twentieth century as a vital part of urban life: "In a large and ever-increasing city many people are turning night into day, not only for pleasure, but for important business transactions. Calls are made by reporters, police, hospitals, doctors, and in fire and ambulance cases." She was proud to facilitate a technology that saved "many journeys, many postage stamps and, in some cases, a life." Neither operator divulged any information on the more scintillating leisure practices of afterhours London, but Laing did describe how the telephone was occasionally used to monitor others' social life: "A lady rang up one night saying: 'Are you there, Central? Will you ring me such and such a number? Please give them a good ring as they are having a party and my daughter is there, and it is getting late.'" For Laing, "some of the most important calls [were] made during the night," and she reflected on how "wonderful" it was that "people depend on the telephone."[91]

A poem published in the October 1909 edition of the *National Telephone Journal* attempted to capture women operators' vital capacities as conduits of orderly communications:

Sweet Maid . . . .
Who standest at the meeting of the ways
Like to the keeper of a toll-gate old
Or like a modern officer of law
Wielding a fair white hand to regulate
The busy traffic . . .[92]

The two metaphors cast operators as at once vestiges of the old private road network and analogues of modern state policemen. Telephone operators usually described how they facilitated connections between private and public interests in prose: "Questions such as the following are put to us: 'Are you there, Central? Can you tell us who has won the boat race?' Or 'Have you heard the latest news of the Druce Case?' Or 'Can you tell us who has won the match?' Or 'Can you tell us where the fire is, for the engine has just passed our house?' . . . . We are taken not for operators but for walking newspapers."[93] As subscribers rented lines for set periods and did not pay for the initial connection to the exchange, using operators as general information sources became a fairly common practice. This tendency was exacerbated by the design of public call boxes (precursors to the iconic red GPO telephone boxes). Telephone users had to insert money only after making contact with the operator.[94]

Telephone operators also found themselves drawn into the domestic routines of subscribers. Karolina Laing's example of being asked to call a house party to check up on a subscriber's daughter reflected the ready conscription of telephone operators into multiple forms of service. *Judy* satirized this relationship in 1898 with mock "telephonic instructions" that included a "telephone nymph" who made daily morning calls to a private home to "know if you can hear her all right" and forced the subscriber to waste time waiting by the receiver.[95] The disruptive, inefficient operator was nonetheless part of the servicing of private life. Telephone companies wanted to encourage this mindset. A National Telephone Company salesman writing for the *Journal* in 1906 argued that it was crucial for private subscribers to embrace the technology "as part of a service, available day and night, weekdays and Sundays, for all sorts of convenient labour and time-saving purposes."[96] Like telegraph boys, telephone operators redefined the role of public servant. For many telephone users, women operators were the wired help.

NUMBER, PLEASE?

The GPO's employee magazine, the *Telegraph and Telephone Journal,* established only in 1914, was more overtly disciplinarian than the *National Telephone Journal.* It devoted substantial column space to war-related communications scenarios: the second issue featured a story about the heroic exploits of Belgium's female telephone operators, who "stood bravely at the switchboard during the destruction of Louvain."[97]

Female telephone operators' first contributions to the *Telegraph and Telephone Journal,* in 1915, concerned elocution. In response to new regulations insisting that telephone operators answer subscribers' calls with a rising inflection in the phrase, "Number, please?," Agnes Avlott, an operator from the Greenwich exchange, argued that this did not go far enough in eradicating connection difficulties. A telephonist had to "convey to her subscriber by her voice the idea that she is anxious to please, and that she understands his difficulties." Avlott felt that the current system of rote phrase repetition and scripted inflections impeded these abilities. Although she also called for elocution and breath training for operators, her article was ultimately a carefully worded call for the GPO to entrust operators with greater responsibility and agency as active mediators. "Could not the telephonist be allowed a little more scope, to be treated more as a human being and less as a machine?" she asked. "Why should not her intelligence and capabilities be recognized and used? Could she not be trusted and allowed to use her own discretion?" She noted that the "present splendidly organized system of observation" would root out any individual indiscretions, furthering the development of "those delightful and desirable qualities, personality and tact."[98]

By advocating for more intensive training to enable the operator to use her own judgment, Avlott was making a case for professionalism in her occupation. The lead editorial on the front page of the following month's *Telegraph and Telephone Journal* responded to this challenge. It agreed wholeheartedly with Avlott on elocution training, noting that "something is already being done in this direction." But while the editor sympathized with her plea for fewer blanket regulations, he countered that "complete freedom of expression could obviously not be allowed to telephonists." The article ended on a note of mildly ominous conciliation: "As long as manual telephony exists we believe that the tact and discretion of experienced operators will be a valuable asset to the Administration."[99] Tact and discretion remained central to the telephone's human network, its strengths as well as its flaws, well into the twentieth century. Battles over the value of operators' work hinged on the extent to which it was seen as menial or professional. In these battles, administrators had the advantage. Despite the many ways in which operators demonstrated their skills, their contribution to electric communications did not result in greater remuneration or status. The fiscal and cultural marginalization of telecommunicative mediation was a hallmark of the new information service work.

Epilogue

FROM THE GREENWICH TELEPHONE EXCHANGE to the Central Telegraph Office, from St Martin's-le-Grand to Cleveland Street, and from silent protests to assertive self-fashioning in print media, telecommunications workers' configuration of modern networks was often at variance with the agendas of administrators. Low wages, gendered labor divisions, and policed movements through the capital were manifestations of the GPO's vision of efficient, secure communications networks in civil society. Telegraphists, telephone operators, and telegraph boys mediated consumers' cultivation of worldly expertise, urban knowledge, and fiscal success. They were gatekeepers of information flows and guards of the boundaries of respectability and discretion. As such, they fought a losing war to gain social status from their work, and they created their own disruptive exchanges. Some relied on liminal forms of mobility; others participated in collective disruptions or appropriated bounded forms of corporate discourse. Their responses to the ordering imposed on their working lives were indicative of the opportunities and pitfalls, aspirations and exclusions inherent in telecommunications systems and the values they were designed to foster.

By the first decades of the twentieth century, the control and disruption of information flows became powerful political tools wielded by women's suffrage advocates, political dissidents in Ireland, and organized labor. In all three cases telecommunications workers were symbolically resonant or active participants—and occasionally both. Women's suffrage, Irish nationalism, and workers' militancy also happen to be the causal factors in an old thesis outlining the "strange death" of England's Liberal Party and the Victorian liberal consensus, put forth by George Dangerfield in 1935.[1] Liberalism's malcontents embraced civil disobedience and violence in response to their political marginalization, and their actions challenged deeply ingrained social and political norms.

Using Freudian tropes to make sense of his actors' spectacular protests and violent agitation, Dangerfield described prewar England as pulsing with released energy. We can downplay Freud while acknowledging that Dangerfield's basic point is still valid: prewar Britain went through an ideological watershed in which liberal political structures faltered in the face of democratic and anti-imperial demands. Liberalism's contradictions, especially the different views of political freedom embraced by different actors, became more tangible and unsustainable.[2] In this moment, agitators, including marginalized members of society, created new possibilities for political action.

In my rendering of this transition, I focus on how rebellious constituencies targeted and channeled modern communications systems and their workers. The telegraph and telephone manifested the social and political order of Britain, and those eager to dismantle the status quo took on the state communications machinery and incorporated the GPO's information technology workers into multiple practices of defiance and refashioning.

THE WOMEN'S REBELLION

In her fond memoir of the militant women's suffrage campaign, Ray Strachey recorded the upending of London's orderly street flows by the sudden appearances of Women's Social and Political Union (WSPU) members.

> They arrived in all sorts of guises, and appeared in all sorts of places. Now one would appear as a messenger boy. . . . They sprang out of organ lofts, they peered through roof windows, and they leapt out of innocent-looking furniture vans; they materialized on station platforms, they harangued the terrace of the House from the river, and wherever they were least expected, there they were.[3]

After 1905, the suffrage movement had picked up momentum and had split into a number of camps, with the WSPU gaining notoriety for its strident militancy. The WSPU's members, dubbed suffragettes, captured the public's attention with their escapades and disturbances. They staged street protests, harangued MPs, interrupted parliament, defaced paintings at the National

Gallery, and destroyed public and private property. Imprisoned suffragettes staged hunger strikes and endured forced feedings, and they publicized these state-inflicted indignities in provocative and conspicuous posters.[4] There is a wonderful irony at the heart of the WSPU's tactics: in their attempt to force the government to give women the most liberal of political demands—the vote—the WSPU's leaders and followers undermined the very systems of governance that enabled self-regulating public life. Their actions were willful challenges to material environments that manifested yet denied freedom.[5]

As a physical representation of paternalist state power, the GPO was a prime target for suffragette activism. Its ubiquitous presence, including street pillar boxes, branch offices, and receiving houses, made it particularly vulnerable to dispersed, anonymous, and repetitive attacks. The GPO had prided itself on its progressive stance on female employment since the 1870s and remained structurally reliant on women's low wages. For militants, the GPO may well have encapsulated the political order's reliance on female complicity.

The first suffragette attack on GPO property occurred in Bristol in 1909, following the forced feeding of an imprisoned suffragette in Birmingham.[6] The geographic distance between these actions reflected the nationwide networks of militant suffragists (made possible in no small part by the services of the GPO). Subsequent actions occurred across the country but were concentrated in London. In 1911, the militant suffragettes' activities intensified, with Emily Wilding Davison leading a nuisance campaign that targeted the capital's mail. Davison (who died a year later after throwing herself in front of the king's horse in the Derby at Epsom Racecourse) began slipping kerosene-soaked rags and flaming matches into the letter slots of pillar boxes. The WSPU never officially sanctioned GPO destruction, however much its leaders aided and abetted its practice.[7] Despite the leadership's formal disapproval, the pillar-box destruction campaign spread through London and beyond. Militants also slipped substances such as ink, treacle, jam, tar, and corrosive chemicals through pillar-box slots. For aspiring militants, such attacks were an easy initiation into direct action: pillar boxes were ubiquitous and designed for quick and efficient urban access. After 1912, post offices also became repeated targets of window smashing and arson throughout Britain. The Investigations Branch (the Confidential Enquiry Branch had changed its name again in 1907) kept a list of women their officers had apprehended for damaging GPO property. Between 1913 and 1914 the Investigations Branch successfully prosecuted eight militant suffragists in London.[8]

Not surprisingly, this postal tactic did not improve the suffragettes' public image. The Postal Archives in London still holds a file containing hundreds of designs for "impermeable" pillar-boxes sent in by outraged postal consumers determined to help the GPO.[9] Letter sorters—many of whom were women at this point—were likely infuriated as well, as they had to manage soiled letters and decipher blemished addresses.

Despite their assaults on GPO property, the WSPU used the gender segregation in postal work to their advantage. Between 1906 and 1912, their headquarters at Clements Inn featured a telephone system with three external lines and an internal switchboard. The historian Krista Cowman notes that the switchboard and its female operators occupied a prominent place in the outer office, a celebration of female technological expertise. But the women who used the telephones knew that police and postal authorities had tapped the lines.[10] The WSPU's telephone and the women who worked the switchboard represented a facet of the politics of urban feminine display, using the telephone sparingly for innocuous calls and perhaps the occasional coded message.

In 1909, another WSPU member, Jessie Kenney, disguised herself as a telegraph boy in an attempt to sneak into the Houses of Parliament. She failed, but her exploit was widely remembered, as the above quotation, other suffragists' memoirs, and Dangerfield's account of the radical suffragist period make apparent.[11] Kenney's subterfuge was a particularly daring performance of gender nonconformity on the streets of Edwardian London, one that took advantage of telegraph boys' mobility, ubiquity, and anonymity. Telegraph boys were potent symbols for women invested in political representation and the politics of mobility.[12]

Kenney's masquerade may also have been the inspiration for fin-de-siècle London's best-known theatrical male impersonator. Until her retirement in 1919, Vesta Tilley's soldiers, swells, sailors, and men around town were music-hall sensations. A postcard in the Victoria & Albert Museum's theater collection, probably created between 1910 and 1914, depicts one of her lesser-known characters, a messenger boy. Flagrantly defying GPO rules, Tilley's messenger has opened a telegram he was meant to deliver, and judging by the look on his face, he is now party to some salacious information.

Tilley's performance toyed with gendered conventions of youthful innocence and, as queer historians remind us, was evocative on multiple erotic

"Jessie Kenney as she tried to gain admittance to Mr. Asquith's meeting on Dec. 10, 1909, disguised as a telegraph boy." Sylvia Pankhurst, *The Suffragette,* 476. Courtesy of Alamy.

Autographed postcard of Vesta Tilley as a boy messenger, ca. 1910.
Rotary Photo Company. Reprinted with kind permission from the
Victoria and Albert Museum.

levels, even harking back to the Cleveland Street scandal.[13] It also foreshad-
owed the presence of female telegraph messengers during the Great War.

THE IRISH REBELLION

Disruption of communications infrastructure also played a role in a different
form of rebellion. On Easter Monday, April 24, 1916, militant Irish republi-
cans attempted to wrest control of Dublin from Britain. That morning, while
many Dubliners were enjoying the holiday, leaders of the revolt stood on the
portico of Dublin's grand GPO headquarters and read a proclamation for the

new republic, identifying the post office as its seat of government. Meanwhile, nationalist soldiers entered the post office and commandeered a number of other buildings throughout the city. For the ensuing week, Irish rebels and British soldiers fought in the streets. The rebellion was finally suppressed when the British launched a sustained artillery attack on the GPO, forcing the surrender of the nationalist leaders and gutting the building. These events became known as the Easter Rising. It is the most iconic event in modern Irish history. Although most Irish people felt ambivalent about the rising itself, the subsequent execution of its leaders by firing squad at drawn-out intervals and their burial in unconsecrated ground turned Irish popular sentiment toward militancy and created martyrs out of the "heroes of '16." The occupation of the GPO was a formative event in Ireland's path toward the overthrow of British rule (except in the six Ulster counties that now make up Northern Ireland). One of the rising's symbolic legacies is an association between Irish republicanism and "blood sacrifice" as an expression of patriotism and as a quasi-mystical means of achieving nationalist ends.[14]

Why the GPO was selected as the site of the rising is still a matter of speculation. Historians debate whether its leaders—particularly Padraig Pearse—intended to martyr themselves all along or whether they truly believed that their insurrection would be successful. Few documents exist outlining the rebel leaders' Dublin strategy, since secrecy was essential to their cause.[15] Many contemporaries and historians assumed that the leaders chose the GPO because of its imposing presence and central location. Built in 1818, it was a massive granite structure, with six Ionic columns of Portland stone facing Sackville (now O'Connell) Street.[16] Other historians suggest that the choice was informed by the strategic and symbolic importance of the GPO as Dublin's communications hub.[17] As the urban geographer Andrew Kincaid puts it, the GPO symbolized "the worldwide network of information that colonialism helped produce and regulate," and was thus a "physical manifestation . . . of a hegemonic colonial attempt to . . . put the modern state and its institutions on display."[18] If the rising's leaders intended to go down in a blaze of patriotic glory, their decision to take the GPO down with them can be read as an attack on one of the many visible forms of imperial order inflicted on Ireland.

If, however, the leaders truly believed they could succeed, the choice of the GPO as the birthplace of a republican state demands a more nuanced explanation. Recent research on postal workers' experience of the Easter Rising suggests that the rebels targeted the GPO both to cripple British communications and to appropriate it as a base for insurrectionary networks.[19] From a tactical point of view, the GPO presented a soft target, lightly defended; but it also may have represented a form of positive state power that could be incorporated into the vision of a modern Irish republic. As in London, insurrectionary forces invested the GPO with contradictory meanings. For Irish nationalists it was both symbolic of imperialism and a center of the effective communications essential to a modern state. As headquarters of the Easter Rising, it signaled that an Irish republic could be fashioned out of the infrastructural legacy of British rule.

Postal workers were part of this legacy, playing roles both in maintaining and in undermining Dublin's imperial communications networks. GPO telegraphists, telephone operators, sorters, postmen, and engineers served both sides during the conflict. Most of Dublin's GPO employees were not actively involved in revolutionary politics, but eighteen men and one youth— an apprentice GPO engineer—were later held in military custody on suspicion of passing on logistical information to the rebels. Many GPO employees, especially in the engineering department, reportedly took part in cutting telegraph and telephone wires in and around Dublin. Their expertise was particularly crucial, for, as in London, most of Dublin's telegraph and telephone lines lay underground.[20] Postal engineers guided rebel soldiers to manholes leading to key junctions.

The rising's leaders synchronized the wire cutting with the reading of the proclamation at the GPO. The telegraphists working on the top floor of the post office were unaware of the events outside and were first alerted to the rising when they noticed that certain lines were inexplicably disconnected. They promptly alerted Dublin Castle that an insurrection was under way. When nationalist soldiers stormed the GPO sorting galleries and instrument rooms, some staff members attempted to barricade the doors. A female telegraphist reportedly tended to one of the rising's first casualties, a soldier guarding the instrument room with an unloaded rifle. The GPO staff were escorted from the building, and a handful of telegraphists immediately headed for the telegraph office on Amiens Street. By rerouting some circuits there they were able to contact London, thereby enabling a swift British response and circumventing the nationalists' attempts to force an information blackout.[21]

The nationalists were further hampered by their inability to shut down Dublin's central telephone exchange on Crown Alley. Along with Amiens Street, Crown Alley became the communications headquarters of the counterinsurgency, where engineers rerouted hundreds of connections to maintain military and government communications. The rebels set up snipers around the building and reportedly shot into the switchboard rooms where female tele-phone operators were managing the improvised lines.[22] The women spent most of the week in the building but were still, despite all the unrest, duly replaced at night by male operators. British authorities commented on the female opera-tors' bravery in terms reminiscent of the descriptions of the Belgian women who kept the telephone lines open to the last minute at Louvain.[23]

The nationalists did not destroy only wires. On at least one occasion during the Rising, post offices in other parts of Ireland received cables straight from the Dublin GPO proclaiming the republican insurgency.[24] However, British forces' use of incendiary bombs prevented any further use the nationalists could have made of the GPO's connections. By April 29, the Rising ended in the nationalists' unconditional surrender. The GPO's severely damaged facade was almost all that remained of the building. The harsh punishments meted out to the Rising's leaders by British authorities ultimately resulted in the Dublin GPO's symbolic import to republican nationalism, but GPO employ-ees quietly shaped the Rising's contours, demonstrating that telecommunica-tions workers' personal allegiances mattered in the conflict's outcome.

A few of the postal workers who disrupted Dublin's information flows that week went on to govern the Free State, then the Republic, of Ireland. Richard Mulcahy was a GPO engineer who cut the wires to Belfast on Easter Monday.[25] In 1922 he became a leader of the pro–Anglo-Irish treaty contin-gent in Ireland's civil war and spent most of the next forty years in the Irish Parliament. In an ironic twist, one participant in the rising, Sean T. O'Kelly, preserved an original copy of the proclamation by, as historian Stephen Ferguson notes, "put[ting] his trust in the Post Office."[26] Shortly after the proclamation was read, O'Kelly mailed a printed version to his aunt using the pillar box outside the GPO headquarters. It is one of the very few copies that survives, and it is currently on display in the main foyer of the Irish Parliament at Leinster House, gifted to the Irish people when O'Kelly served as president of the republic. Another copy is on display in the rebuilt GPO building on present-day O'Connell Street. It is one of the artifacts that make it the world's most nationally sanctified working post office.

THE WORKERS' REBELLION

In another fractious corner of the British Empire, India's telegraphists staged a strike in 1908 that, though unsuccessful in achieving its aims, was highly effective in demonstrating the potential of "a single disruptive action emanating from multiple centers."[27] In Britain, meanwhile, GPO workers continued to harness the flows of wires for their own ends. Despite all the drilling, uniform inspections, army recruitment schemes, Messenger Institute classes, and fitness regimes, telegraph boys persisted in growing up to become unionized postmen. The "better class of boy" was not turning out the way administrators had hoped. In 1919, telegraphists, sorters, and postmen put their long-standing differences aside and formed a combined Union of Post Office Workers (UPW). The UPW was Britain's largest civil service union for much of the twentieth century and effected institutional welfare reform until the late 1970s. Renamed the Union of Communications Workers (UCW) in 1980, and then the Communications Workers Union (CWU) in 1995, it still exists today. Its current membership of 197,000 includes employees of Britain's privatized telecommunications companies, such as BT, as well as the Royal Mail. It devotes much of its effort to stemming the tide of further privatizations and post office closures, and promoting unionizing in privately held communications corporations.[28]

One of the UPW's first targets of reform was telegraph boys' drill. In 1920, using language that echoed the pacifist sentiments of the International Arbitration League's deputation almost thirty years previously, UPW members argued that drill "was conducive to militarism" and "alien to the general administration of the Post Office." The postmaster general agreed as a conciliatory gesture to end drill. With the passing of the Education Act in 1918, telegraph boys had to attend eight hours of educational classes a week, which included exercises. The GPO initially negotiated with the London County Council to have the boys' drill count toward those hours, but the LCC balked at the use of rifles during drill.[29] The GPO backed down, reasoning that London telegraph boys would receive satisfactory fitness training unarmed and in partnership with state schooling.

The growth of state welfare and union pressures had palpable effects on London's communications workers: messengers no longer marched in formation, nor did they have to salute their "commanding officers." In 1921, this policy was extended across Britain. According to the GPO secretary, this decision, was a "measure of economy" and testament to the fact that the post office offered "very good prospects" and attracted "a good type of boy," as opposed to the "indifferent type" of bygone years "to whom the Department offered practically no prospects and . . . was almost certain to be dismissed at the age of 16."[30]

Telegraph boys were still encouraged to attend extra fitness classes and make use of the GPO's in-house gymnasiums, a legacy of their enthusiastic physical training instructor, Henry Rippon-Seymour. His fervor for virile display persisted into the interwar era and deserves a small mention. After serving as a lieutenant colonel in the Great War, he published a collection of poems celebrating his experiences in the trenches, titled *Songs of the Somme*.[31] In 1925 he became the president of the National Fascisti (NF), a splinter group of Britain's first self-proclaimed fascist party, the British Fascisti.[32] Regarding its parent group as too soft, the NF favored direct action, usually involving fistfights with communists and the destruction of left-wing media. Its members wore black shirts and brandished swords through the streets of London (much to the amusement of passers-by), and they provided fencing and boxing training for teenage boys.[33] Rippon-Seymour's first secretary, Colonel Victor Barker, worked under Rippon-Seymour for a year and left the organization after Rippon-Seymour used Barker's gun to threaten another NF member. Two years later, Barker's bankruptcy trial became a sensation when court proceedings revealed that he had been named Valerie Arckell-Smith at birth and had served as a woman ambulance driver in World War I. Barker's success as an NF member shocked Rippon-Seymour and contributed to public ridicule of the nascent fascist movement.[34]

Rippon-Seymour's influence at the post office was more enduring than his contribution to far-right politics. Telegraph boys' fitness regimens persisted at the GPO. The waiting rooms, lockers, and meal portions provided for them grew more generous, and GPO-sponsored leisure options also increased. In the interwar period, telegraph boys had pool and billiards clubs as well as football and cricket teams. They spent eight hours a week attending classes, and so long as they did not commit major infractions, they were carefully absorbed into the GPO establishment on turning eighteen.

One unpardonable offense continued to cause problems for the GPO. In August 1915, four indoor telegraph messengers, all working in the same accounting office at central headquarters in St Martin's-le-Grand, were dismissed for "indecency between male persons." The Investigations Branch ran the enquiry, one of many; the year 1915 was notable for telegraph boys' sexual transgressions. Six telegraph boys were dismissed from Brighton's branch office for same-sex transgressions in May, and two Gloucester telegraph boys were similarly dismissed that October.[35] Networks of telegraph boy rent and homoerotic encounters between messengers continued to trouble the GPO's twentieth-century ordering. Incidentally, the BT tower (formerly the Post Office Tower), a phallic icon of modern London's wireless telecommunications, rises up from 50 Cleveland Street, just a short walk up the road from the site of late-Victorian telegraph boy sexual exchanges.

While few Londoners now associate it with a late-Victorian telegraph boy sex scandal, the BT tower stands as a reminder of the British Post Office's divestment of many of its assets in the 1980s. Much of what was once the GPO is now privatized, but the Royal Mail still has its own internal investigation department. A commemorative website launched in 2016 to celebrate "500 years of Royal Mail" proudly declares, "It is one of the few remaining organizations in the UK authorized to investigate and prosecute crimes committed against itself."[36] A distinct postal security apparatus endures into the twenty-first century. Nineteenth-century telegraph boys' involvement with prostitution quietly contributed to this particular legacy.

Before the final demise of the telegraph service in 1982, London's telegraph messengers still had to balance their delivery duties, their public display, and the excitements, opportunities, and distractions of urban life. In an unpublished memoir, Bob Gibbons reminisced about his days as a central London telegraph boy in the early 1930s. Although military drill was a thing of the past, his daily work regime began with exercises and a uniform inspection. Those boys displaying the most "smartness" were approvingly named "dazzers" by their supervisors. On the job, Gibbons became an efficient urban traveler and guide: "I got to know every street in the westend [sic], and was often asked by people who were lost, and I always knew where to direct them." He enjoyed his ability to cross boundaries and peek into London's exclusive cultural venues, including the interiors of the grand hotels and the BBC's headquarters, even though "you never got beyond the reception desk." "It was also good to get messages for stars at theatres," he noted, "because going round to the stage door you would sometimes meet the stars."[37] Celebrity encounters existed alongside London microeconomies which appealed to messengers. Gibbons recalled that he and his fellow messengers "always want[ed] to take the messages to one bookies (Turf Accounts) in Bond Street because we were always given 3 cigarettes upon delivery of the messages."

Gibbons also described more intimidating deliveries, particularly in Soho, which he remembered as "a little scary at times." On one memorable occasion he had to deliver a message to "a 'Lady of the Streets'" in this district: "When I knocked at her door she called out 'I am here' a door opened on the landing and she was sitting on the Loo and calmly held out her hand for the message." Such boundary-defying encounters remind us of telegraph boys' liminality.

But Gibbons's official capacities prevented him from becoming too engrossed in the urban spectacles and possibilities surrounding him. He was "frightened to take too long" out on delivery, because if he did so his pay docket would be marked "excess," a fineable offense.[38] Telegraph boys routinely managed London's urban excesses, remaining knowing and potentially troubling icons of the intersections between orderly information flows and urban misrule.

NOTES

ABBREVIATIONS

BTA   BT (British Telecom) Archives
NA   National Archives of the United Kingdom
PM   Postal Museum
UWMRC   University of Warwick Modern Records Center

INTRODUCTION

1. Charles Whibley, *Scots Observer,* July 5, 1890, quoted in H. Montgomery Hyde, *The Cleveland Street Scandal* (London: W. H. Allen, 1976), 240.

2. Henry James, *In the Cage* (London: Martin Secker, 1924 [1898]), 10.

3. "The Telephone Exchange," *Chambers's Journal,* March 16, 1889, 175.

4. Lyon Playfair's comments in Report from the Select Committee on Post Office (Telegraph Department); Together with the Proceedings of the Committee, Minutes of Evidence, and Appendix, HC 357 Vol. 13.1, 1876 (hereafter Playfair Report).

5. Telegraphy was a government business from the 1870s onward, and the telephone system came under direct state control in the early twentieth century. I am indebted to the thematic explorations of the few existing studies of this topic, particularly the attention to administrative rationalities of public and private services in Martin Daunton, *Royal Mail: The Post Office since 1840* (London: Athlone, 1985) and *The Victorian Post Office: The Growth of a Bureaucracy* (Woodbridge, Suffolk: Boydell Press, 1992), as well as to Alan Clinton's careful delineation of GPO labor practices in *Post Office Workers: A Trade Union and Social History* (London: George Allen and Unwin, 1984). Clinton relied on the extensive archival collections held at the Union of Communications Workers House on Crescent Lane in London, which reportedly provided "virtually continuous records" of GPO trade associations from 1881. This archive was transferred to the University of Warwick's Modern Records

Centre and was subsequently reorganized. In instances where the original document trail is unclear, I have relied on Clinton's synthesis.

6. This insight taps into a vein of scholarship I loosely define as "liberal materialism." Foundational texts include Patrick Joyce, *The Rule of Freedom: Liberalism and the Modern City* (New York: Verso, 2003), and John Law, *Organizing Modernity: Social Ordering and Social Theory* (Oxford: Blackwell, 1994). Influential histories that explicitly address technology and liberalism include Chris Otter, *The Victorian Eye: A Political History of Light and Vision in Britain, 1800–1910* (Chicago: University of Chicago Press, 2008). These studies are in turn historical explorations of Michel Foucault's concept of governmentality and Bruno Latour's insistence on the agency of objects. See Foucault, "Governmentality," trans. Rosi Braidotti, in *The Foucault Effect: Studies in Governmentality,* ed. Graham Burchell, Colin Gordon, and Peter Miller (Chicago: University of Chicago Press, 1991): 87–104; Latour, "Technology Is Society Made Durable," in *A Sociology of Monsters: Essays on Power, Technology, and Domination,* ed. John Law (London: Routledge, 1991). An example of recent work that engages with but challenges some of the more determinist trends in this scholarship and acknowledges inequality of agency between people and the artifacts they make is James Vernon, *Distant Strangers: How Britain Became Modern* (Berkeley: University of California Press, 2014).

7. I am incorporating both Elaine Hadley's identification of the processes involved in liberal cognition and Stephan Collini's definition of Victorian character, particularly its characterization as "an ascribed quality, possessed and enjoyed in public view." See Hadley, *Living Liberalism: Practical Citizenship in Mid-Victorian Britain* (Chicago: University of Chicago Press, 2010), introduction; and Stefan Collini, "The Idea of 'Character' in Victorian Political Thought," *Transactions of the Royal Historical Society* 35 (1985): 40, doi:10.2307/3679175.

8. Lauren Goodland, *Victorian Literature and the Victorian State* (Baltimore: Johns Hopkins University Press, 2003), viii.

9. I am particularly indebted to David Vincent's work: see *The Culture of Secrecy: Britain, 1832–1988* (Oxford: Oxford University Press, 1998); *I Hope I Don't Intrude: Privacy and Its Dilemmas in Nineteenth-Century Britain* (Oxford: Oxford University Press, 2015); *Privacy: A Short History* (Cambridge: Polity, 2016). See also Deborah Cohen, *Family Secrets: Shame and Privacy in Modern Britain* (Oxford: Oxford University Press, 2017).

10. In recent years, attention to the meaning of work has receded. See John McIlroy, "Waving or Drowning? British Labor History in Troubled Waters," *Labor History* 53, no. 1 (2012): 91–119, doi:10.1080/0023656X.2012.650435; Patrick Joyce, "The End of Social History?" *Social History* 20, no. 1 (1995): 73–91, www.jstor.org /stable/4286248; Mike Savage, "Class and Labour History," in *Class and Other Identities: Gender, Religion and Ethnicity in the Writing of European Labour History,* ed. Lex Heerma van Voss and Marcel van der Linden (Oxford: Berghan, 2002) 55–72; and Joan Allen, Alan Campbell, Eric Hobsbawm, and John McIlroy, eds., *Histories of Labour: National and International Perspectives* (Pontypool, Wales: Merlin, 2010).

11. John Munro, "At the Central Telegraph Station, St Martins-le-Grand," *Time,* July 1879, 485.

12. The development of electronic communications technologies has received considerable attention in recent years, for obvious reasons. One popular historian has heralded the nineteenth century's telegraph system as "the Victorian Internet" (T. Standage, *The Victorian Internet: The Remarkable Story of the Telegraph and the Nineteenth Century's Online Pioneers* [New York: Walker, 1998]). For a comprehensive technical history of telegraphy, see Ken Beauchamp, *History of Telegraphy* (London: Institution of Engineering and Technology, 2001). For international perspectives, see Roland Wenzlhuemer, "The Development of Telegraphy, 1870–1900: A European Perspective on a World History Challenge," *History Compass* 5 (2006): 1720–42, doi:10.1111/j.1478-0542.2007.00461.x; Peter J. Hugill, *Global Communications Since 1844: Geopolitics and Technology* (Baltimore: Johns Hopkins University Press, 1999); and D. Headrick and Pascal Griset, "Submarine Telegraph Cables: Business and Politics, 1838–1939," *Business History Review* 75, no. 3 (2001): 543–78, www.jstor.org/stable/3116386.

13. D. Headrick, *The Tools of Empire: Technology and European Imperialism in the Nineteenth Century* (Oxford: Oxford University Press, 1981); D. Headrick, *The Invisible Weapon: Telecommunications and International Politics, 1851–1945* (Oxford: Oxford University Press, 1991); Ben Marsden and Crosbie Smith, *Engineering Empires: A Cultural History of Technology in Nineteenth-Century Britain* (Basingstoke: Palgrave Macmillan, 2005); Simon J. Potter, "Webs, Networks, and Systems: Globalization and the Mass Media in the Nineteenth- and Twentieth-Century British Empire," *Journal of British Studies,* 46, no. 3 (2007): 621–46, www.jstor.org /stable/10.1086/515446; Bruce J. Hunt, "Doing Science in a Global Empire: Cable Telegraphy and Electrical Physics in Victorian Britain," in *Victorian Science in Context,* ed. Bernard Lightman (Chicago: University of Chicago Press, 1997), 311–33. On resistance and appropriation, see, for example, E. Thomas Ewing, "'A Most Powerful Instrument for a Despot': The Telegraph as a Transnational Instrument of Imperial Control and Political Mobilization in the Middle East," in *The Nation State and Beyond,* ed. Roland Wenzlhuemer and Isabella Löhr (Berlin: Springer-Verlag, 2013), 83–100; D. K. Lahiri Choudhury, "Sinews of Panic and the Nerves of Empire: The Imagined State's Entanglement with Information Panic, India c. 1880–1912," *Modern Asian Studies* 38, no. 4 (2004): 965–1002, doi10.1017/S0026749X0400126X; and Yakup Bektas, "The Sultan's Messenger: Cultural Constructions of Ottoman Telegraphy, 1847–1880," *Technology and Culture* 41, no. 4 (2000): 669–96. doi:10.1353/tech.2000.0141.

14. Iwan Rhys Morus, "The Nervous System of Britain: Space, Time and the Electric Telegraph in the Victorian Age," *British Journal for the History of Science* 33, no. 4 (2000): 455–75, www.jstor.org/stable/4028030.

15. The geographer Nigel Thrift has detected processes of "technological determinism" in such responses, one of the most pernicious effects of which is to imagine telecommunications "to have the same effects everywhere and rapidly." This totalizing mindset leads to "fantasies about the control of information spaces," leaving

little interpretative space for alternative information practices and aspirations. Moreover, homogeneous models of technology-driven social transformation obscure patterns of information technology distribution and production that reaffirm social inequities. Nigel Thrift, "New Urban Eras and Old Technological Fears: Reconfiguring the Goodwill of Electronic Things," *Urban Studies* 33, no. 8 (1996): 1485–86, doi:10.1080/0042098966754.

16. Much recent work on imperial communications is influenced by Christopher Bayly's concept of "information panics," which posits that imperial expansion and maintenance lead to continual crises over the control of information flows. See C. A. Bayly, *Empire and Information: Intelligence Gathering and Social Communication in India, 1780–1870* (Cambridge: Cambridge University Press, 1996). D.K. Lahiri Choudhury uses this insight to examine telegraphy in the Indian subcontinent: see Choudhury, *Telegraphic Imperialism: Crisis and Panic in the Indian Empire, c. 1830* (Basingstoke: Palgrave Macmillan, 2010). In a different vein, Jeffrey Sconce has related the imperial resonances of telegraphy to spiritualism, suggesting that the "haunted" electronic networks of telegraphy and other early telecommunications systems encouraged both "exploratory" crossings of frontiers and "an all-enveloping force occupying the ether." Sconce, *Haunted Media: Electric Presence from Telegraphy to Television* (Durham, NC: Duke University Press, 2000), 10–11.

17. I am not making the case for London as an early incarnation of the "informational city," Manuel Castells's evocative label for the current concentration of tech-industry capital and labor in a handful of global urban centers (London among them). The current knowledge economy has arisen not only from the swift transfer of information but also from technologies of mass data accumulation, collation, processing, and selling. In this respect, the late Victorian and Edwardian "information economy" is markedly different from our own. Castells, *The Informational City: Information Technology, Economic Restructuring, and the Urban-Regional Process* (Oxford: Blackwell, 1989).

18. John Tully, "A Victorian Ecological Disaster: Imperialism, the Telegraph, and Gutta Percha," *Journal of World History* 20, no. 4 (2009): 570, www.jstor.org /stable/40542850; Roland Wenzlhuemer, *Connecting the Nineteenth-Century World: The Telegraph and Globalization* (Cambridge: Cambridge University Press, 2013), chapter 7.

19. Stephen Graham and Simon Marvin, *Splintering Urbanism: Networked Infrastructures, Technological Mobilities and the Urban Condition* (London: Routledge, 2001), 318–19.

20. What has intrigued economic and imperial historians in recent years is the importance of British fiscal services to the national and imperial economy. The individuals working in commerce and its related industries represent the aristocracy of service labor; their wealth and political clout put financial service providers in entirely different socioeconomic categories from most other service workers.

21. C.H. Lee, "The Service Sector, Regional Specialization, and Economic Growth in the Victorian Economy," *Journal of Historical Geography* 10, no. 2 (1984): 139, doi: 10.1016/0305–7488(84)90115–4.

22. By the latter half of the nineteenth century, social investigators and observers had shifted their gaze away from the industrial boomtowns in the North of England and back to the capital. See Asa Briggs, *Victorian Cities* (Berkeley: University of California Press, 1965); Gareth Stedman Jones, *Outcast London: A Study in the Relationship between Classes in Victorian Society* (London: Penguin, 1984); Judith Walkowitz, *City of Dreadful Delight: Narratives of Sexual Danger in Late-Victorian London* (Chicago: University of Chicago Press, 1992); Lynda Nead, *Victorian Babylon: People, Streets, and Images in Nineteenth-Century London* (New Haven: Yale University Press, 2000); and Tristam Hunt, *Building Jerusalem: The Rise and Fall of the Victorian City* (London: Weidenfeld and Nicolson, 2004).

23. In contrast to fin-de-siècle Berlin, which Andreas Killen has characterized as an innovative, hypermodern "site of anxiety and shock," London simultaneously embraced the new and fetishized the old. The capital's contributions to electric information networks and their cultural impact were similarly contradictory. See Andreas Killen, *Berlin Electropolis: Shock, Nerves, and German Modernity* (Berkeley: University of California Press, 2006), 8.

24. Walkowitz, *City of Dreadful Delight;* Nead, *Victorian Babylon;* Pamela Gilbert, *Mapping the Victorian Social Body* (Albany: SUNY Press, 2004); Frank Mort, *Dangerous Sexualities: Medico-moral Politics in England since 1830* (London: Routledge, 1987), chapter 8.

25. Different state communications systems have dealt with this problem in different ways. In Germany, for example, telecommunications workers were designated "mental laborers," which gave them a particular social status, salary level, and standing in the German bureaucracy. This designation also had unintended consequences, producing a nationally specific relationship between "brain work," mental disease, and Germany's welfare provisions. See Killen, *Berlin Electropolis,* 171–75.

26. Lee, "Service Sector," 139–55.

27. The sociologist Linda McDowell has dealt with the problem of past and present service-sector hierarchies by defining high-status "producer" and mostly low-status "consumer" services. Linda McDowell, *Working Bodies: Interactive Service Employment and Workplace Identities* (Chichester: Wiley-Blackwell, 2011), 30–31.

28. On this point I am indebted to Jessica P. Clark, "Pomeroy v. Pomeroy: Beauty, Modernity, and the Female Entrepreneur in Fin-de-Siècle London," *Women's History Review* 22, no. 6 (2013): 877–903, and Amanda Herbert, "Gender and the Spa: Space, Sociability, and the Self at British Health Spas, 1670–1714," *Journal of Social History* 43, no. 2 (2009): 361–83, doi:10.1353/jsh.0.0260.

29. For a recent British study engaged with the contestations inherent to the growth of middle-class women's professional work, see Gillian Sutherland, *In Search of the New Woman: Middle-Class Women and Work in Britain, 1870–1914* (Cambridge: Cambridge University Press, 2015).

30. The regulation, commodification, and monetization of affect have lately engaged sociologists and social theorists interested in labor. Linda McDowell, Michael Hardt, Antonio Negri, Kathi Weeks, and many others have delved into

modern capitalism's interest in the "creation and manipulation of affect" by workers for profit in the postindustrial West. These studies are understandably guided by presentist concerns with the types of estrangement and alienation attendant on such personalized labor appropriations, particularly in relation to gender inequities and in postcolonial spaces. Sociologists should not be expected to do double duty as historians, but historical processes are both crucial to and absent from most of this recent theorizing. See Michael Hardt, "Affective Labor," *Boundary* 2, no. 2 (1999): 89–100, www.jstor.org/stable/303793; Michael Hardt and Antonio Negri, *Empire* (Cambridge, MA: Harvard University Press, 2009); Kathi Weeks, "Life within and against Work: Affective Labor, Feminist Critique, and Post-Fordist Politics," *Ephemera: Theory and Politics in Organization* 7, no. 1 (2007): 233–49. See also Emma Dowling, Rodrigo Nunes, and Ben Trott, "Immaterial and Affective Labor: Explored," *Ephemera: Theory and Politics in Organization* 7, no. 1 (2007): 1–7; Manuel Castells, *End of Millennium: The Information Age: Economy, Society, and Culture*, vol. 3 (Chichester: John Wiley & Sons, 2010).

31. The cultural critic John Durham Peters has argued that prior to the nineteenth century, *medium* in European intellectual circles "had always meant an element, environment, or vehicle in the middle of things." It was the telegraph—and Victorian spiritualism, which derived much of its legitimation and influence from telegraphy—that changed the word *medium* "into a conveyance" of "human signals and meanings." This book both acknowledges this historical trajectory and changes its tack: I look closely at the people who performed telecommunications mediations and the environments in which they did so. This was not exactly what Peters had in mind, interested as he is in breaking down boundaries between human and natural phenomena and ascribing complex agencies to all aspects of the material world. While I believe these lines of inquiry are invaluable as we head into a very uncertain material future, the "shrinkage of the notion of communications to mean intentional sendings among humans," often encapsulated in the figure of a woman, still merits study on those very terms. John Durham Peters, *The Marvelous Clouds: Toward a Philosophy of Elemental Media* (Chicago: University of Chicago Press, 2015), 46–48. See also John Durham Peters, *Speaking into the Air: A History of the Idea of Communication* (Chicago: University of Chicago Press, 1999) 94–101.

32. See Gregory Anderson, "The White Blouse Revolution," in *The White Blouse Revolution: Female Office Workers since 1870*, ed. Gregory Anderson (Manchester: University of Manchester Press,1988), 1–26; Meta Zimmeck, "Jobs for Girls: the Expansion of Clerical Work for Women, 1870–1930," in *Unequal Opportunities: Women's Employment in England, 1800–1918*, ed. Angela John (Oxford: Oxford University Press,1986), 153–78; David Rubenstein, *Before the Suffragettes: Women's Emancipation in the 1890s* (Brighton: Harvester, 1986); Elaine Showalter, *Sexual Anarchy: Gender and Culture in the Fin de Siècle* (London: Bloomsbury, 1991); Anna Davin, "Women Telegraphists and Typists, 1870–1890," in *Women in Industry and Technology,* ed. Amanda Devonshire and Barbara Wood (London: Museum of London, 1986) 214–15; Davin, "City Girls: Young Women, New Employment, and the City, London 1880–1910," in *Secret Gardens, Satanic Mills: Placing Girls in*

European History, 1750–1960, ed. Mary Jo Maynes, Birgitte Søland, and Christina Benninghaus (Bloomington: Indiana University Press, 2005) 209–23; Dina Copelman, *London's Women Teachers: Gender, Class and Feminism, 1870–1930* (London: Routledge, 1996). For recent scholarship, see Helen Glew, *Gender, Rhetoric, and Regulation: Women's Work in the Civil Service and London County Council, 1900–1955* (Manchester: University of Manchester Press, 2016). For women's work in relation to shifts in masculinity, see John Tosh, *A Man's Place: Masculinity and the Middle-Class Home in Victorian England* (New Haven: Yale University Press, 1999) chapters 7–8; Peter Bailey, "White Collars, Gray Lives? The Lower Middle Class Revisited," *Journal of British Studies* 38, no. 3 (1999): 273–90, www.jstor.org/stable/176057; and A. James Hammerton, "Pooterism or Partnership? Marriage and Masculine Identity in the Lower Middle Class, 1870–1920," *Journal of British Studies* 38, no. 3 (1999): 291–321, www.jstor.org/stable/176058.

33. This is a process first documented in the Canadian telegraph industry in the early twentieth century by Shirley Tillotson: "'We May All Soon Be 'First-Class Men': Gender and Skill in Canada's Early Twentieth Century Urban Telegraph Industry," *Labour/Le Travail* 27 (1991): 97–125, www.jstor.org/stable/25130246.

34. Feminist historians and economists have charted similarly contentious patterns elsewhere of work segregation, gendered workplace respectability, and the devaluation of women's skills. See foundational scholarship such as Heidi Hartman, "Capitalism, Patriarchy, and Job Segregation by Sex," *Signs* 1, no. 3 (1976): 137–69, www.jstor.org/stable/3173001; Barbara Taylor and Anne Phillips, "Sex and Skill: Notes towards a Feminist Economics," *Feminist Review* 6, no. 1 (1980): 1–15. See also Sonya Rose, *Limited Livelihoods: Gender and Class in Nineteenth-Century England* (Berkeley: University of California Press, 1992), chapters 2, 6. For an account of multiple gender arrangements in industrializing Britain that predates this study, see Anna Clark, *The Struggle for the Breeches: Gender and the Making of the British Working Class* (Berkeley: University of California Press, 1995), chapters 7, 11, and 13. Recently Mar Hicks has demonstrated the deleterious consequences of gender segregation in the information technology sector in mid-twentieth-century Britain in *Programmed Inequality: How Britain Discarded Women Technologists and Lost its Edge in Computing* (Cambridge, MA: MIT Press, 2017).

35. Advice to Telephone Supervising Officers, 1909: 3, POST 68/241, BTA.

36. "Curiosities of the Wire," *Chambers's Journal*, September 2, 1876, 568.

37. Kate Thomas, *Postal Pleasures: Sex, Scandal, and Victorian Letters* (Oxford: Oxford University Press, 2012), 1. For the sexual dynamics of information transmission, see also Kate Mullin, *Working Girls: Fiction, Sexuality, and Modernity* (Oxford: Oxford University Press, 2016).

38. "Curiosities of the Wire."

39. "Curiosities of the Wire."

40. Kate Thomas has compellingly located the more subversive possibilities of a "deliciously intermediated" communications system. But the desires of the mediators in this instance—and expressed in other journalistic accounts—resembled parasexuality, Peter Bailey's characterization of Victorian sexual norms produced

through mixed-gender service economy interactions (here adapted from the public house to the telegraph office). Thomas, *Postal Pleasures,* 2; Peter Bailey, "Parasexuality and Glamour: the Victorian Barmaid as Cultural Prototype," *Gender and History* 2, no. 2 (1990): 148–72, doi: 10.1111/j.1468–0424.1990.tb00091.x.

41. H. Montgomery Hyde, *The Cleveland Street Scandal* (London: W.H. Allen, 1976); Colin Simpson, Lewis Chester, and David Leitch, *The Cleveland Street Affair* (Boston: Little, Brown, 1976); Morris B. Kaplan, *Sodom on the Thames: Sex, Love, and Scandal in Wilde Times* (Ithaca, NY: Cornell University Press, 2005), chapter 3; Jeffrey Weeks, *Sex, Politics, and Society: the Regulation of Sexuality since 1800* (London: Longman, 1981), chapter 5; Theo Aronson, *Prince Eddy and the Homosexual Underworld,* 2nd ed. (London: John Murray, 1996); Trevor Fisher, *Scandal: Sexual Politics in Late Victorian Britain* (Stroud: Sutton, 1995); H.G. Cocks, *Nameless Offences: Homosexual Desire in the Nineteenth Century* (London: I.B. Tauris, 2003), 144–53.

42. Stephen Humphries, *Hooligans or Rebels? An Oral History of Working-Class Childhood and Youth, 1889–1930* (Oxford: Oxford University Press, 1981); John Springhall, *Coming of Age: Adolescence in Britain, 1860–1960* (Dublin: Gill and Macmillan, 1986); John Springhall, *Youth, Empire and Society: British Youth Movements, 1883–1940* (London: Croom Helm, 1977); John Gillis, *Youth and History: Tradition and Change in European Age Relations, 1770–Present* (London: Academic Press, 1981); Michael Childs, *Labour's Apprentices: Working-Class Lads in Late Victorian and Edwardian England* (Montreal: McGill University Press, 1992); Harry Hendrick, *Images of Youth: Age, Class, and the Male Youth Problem, 1880–1920* (Oxford: Clarendon Press, 1990); and Seth Koven, "From Rough Lads to Hooligans: Boy Life, National Culture, and Social Reform," in *Nationalisms and Sexualities,* ed. Andrew Parker, Mary Russo, Doris Sommer, and Patricia Yaeger (New York: Routledge, 1992), 365–91.

43. I am indebted to Mary Fissell for this phrasing; in a discussion about this project she described our current moment as "the age of mass intimacies."

CHAPTER ONE. DISPATCHES FROM UNDERGROUND

1. W. Johnson, "Telegraph Street," *Temple Bar,* July 1871.

2. Johnson, "Telegraph Street."

3. Jerry White, *London in the Nineteenth Century: "A Human Awful Wonder of God"* (London: Vintage, 2008), chapters 2 and 3.

4. Chris Otter, "Making Liberal Objects: British Techno-Social Relations, 1800–1900," *Cultural Studies* 21, no. 5 (2007): 575, doi: 10.1080/09502380701278962.

5. Johnson, "Telegraph Street."

6. John Munro, "At the Central Telegraph Station, St. Martins-le-Grand," *Time,* July 1879, 485.

7. Iwan Rhys Morus, "The Nervous System of Britain: Space, Time and the Electric Telegraph in the Victorian Age," *British Journal for the History of Science* 33, no. 4 (2000): 470, www.jstor.org/stable/4028030.

8. Morus, "The Nervous System of Britain," 456.

9. C. R. Perry, *The Victorian Post Office: The Growth of a Bureaucracy* (London: Royal Historical Society, 1992), 87–88; "Art. VIII: Special Report from the Select Committee on the Electric Telegraph Bill; together with Minutes of Evidence," *Edinburgh Review*, July 1870, 225.

10. "Art. VIII," 225.

11. For a detailed study of the system before nationalization, see Simone Fari, *Victorian Telegraphy before Nationalization* (Basingstoke: Palgrave Macmillan, 2015).

12. "The Telegraph and the Post Office," *Times*, November 12, 1867.

13. Perry, *The Victorian Post Office*, 88.

14. W. S. Jevons, "On the Analogy between the Post Office, Telegraphs, and Other Systems of Conveyance of the United Kingdom as Regards Government Control," *Methods of Social Reform*, 2nd ed. (London: MacMillan, 1904).

15. Perry, *The Victorian Post Office*, 104–5.

16. A Report to the Postmaster General upon Certain Proposals which Have Been Made for Transferring to the Post Office the Control and Management of the Electric Telegraphs throughout the United Kingdom; Supplementary Report to the Postmaster General upon the Proposal for Transferring to the Post Office the Control and Management of the Electric Telegraphs Throughout the United Kingdom, British Parliamentary Papers, 1867–68, HC 202 Vol. 41.555.

17. "The Telegraphs and the Post Office," *Pall Mall Gazette*, March 11, 1868.

18. Perry, *The Victorian Post Office*, chapter 4.

19. Patrick Joyce, *The Rule of Freedom* (London: Verso, 2003), chapters 3–5; Chris Otter, *The Victorian Eye: A Political History of Light and Vision in Britain, 1800–1910* (Chicago: University of Chicago Press, 2008); Simon Gunn, *The Public Culture of the Victorian Middle Class: Ritual and Authority in the English Industrial City, 1840–1914* (Manchester: Manchester University Press, 2000).

20. Joyce, *The Rule of Freedom*; Otter, *The Victorian Eye*. See also David Pike, *Metropolis on the Styx: The Underworlds of Modern Urban Culture, 1801–2001* (Ithaca, NY: Cornell University Press, 2007), chapters 1 and 3.

21. The company's success was due to an earlier merger between Silvertown and the West Ham Gutta-Percha Company, whose owner, Thomas Hancock, had developed a lucrative hold on the export of gutta-percha from Southeast Asia. A close relative of rubber, gutta-percha is a naturally occurring resin. It was much better suited to insulating underwater cables than was rubber from Africa and South America, as the latter degrades in salt water. Gutta-percha extraction drove the international telegraph industry, resulting in the near extinction of gutta-percha-producing trees in British Malaya and Sarawak by the end of the nineteenth century. In England, gutta-percha was incorporated into the manufacture of products from toys and clothing to pipes and roof tiles. Until it was supplanted by synthetic rubbers and plastics in the early twentieth century, it was a staple of both communications and the modernizing consumer economy. See John Tully, "A Victorian Ecological Disaster: Imperialism, the Telegraph, and Gutta-Percha," *Journal of World*

History 20, no. 4 (2009): 559–79. www.jstor.org/stable/40542850; Amarjit Kaur, "A History of Forestry in Sarawak," *Modern Asian Studies* 32 (1998): 117–47, www.jstor .org/stable/312971.

22. Howard Robinson, *The British Post Office: A History* (Princeton: Princeton University Press, 1948), 403.

23. Robinson, *The British Post Office*, 403.

24. Annual Reports of the Postmaster General, 1871–75, PM.

25. White, *London in the Nineteenth Century*, 27.

26. Perry, *The Victorian Post Office*, 4.

27. Munro, "At the Central Telegraph Station," 485.

28. Johnson, "Telegraph Street."

29. "The Electric Telegraph of London," *Bow Bells,* November 30, 1870, 451.

30. "Our Postal Telegraphs," special issue, *The Engineer,* 1891.

31. Based on floor plan from "Our Postal Telegraphs."

32. Residents in more affluent eastern areas stubbornly clung to their former designation, giving their addresses as "NE," and the GPO indulged this practice. In 1866 the NE district was abolished: N and E, the Bethnal Green office (head office), became an eastern branch office. S. G. Dawkins and J. W. A Lowder, "London: Origin and Development of the Districts and Postal Services," 1969, reference library, PM.

33. These numbers are derived from the appendix of the *British Postal Guide* (London: George E. Eyre and William Spottiswoode, 1875), which listed all publicly accessible telegraph offices and receiving houses in London.

34. *British Postal Guide,* 1890.

35. Roland Wenzlhuemer, *Connecting the Nineteenth-Century World: The Telegraph and Globalization* (Cambridge: Cambridge University Press, 2013), chapter 7.

36. Perry, *The Victorian Post Office*, chapters 4 and 5.

37. "A Year's Telegraphy," *Pall Mall Gazette,* February 13, 1871.

38. "Postal Telegraphs," *Daily News,* July 25, 1876.

39. George Leeman, Electric Telegraphs Bill [Bill 82], 2nd reading, 9 June, 192 Parl. Deb. (3rd ser.) (1868), col. 1307.

40. Thomas Crook, "Secrecy and Liberal Modernity in Victorian and Edwardian Britain," in *The Peculiarities of Liberal Modernity in Imperial Britain,* ed. Simon Gunn and James Vernon, (Berkeley: University of California Press, 2011), 167; David Vincent, *The Culture of Secrecy: Britain, 1832–1998* (Oxford: Oxford University Press, 1998), chapter 2.

41. Vincent, *The Culture of Secrecy,* 45.

42. "The Telegraph Bill," *Saturday Review of Politics, Literature, and Art,* June 13, 1868, 780–81; "The Electric Telegraphs," *Lloyds Weekly Newspaper,* June 14, 1868; *Occasional Notes, Pall Mall Gazette,* 10 June 1868; "The Debate on the Electric Telegraphs Bill," *Economist,* June 13, 1868.

43. David Vincent, *I Hope I Don't Intrude: Privacy and its Dilemmas in Nineteenth-Century Britain* (Oxford: Oxford University Press, 2015), introduction, chapters 5–7.

44. Mary Poovey, "Writing about Finance in Victorian England: Disclosure and Secrecy in the Culture of Investment," *Victorian Studies* 45, no. 1 (2002): 17–41, www.muse.jhu.edu/article/43751.

45. I am indebted to Victor McVey for his comprehensive online collections and links to telegraph code manuals. McVey, "Telegraphic and Signal Codes: Annotated Directory of Scans, Transcriptions," last updated April 26, 2013, www.jmcvey.net /cable/scans.htm.

46. McVey, "Telegraphic and Signal Codes."

47. W. Clausen-Thue, *The ABC Universal Commercial Electronic Telegraphic Code* (London: Rock Terrace, 1873), 48.

48. Clausen-Thue, *The ABC Telegraphic Code,* 3rd ed. (London: Eden Fisher, 1876), vii.

49. Clausen-Thue, *The ABC Telegraphic Code,* vii.

50. "Fenians' Telegram to Their Friends," *Punch,* 18 June 1870, 249.

51. The introduction of greetings telegrams in the twentieth century was a response to this long-standing association, which waned in the late nineteenth and early twentieth centuries but returned in full force with the onset of the Great War.

52. "Curiosities of the Wire," *Chambers's Journal,* September 2, 1876.

CHAPTER TWO. THE PUBLIC SERVICE OF DISCRETION

1. Frank Ives Scudamore to Postmaster General William Monsell, 30 December 1871, The Telegraphists' Strike, file XX, POST30/215, BTA. London's telegraphists were involved in the agitation: the GPO's internal security force, the Missing Letter Branch, recorded clandestine after-work meetings at a house in Highbury in the build-up to the strike, for example, and London telegraphists were aware they were being spied on by their superiors. But they did not ultimately follow the example of their northern, Scottish, and Irish colleagues: The Telegraphists' Strike, file IV, POST 30/215 BTA. See also Henry Swift, *A History of Postal Agitation: From Fifty Years Ago to the Present Day* (London: C. Arthur Pearson, 1900), 135–53.

2. Telegraph Act, 1868, 31 & 32, Vict. C.110: 1063.

3. W. E. Gladstone to Lord John Russell, June 20, 1854, cited in David Vincent, *The Culture of Secrecy: Britain, 1832–1998* (Oxford: Oxford University Press, 1999), 43.

4. Vincent, *Culture of Secrecy,* chapter 2. On the ways this ordering "mechanized" government hierarchies, see Jon Agar, *The Government Machine: A Revolutionary History of the Computer* (Cambridge, MA: MIT Press, 2003), 52–66.

5. Kate Thomas, *Postal Pleasures: Sex, Scandal, and Victorian Letters* (Oxford: Oxford University Press, 2012), 1, 4.

6. Alan Clinton, *Post Office Workers: A Trade Union and Social History* (London: George Allen & Unwin, 1984), 49–50.

7. Clinton, *Post Office Workers,* 49–59; M. J. Daunton, *Royal Mail: The Post Office since 1840* (London: Athlone, 1985), chapter 6.

8. Daunton, *Royal Mail,* 214.

9. Patrick Joyce, *The State of Freedom: A Social History of the British State since 1800* (Cambridge: Cambridge University Press, 2013), 129. Post office uniforms had undergone a number of transformations since their inception in the eighteenth century, in some senses going full circle from regulatory spectacle to status symbol to emblems of a well-managed bureaucratic working-class. Uniforms were instituted in the eighteenth century to better monitor King's Messengers and their supposed propensity to linger in drinking establishments. In the early nineteenth century the elaborate bright red uniform was a sign of pride and a marker of state authority. Both the uniform and postal workers' social standing changed dramatically in the Victorian era. As the post office developed into a ubiquitous and affordable network of communication, the postman became common, in both senses of the word.

10. In 1870, the GPO created a class of "boy sorters," which led to further resentments among the adult sorting staff. Swift, *A History of Postal Agitation,* 155–56.

11. Clinton, *Post Office Workers,* 3–4, 81–82.

12. Clinton, *Post Office Workers,* 52–53, 118–21.

13. Swift, *A History of Postal Agitation,* 135–36.

14. I use the appendixes from Clinton, *Post Office Workers,* for these figures. Elsewhere I have drawn directly from GPO establishment records.

15. Swift, *A History of Postal Agitation,* 142.

16. Memorandum from E. Cooper to T. Johnson, November 30, 1871, The Telegraphists' Strike, 1871 file IV, POST 30/215, BTA.

17. Memorandum from Scudamore, November 21, 1871, The Telegraphists' Strike, 1871, file IV, POST 30/215, BTA.

18. *Daily News,* December 9, 1871.

19. "Official Interception of Telegrams," *Saturday Review,* December 16, 1871.

20. First Report of the Civil Service Inquiry Commission; With Correspondence (1875), C. 1113.HMSO 14 (hereafter Playfair Commission).

21. *Telegraph Clerks' Agitation,* pamphlet, March 16, 1882, Postal Telegraph Clerks' Association: Conferences and Deputations (1), 148/PT/1/2/1, UWMRC.

22. Report from the Select Committee on Post Office (Telegraph Department); Together with the Proceedings of the Committee, Minutes of Evidence, and Appendix (1876), HC 357–13: 52 (hereafter Playfair Report).

23. Joyce, *State of Freedom,* 97.

24. D.K. Lahiri Choudhury, *Telegraphic Imperialism: Crisis and Panic in the Indian Empire* (Basingstoke: Palgrave MacMillan, 2010), 21; Playfair Report, 50. In *The Telegraphist: A Monthly Journal of Popular Electrical Science* (1880–89), a regular column, *The Telegraphist in the Field,* described the work of imperial telegraphy performed by British telegraphists in India and elsewhere.

25. Playfair Report, 50.

26. "History of Dual Training," 1905, File I Post 63/4, PM.

27. *Telegraph Clerks' Agitation.*

28. "The Duties of a Telegraph Clerk," *The Telegraphist,* December 1, 1885: 5.

29. Address of the Provincial Postal Telegraph Male Clerks to Candidates at the General Election, 1892, 7; Postal Telegraph Clerks' Association: Petitions, 148/PT/2/1/4; Statements of the Senior, First, Second, and Female Clerks of the Central Telegraph Office: Conferences and Deputations, (1) 148/PT/1/2/1, UWMRC.

30. Address of the Provincial Postal Telegraph Male Clerks.

31. Statements of the Senior, First, Second, and Female Clerks, 7.

32. Statements of the Senior, First, Second, and Female Clerks, 17.

33. "Duties of a Telegraph Clerk."

34. Address of the Provincial Postal Telegraph Male Clerks.

35. Evidence of R. C. Tombs, Report of Committee: Postmen, Their Duties and Pay, 1891, appendix 138, POST 30/598, PM.

36. "Mr Scudamore and the Telegraph Department," *Spectator,* December 16, 1871.

37. Dublin GPO secretary to Frank Scudamore, December 11, 1871, Strike of the Telegraphists: Dublin and Cork, folder XI, POST 30/215, part 2, BTA.

38. Limerick postmaster to Postmaster General William Monsell, December 11, 1871, Strike of the Telegraphists: Dublin and Cork, folder XI, POST 30/215, part 2, BTA.

39. Clinton, *Post Office Workers,* 119; "Telegraph Street," *Temple Bar,* July 1871, 516.

40. Swift, *A History of Postal Agitation,* 155. For the relative numbers of men and women telegraphists in the 1870s, I have used post office establishment records, as well as summaries commissioned in 1878 that are part of the report "Further Substitution of Male for Female Telegraphists at the Central Telegraph Office," 1878–1880, POST 30/364C, BTA.

41. "Telegraph Street."

42. "Art VI: The Electric Telegraph," *British Quarterly Review,* April 1874, 467.

43. Anthony Trollope, "The Young Women at the Central Telegraph Office," *Good Words,* December 1877, 379.

44. Susan Shelangoskie, "Anthony Trollope and the Social Discourse of Telegraphy after Nationalization," *Journal of Victorian Culture* 14, no. 1 (2009): 72–93, doi: 10.3366/E1355550209000605.

45. Shelangoskie, "Anthony Trollope."

46. Elizabeth Banks, *Campaigns of Curiosity: Journalistic Adventures of an American Girl in London* (Chicago: F. Tennyson Neely, 1894), 4.

47. From the later Victorian period through the mid-twentieth century, domestic service remained the largest sector of female employment. For recent work on the continuities of service, see Lucy Delap, *Knowing Their Place: Domestic Service in Twentieth-Century* Britain (Oxford: Oxford University Press, 2011).

48. I am drawing on Stefan Collini's insights about nineteenth-century "character," particularly his observation that it was "an ascribed quality, possessed and enjoyed in public view." Collini, "The Idea of 'Character' in Victorian Political Thought," *Transactions of the Royal Historical Society* 35 (1985): 40, doi:10.2307/3679175.

49. To middle-class elites, the landed gentry's extravagant household staffs may have signaled immoral indulgences, but they remained crucial markers of status that

were readily embraced by those merchants and bankers who bought their way into landed estates.

50. I draw inspiration here from Elaine Hadley's application of "liberal cognition" to the daily practices of Victorian cultivation. Hadley, *Living Liberalism: Practical Citizenship in Mid-Victorian Britain* (Chicago: University of Chicago Press, 2010), 12–17.

51. Andrew Lang, *Longman's Magazine* XIII, 1899, 659–60, quoted in Margaret Beetham, "Domestic Servants as Poachers of Print: Reading, Authority and Resistance in Late Victorian Britain," in *The Politics of Domestic Authority in Britain since 1800*, ed. Lucy Delap, Ben Griffin, and Abigail Wills (Basingstoke: Palgrave Macmillan, 2009), 196.

52. Deborah Cohen, *Family Secrets: Shame and Privacy in Victorian Britain* (Oxford: Oxford University Press, 2017), 3, 4.

53. Brian McCuskey, "The Kitchen Police: Servant Surveillance and Middle-Class Transgression," *Victorian Literature and Culture* 28, no. 2 (2000): 362, www.jstor.org/stable/25058524.

54. *Beeton's Book of Household Management,* (London: S.O. Beeton, 1861), 977.

55. Beetham, "Domestic Servants."

56. David Vincent, *I Hope I Don't Intrude: Privacy and its Dilemmas in Nineteenth-Century Britain* (Oxford: Oxford University Press, 2015), 191.

57. William Lynd, *The Telegraphist,* January 1, 1886, 18.

58. F.E. Baines, *Forty Years at the Post Office: A Personal Narrative,* vol. 2 (London: Richard Bentley & Son, 1895), 76–77.

59. See, for example, "The Electric Telegraph of London," *Bow Bells,* December 1, 1870, 451; John Munro, "At the Central Telegraph Station, St Martins-le-Grand," *Time,* July 1879, 485, 486.

60. Scholarship on the Victorian female body and medical discourse is extensive. See, for example, Ludmilla Jordanova, *Sexual Visions: Images of Gender in Science and Medicine between the Eighteenth and Twentieth Centuries* (Madison: University of Wisconsin Press, 1989); Frank Mort, *Dangerous Sexualities: Medico-moral Politics in England since 1830* (New York: Routledge, 1987); Ornella Moscucci, *The Science of Woman: Gynaecology and Gender in England, 1800–1929* (New York: Cambridge University Press, 1990); Mary Poovey, *Uneven Developments: The Ideological Work of Gender in Mid-Victorian England* (Chicago: University of Chicago Press, 1988), chapter 2; Judith Walkowitz, "Science and the Séance: Transgressions of Gender and Genre in Late-Victorian London," *Representations* 22 (1988): 3–29.

61. Jill Galvan, *The Sympathetic Medium: Feminine Channeling, the Occult, and Communications Technologies, 1859–1919* (Ithaca, NY: Cornell University Press, 2010) 12.

62. See Leah Price and Pamela Thurschwell, eds., *Literary Secretaries/Secretarial Culture* (Aldershot: Ashgate, 2005); and Jeffry Sconce, *Haunted Media: Electric Presence from Telegraphy to Television* (Durham, NC: Duke University Press, 2000). For the broader social resonances of female mediums and spiritualism in the Victorian era, see Walkowitz, "Science and the Séance."

63. Jeffery Sconce conflates spiritual mediums with the telecommunications infrastructure surrounding their ascent, describing them as "wholly realized cybernetic beings—electromagnetic devices bridging flesh and spirit, body and machine, material reality and electronic space." Sconce, *Haunted Media,* quoted in Galvan, *Sympathetic Medium,* 27.

64. Scudamore, quoted in "Telegraph Street."

65. "The Central Telegraph Office," *Capital and Labour,* April 7, 1875.

66. "Special Report from the Select Committee on the Electric Telegraph Bill; Together with Minutes of Evidence," *Edinburgh Review,* July 1870, 219–20.

67. "Woman's Work at the Postal Telegraph," *Englishwoman's Domestic Review,* January 1, 1872, 24 (emphasis in original).

68. "The Electric Telegraph of London."

69. Trollope, "Young Women at the Central Telegraph Office," 383.

70. "The Central Telegraph Office," *Capital and Labour.*

71. "The Central Telegraph Office," part 1 of 4, *Illustrated London News,* November 28, 1874.

72. "Telegraph Street."

73. "Telegraph Street."

74. Richard Menke, *Telegraphic Realism: Victorian Fiction and other Information Systems* (Stanford, CA: Stanford University Press, 2008), 165.

75. Munro, "At the Central Telegraph Station," 486.

76. "At the Central Telegraph Office," *Capital and Labour.*

77. Munro, "At the Central Telegraph Station," 486–87.

78. Henry James, *In the Cage* (London: Martin Secker, 1924 [1898]), 10.

79. Eric Savoy, "'In the Cage' and the Queer Effects of Gay History," *Novel* 28, no. 3 (1995): 284–307, www.jstor.org/stable/1345925; Hugh Stevens, "Queer Henry in the Cage," in *The Cambridge Companion to Henry James,* ed. Jonathan Freedman (Cambridge: Cambridge University Press, 1998): 120–38; Eric Haralson, *Henry James and Queer Modernity* (Cambridge: Cambridge University Press, 2003). This scholarship relies heavily on Eve Kosofsky Sedgwick's reading of male homoerotics in fin-de-siècle British literature. See Sedgwick, *The Epistemology of the Closet* (Berkeley: University of California Press, 1990) and "Queer Performativity: Henry James's *The Art of the Novel,*" *GLQ: A Journal of Lesbian and Gay Studies* 1, no. 1 (1993): 1–16, doi:10.1215/10642684-1-1-1. For a more recent study, see Thomas, *Postal Pleasures,* postscript.

CHAPTER THREE. GENDERING THE CENTRAL
TELEGRAPH OFFICE

1. Employment of Women in the Public Service," *Quarterly Review,* 1881, 185.

2. Telegraphs: Report by Mr. Scudamore on the Reorganization of the Telegraph System of the United Kingdom, 1871, 78, C.304, HMSO.

3. F. I. Scudamore, *18th Report of the Postmaster General on the Post Office* (London: HMSO, 1872), 12–13.

4. Edina [pseud.], "The Ethics of Telegraphy," *Telegraphist,* July 1, 1887, 118.

5. W. Johnson, "Telegraph Street," *Temple Bar,* July 1871, 516.

6. Scudamore, *18th Report of the Postmaster General.*

7. "Provincial Notes: Edinburgh," *Telegraphist,* July 1, 1887, 124.

8. Central Telegraph Office, London: Further Substitutions of Male for Female Telegraphists; Statement of Present and Proposed Establishments, 1879, 2; Social Rank of Female Telegraphists, 1878, POST 30/364C, BTA.

9. Social Rank of Female Telegraphists.

10. Dina Copelman, *London's Women Teachers: Gender, Class, and Feminism, 1870–1930* (London: Routledge, 1996), xv.

11. Arthur. J. Munby diaries, April 10, 1863, in Derek Hudson, *Munby: Man of Two Worlds: The Life and Diaries of Arthur J. Munby, 1828–1910* (Boston: Gambit, 1972), 156. Quoted in Anna Davin, "Women Telegraphists and Typists, 1870–1890," in *Women in Industry and Technology,* ed. Amanda Devonshire and Barbara Wood (London: Museum of London, 1986), 214–15.

12. Anna Davin, "Women Telegraphists"; Kate Mullin, *Working Girls: Fiction, Sexuality, and Modernity* (Oxford: Oxford University Press, 2016).

13. Dina Copelman, *London's Women Teachers;* Anna Davin, "Women Telegraphists and Typists." See also Anna Davin, "City Girls: Young Women, New Employment, and the City, London 1880–1910," in *Secret Gardens, Satanic Mills: Placing Girls in European History, 1750–1960,* ed. Mary Jo Maynes, Birgitte Søland, and Christina Benninghaus (Bloomington: Indiana University Press, 2005), 209–23.

14. This gendered division in telegraphy was first analyzed by the Canadian historian Shirley Tillotson, in "'We May All Soon Be 'First-Class Men': Gender and Skill in Canada's Early Twentieth-Century Urban Telegraph Industry," *Labour/Le Travail* 27 (1991): 97–125, www.jstor.org/stable/25130246.

15. One of the best-known renderings of the role of village postmistress is provided in Flora Thompson's three-part memoir *Lark Rise to Candleford* (Oxford: Oxford University Press, 1945).

16. The very uncertain evidence of last names suggests that many telegraphists likely had European backgrounds of some kind, including Jewish origins. The ubiquitous racism of late-Victorian society and the lack of mention of any people of color in archival records imply that London's telegraphists—and the rest of the British GPO workforce—were overwhelmingly white.

17. "Committee Report, Schools of Instruction," 1870, POST 63/13, BTA.

18. ABC machines enabled operators to type messages using a set of lettered keys; the letters were then converted into electronic code.

19. Central Telegraph Office, London: Further Substitutions of Male for Female Telegraphists; Statement of Present and Proposed Establishments, 1879, 2, POST 30/364C, BTA.

20. In the 1870s, third-class female telegraphists started at a weekly wage of eight shillings, rising in increments of one shilling and maxing out at seventeen shillings.

Female telegraphists in nonsupervisory positions could make a maximum of thirty shillings a week. The figures are taken from numerous wage summaries in Central Telegraph Office, London: Further Substitutions.

21. H. C. Fischer memorandum, December 16, 1878, in Central Telegraph Office, London: Further Substitutions, POST 30/364C, BTA. This policy was apparently in effect for some time. See, for example, *National Telephone Journal,* April 1911, 15.

22. Fischer memorandum in Central Telegraph Office, Further Substitutions.

23. Bruce J. Hunt, "Doing Science in a Global Empire: Cable Telegraphy and Electrical Physics in Victorian Britain," in *Victorian Science in Context,* ed. Bernard Lightman (Chicago: University of Chicago Press, 1997), 323, 325.

24. One of the Maligned [pseud.], "Correspondence: Females in the Telegraph Service," *Telegraphist,* February 2, 1885, 36.

25. Pons Ælii [pseud.], "Females in the Telegraph Service," *Telegraphist,* January 1, 1885, 23.

26. "Metropolitan Items, Central Telegraph Office," *Telegraphist,* February 2, 1885, 31.

27. "Metropolitan Items."

28. "Women in the Civil Service," *Civil Service Gazette,* December 1, 1884, quoted by Efel [pseud.] in *Telegraphist,* February 2, 1885.

29. One of the Maligned, "Correspondence: Females in the Telegraph Service," 36.

30. "A Visit to the Central Telegraph Office," *Chums,* November 9, 1892, 141.

31. The relationship between this passage and its readers is complicated by the fact that *Chums* was marketed to public school boys who would never work as telegraph messengers. Identification and voyeurism coexist throughout *Chums.* For a more in-depth look at boys' magazines, class, and identity, see Kelly Boyd, *Manliness and the Boys' Story Paper in Britain: A Cultural History, 1855–1940* (New York: Palgrave, 2003).

32. Post Office Establishments: Return to an Order of the House of Commons, Dated 6 April 1897, for Copy of "Evidence (with Indices, Summaries, and Appendices) Taken before the Committee on Post Office Establishments," HC 163–44. London: HMSO, 189 (hereafter Tweedmouth Commission).

33. "Telegraph Street," 516.

34. Here I draw on a rich vein of feminist urban history, the generative text of which is Judith Walkowitz, *City of Dreadful Delight: Narratives of Sexual Danger in Late-Victorian London* (Chicago: University of Chicago Press, 1992).

35. These complaints emerged in male telegraphists' petitions throughout the late nineteenth century.

36. Special Staff at Race Meetings, November 24, 1911, file XVI, POST 30/2722B, BTA.

37. H. C. Fischer, memorandum to secretary, July 18, 1878, POST 30/364C, BTA.

38. "Female Clerks in the Civil Service," *Daily Chronicle,* October 19 and 23, 1879; "Female Labour in the Post Office," *Standard,* May 27, 1879; "The Employment of Women," *Ipswich Journal,* June 7, 1879.

1. Alan Clinton, *Post Office Workers: A Trade Union and Social History* (London: George Allen & Unwin, 1984), 128, 129.

2. Postal Telegraph Clerks' Association, Odds & Ends, 1881–1905, 148/PT/2/1/1, UWMRC.

3. Clinton, *Post Office Workers,* 129, 130.

4. Patrick Joyce, *The State of Freedom: A Social History of the British State since 1800* (Cambridge: Cambridge University Press, 2013), 134.

5. According to Clinton in *Post Office Workers,* it had two competitors in the later 1880s, the *Postal and Telegraphist Service Gazette* and the *Telegraph Services Gazette,* but I was unable to locate any copies of either. Clinton, *Post Office Workers,* 129, 234, 603, 604.

6. See Bernard Lightman, "The Voices of Nature: Popularizing Victorian Science," in *Victorian Science in Context,* ed. Bernard Lightman (Chicago: University of Chicago Press, 1997), 187–211; Laura Rotunno, "*Blackfriars, the Post Office Magazine:* A Nineteenth-Century Network of the 'Happy Ignorant,'" *Victorian Periodicals Review* 44, no. 2 (2011): 141–64, doi: 10.1353/vpr.2011.0019.

7. Reform [pseud.], "Wanted, a Telegraphist General," *Telegraphist,* June 1, 1885.

8. "Provincial Notes: Belfast," *Telegraphist,* July 1, 1887.

9. Edina [pseud.] "Why Postal and Telegraph Officials Do Not Fraternise," *Telegraphist,* June 1, 1885.

10. Veritas Odium Parit [pseud.], "Sunday Duty at TS and in the Provinces," *Telegraphist,* December 1, 1884.

11. Such gendered contours of sabbatarianism were the result of a combination of religious lobbying to enforce Sunday abstinence from trade and beliefs that women needed more physical rest than men. Duncan Campbell-Bannerman, *Masters of the Post: The Authorized History of the Royal Mail* (London: Penguin, 2012), 149.

12. Clinton, *Post Office Workers,* 269.

13. Cymro [pseud.], "The Female Sex and the Telegraph Service," *Telegraphist,* July 1, 1887.

14. Pons Ælii, "Females in the Telegraph Service," *Telegraphist,* January 1, 1885.

15. Pons Ælii, "Females in the Telegraph Service."

16. Saul [pseud.], "Women's Work," *Telegraphist,* March 2, 1885.

17. See, for example, PTCA Propositions to Be Submitted to the Annual Conference, to Be Held at Cannon Street Hotel, London, the 4th of June, 1892, Postal Telegraph Clerks' Association: Conferences and Deputations, (1) 148/PT/1/2/1, UWMRC.

18. William Lynd, "A Scientific Lady," *Telegraphist,* July 1, 1886.

19. William Lynd, "Editorial Notes: Female Labour in the Telegraph Service," *Telegraphist,* May 1, 1885.

20. Lynd, "Editorial Notes: Female Labour."

21. Lynd, "Editorial Notes: Female Labour."

22. Efel [pseud.], "Females in the Telegraph Service," *Telegraphist*, February 2, 1885.

23. Efel, "Females in the Telegraph Service."

24. Se Defendendo [pseud.], "Female Telegraph Clerks," *Telegraphist*, February 2, 1885.

25. One of the Maligned [pseud.], "Correspondence: Females in the Telegraph Service," *Telegraphist*, February 2, 1885.

26. Seaweed [pseud.], "Female Labour in the Service," *Telegraphist*, July 1, 1887.

27. Se Defendendo. "Female Telegraph Clerks," February 2, 1885.

28. Se Defendendo, "Female Telegraph Clerks." *Telegraphist*, April 1, 1885.

29. Efel, "Females in the Telegraph Service," emphasis in original.

30. Efel, "Females in the Telegraph Service."

31. Pons Ælii, "Females in the Telegraph Service," *Telegraphist*, March 2, 1885.

32. Edward Raymond Barker, "Female v. Male Telegraphists," *Telegraphist*, May 1, 1885.

33. Edina [pseud.], "The Ethics of Telegraphy," *Telegraphist*, July 1, 1887.

34. F. I. Scudamore, *18th Report of the Postmaster General on the Post Office* (London: HMSO, 1872), 13.

35. Edina, "Ethics of Telegraphy"; Edina, "Modern Chivalry," *Telegraphist*, September 1, 1885.

36. "Amateur Dramatic Clubs," *Telegraphist*, April 1, 1885, 59.

37. "Provincial Notes: Edinburgh," *Telegraphist*, October 1, 1886, 154.

38. "Social Notes: Glasgow," *Telegraphist*, June 1885, 86.

39. Se Defendendo, "Female Telegraph Clerks," April 1, 1885.

40. Edina, "Ethics of Telegraphy."

41. Edina, "Ethics of Telegraphy."

42. Edina, "Ethics of Telegraphy."

43. See Henry Swift, *A History of Postal Agitation: From Fifty Years Ago to the Present Day* (London: C. Arthur Pearson, 1900), 225.

44. William Lynd, "Editorial Notes: Pulvermacher's Electrical Appliances," *Telegraphist*, March 2, 1885.

45. Tempus Omnia Revelat [pseud.], "Dangers of Sound-Reading," *Telegraphist*, April 1 1885.

46. Enquirer [pseud.], "Disease among Telegraphists," *Telegraphist*, December 1, 1884.

47. Tempus Omnia Revelat, "Dangers of Sound-Reading."

48. Electricity and telegraphy, heightened sensitivity, and mental strain or illness have been linked by both historians of medicine and literary critics. Important texts include Janet Oppenheim, *"Shattered Nerves": Doctors, Patients and Depression in Victorian England* (Oxford: Oxford University Press 1991); Anson Rabinbach, *The Human Motor: Energy, Fatigue, and the Origins of Modernity* (Berkeley: University of California Press, 1992); Jill Galvan, *The Sympathetic Medium: Feminine Channeling, the Occult, and Communication Technologies, 1859–1919* (Ithaca, NY: Cornell University Press, 2010); Iwan Rhys Morus, *Bodies/Machines* (Oxford: Berg, 2002) Iwan Rhys Morus, *Shocking Bodies: Life, Death and Electricity in Victorian*

England (Stroud: History Press, 2011); Andreas Killen, *Berlin Electropolis: Shock, Nerves, and German Modernity* (Berkeley: University of California Press, 2006); Jeffrey Sconce, *Haunted Media: Electronic Presence from Telegraphy to Television* (Durham, NC: Duke University Press, 2000), chapter 1.

49. Tempus Omnia Revelat, "Dangers of Sound-Reading."

50. Saul [pseud.], "Our Service," *Telegraphist,* December 1 1884.

51. "Music," *Our Girls Column, Telegraphist,* February 1, 1888, 46.

52. Edina, "Ethics of Telegraphy."

53. Tempus Omnia Revelat, "Dangers of Sound-Reading."

54. "Music."

55. Clinton, *Post Office Workers,* 128.

56. Petition to Henry Fawcett, postmaster general, from the Female Supervisors and Clerks of the Central Telegraph Office, 1881, Box 310.4, Labour History, 1/16/5/744, Morten Collection, Haringey Archive Service at Bruce Castle, London.

57. Petition to Fawcett from the Female Supervisors and Clerks.

58. Statements of the Senior, First, Second, and Female Clerks, 1889, 7, Postal Telegraph Clerks' Association: Conferences and Deputations (1), 148/PT/1/2/1, UWMRC.

59. Postal Telegraph Clerks' Association, Report of Proceedings of the Sixth Annual Conference, Belfast, June 9, 1887, Postal Telegraph Clerks' Association: Conferences and Deputations (1), 148/PT/1/2/1, UWMRC.

60. Clinton, *Post Office Workers,* 235.

61. Lynd, "Editorial Notes," *Telegraphist,* November 1, 1886.

62. Clinton, *Post Office Workers,* 134, 135. The Trades Union Congress was (and remains) a broad federation of British trade unions. It was founded in Manchester in 1868.

63. "Latest Labour Movement," *Reynolds's,* May 18, 1890; "A Desirable 'Raikes' Progress," *Punch,* March 15, 1890; "Occasional Notes," *Pall Mall Gazette,* May 5, 1890.

64. *Account of the Celebration of the Jubilee of Uniform Inland Penny Postage* (London: Richard Clay and Sons, 1891), 192.

65. *Account,* 194.

66. Swift, *A History of Postal Agitation,* 233–34; "The Post Office Jubilee Celebration Conversazione," *Times,* July 3, 1890; Henry St John Raikes, *The Life and Letters of Henry Cecil Raikes* (London: Macmillan, 1898), 327.

67. Swift, *A History of Postal Agitation,* 233.

68. "The Post Office Jubilee Celebration Conversazione."

69. Swift, *A History of Postal Agitation,* 234. See also "The Jubilee of the Penny Post," *Times,* July 4, 1890.

70. Clinton, *Post Office Workers,* 134.

71. Minutes of PTCA Conference, Leicester, 1890, 35, PTCA Conferences and Deputations, 1890–1893, Petitions, 148/PT/2/1/4, UWMRC.

72. PTCA: Resolutions and Alterations of Rules, June 6, 1891, Postal Telegraph Clerks' Association: Conferences and Deputations (1), 148/PT/1/2/1, UWMRC.

73. "The Telegraph Clerks' Association," *Women's Penny Paper,* November 15, 1890.

74. "The Telegraph Clerks' Association."

75. Clinton, *Post Office Workers,* 239.

CHAPTER FIVE. UNINTENDED NETWORKS

1. "Transfer of the Telegraphs to the Government," *Post,* February 5, 1870.

2. "Editorial," *Sunday Times,* December 12, 1869.

3. For a comparable study of telegraph boys in the United States, see Gregory Downey, *Telegraph Messenger Boys: Labor, Technology, and Geography, 1850–1950* (New York: Routledge, 2002).

4. Martin Daunton first chronicled GPO attempts to discipline telegraph boys in his comprehensive history of the post office, *Royal Mail: The Post Office since 1840* (London: Athlone, 1985), 198–211.

5. See Matt Cook, *London and the Culture of Homosexuality, 1885–1914* (Cambridge: Cambridge University Press, 2003); Morris Kaplan, *Sodom on the Thames: Sex, Love, and Scandal in Wilde Times* (Ithaca, NY: Cornell University Press, 2005).

6. Seth Koven, *Slumming: Sexual and Social Politics in Victorian London* (Princeton: Princeton University Press, 2004); Erika Rappaport, *Shopping for Pleasure: Women in the Making of London's West End* (Princeton: Princeton University Press, 2001); Simon Gunn, *The Public Culture of the Victorian Middle Class: Ritual and Authority in the English Industrial City, 1840–1914* (Manchester: Manchester University Press, 2000).

7. Candidate Book, December 1868–December 1870, POST 58/194, PM.

8. PO Appointments, Qualifications, Modes of Admission Etc. 1868, POST 57/1, PM.

9. Daunton, *Royal Mail,* 203.

10. Indoor messengers wore dark gray uniforms until the twentieth century.

11. Report by the Controller, London Postal Section on the appearance of Boy Messengers, November 27, 1891, POST 61/7, PM.

12. Letter from Metropolitan district surveyor to London controller Robert Tombs, January 26 1876, Telegraph Messengers' Uniform, London, Proposal to Add District Initials to Tunics, Not Adopted, file IV, POST 30/295A, PM.

13. See Matthew Hilton, "'Tabs', 'Fags,' and the 'Boy Labour Problem' in Late Victorian and Edwardian Britain," *Journal of Social History* 28, no. 3 (1995): 587–607, doi: 10.1353/jsh/28.3.587. Hilton argues that working-class boys' smoking became a serious concern in beginning in the 1880s, when cigarettes became cheap and widely available. This example demonstrates that boys' smoking had a longer history. This telegraph boy was likely smoking a pipe rather than a cigarette.

14. "Christmas Boxes," *Moonshine,* January 8, 1887, 21.

15. "Our Sportsfolio," *Licensed Victualler,* May 20, 1890.

16. "Fast Boys of the Period, II," *British Juvenile,* July 1, 1870.

17. "Fast Boys of the Period."

18. See, for example, *Metropolitan News, Illustrated London News,* May 6, 1871.

19. Telegraphs: Instructions for Telegraph Messengers in London, 1896, POST 68/181, PM.

20. "A Telegraph Boy's Story," *Boy's Own Paper,* no. 697, May 21, 1892, 539.

21. "Law and Police," *Illustrated London News,* March 20, 1875.

22. Downey, *Telegraph Messenger Boys,* 63.

23. For the rules governing telegraph boys' deliveries, see for example Telegraphs: Instructions for Messengers in London, 1887, POST 68/178, PM.

24. "A Visit to the Central Telegraph Office," *Chums,* November 16, 1892, 141.

25. F. E. Baines, *Forty Years at the Post Office: A Personal Narrative,* vol. 2 (London: Richard Bentley and Son, 1895), 75; "A Visit to the Central Telegraph Office," 141.

26. Baines, *Forty Years,* 74.

27. See Matt Houlbrook, "Soldier Heroes and Rent Boys: Homosex, Masculinities, and Britishness in the Brigade of Guards, 1900–1960," *Journal of British Studies* 42, no. 3 (2003): 351–88.

28. Houlbrook, "Soldier Heroes and Rent Boys," 353.

29. Cook, *London and the Culture of Homosexuality,* introduction and chapter 1. See also Katie Hindmarch-Watson, "Lois Schwich, the Female Errand Boy: Narratives of Female Cross-Dressing in Late Victorian London," *GLQ* 14 (2008): 77, 92, 93.

30. Memorandum to postmaster general John Manners, February 8, 1876, Metropolitan Telegraph Circuits, Rearrangement of 1869 Plan, POST 30/289B, BTA.

31. Postmaster General John Manners to GPO Secretary John Tilley, minute 3368, May 26, 1875, Secretary's Minutes to the Postmaster General, May 3-June 7, 1875, vol. 143, POST 35/350, PM.

32. Telegraph Messengers: Immoral Conduct; Mr. Jeffery's Report, minute 5521, September 5, 1876, Secretary's Minutes to the Postmaster General, August 28–October 11, 1876, vol. 158, POST 35/365, PM.

33. Response of postmaster general to minute 5521, September 6, 1876, Secretary's Minutes to the Postmaster General, August 28–October 11, 1876, vol. 158, POST 35/365, PM.

34. Charles Upchurch, *Before Wilde: Sex between Men in the Age of Reform* (Berkeley: University of California Press, 2009), chapter 4.

35. H. G. Cocks, *Nameless Offences: Homosexual Desire in the Nineteenth Century* (London: I. B. Tauris, 2003), introduction, chapters 1–2. On this phenomenon in relation to Victorian masculinities, see Sean Brady, *Masculinity and Male Homosexuality in Britain, 1861–1913* (Basingstoke: Palgrave MacMillan, 2005). This culture of secrecy around homosexual practices most likely explains the absence of Tilley's initial report.

36. Stefan Petrow, *Policing Morals: The Metropolitan Police and the Home Office, 1870–1914* (Oxford: Clarendon, 1994), 130.

37. Telegraph Boy Messengers: Immoral Conduct; Reply to Report from the Home Office, minute 6898, November (n.d.), Secretary's Minutes to the Postmaster General, October 11–November 20, 1876, vol. 158, POST 35/366, PM.

38. Immoral Conduct of Boy Messengers: Assessment of Mr. Jeffery's Report, minute 149, January 5, 1877, Secretary's Minutes to the Postmaster General, December 28, 1876–January 31, 1877, vol. 161, POST 35/368, PM.

39. Immoral Conduct and Dismissal of Certain Boys, minute 549, n.d. Secretary's Minutes to the Postmaster General, December 28, 1876–January 31, 1877, vol. 161, POST 35/368, PM.

40. Thomas Jeffery, "Immorality among Boys: Mr. Jeffery's Report and Recommendation," March 31, 1877, Telegraph Messengers, London, Immorality among Boys, file 1, POST 30/1052, PM.

41. Jeffery, "Immorality among Boys."

42. Jeffery, "Immorality among Boys."

43. This is a standard trope among Victorian historians. For a study dealing specifically with the sexual contexts of environmental contagion, see Frank Mort, *Dangerous Sexualities: Medico-moral Politics in England since 1830* (London: Routledge, 1987) introduction and 49–54, 64–66.

44. Jeffery, "Immorality among Boys."

45. Jeffery, "Immorality among Boys."

46. Jeffery, "Immorality among Boys." On late Victorian London's streets as portals to social and sexual underworlds, see Judith Walkowitz, *City of Dreadful Delight: Narratives of Sexual Danger in Late-Victorian London* (Chicago: University of Chicago Press, 1992), chapters 1, 3, 7; Deborah Nord, "The Social Explorer as Anthropologist: Victorian Travelers among the Urban Poor," in *Visions of the Modern City: Essays in History, Art, and Literature,* ed. William Sharpe and Leonard Wallock, 122–34 (Baltimore: Johns Hopkins University Press, 1987).

47. Jeffery, "Immorality among Boys."

48. Jeffery, "Immorality among Boys."

49. Jeffery, "Immorality among Boys."

50. Smith's case appears in Cocks, *Nameless Offences,* 35–36, 61–63.

51. For more examples and analysis of how the legal system and those accused of sodomy grappled with issues of evidence and corroboration, see H. G. Cocks, "Making the Sodomite Speak: Voices of the Accused in English Sodomy Trials, c. 1800–98," *Gender and History* 18 (2006): 87–107, doi: 10.1111/j.1468-0424.2006.00416.x.

52. Sean Brady has argued that Smith's treatment is an example of the "culture of resistance" in Britain to public discussion of sex and sexuality between men. To Brady, the Victorian and Edwardian period was significant for its inflexible codes of manhood. "Alternative" masculinities were suspect in a culture that required men to be breadwinning husbands above all else. Brady offers the reluctance of some of the state's attorneys to go after Smith as proof of the official unwillingness to expose a respectable and supposedly well-connected member of the masculine establishment. My reading differs somewhat from Brady's: while I acknowledge his point about secrecy, respectability, and Victorian crises of masculinity, I see the evidence

in this case pointing less toward a concern about Smith's respectability (and masculine respectability in general) and more toward an all-out effort to corral flexible notions of Victorian boyhood into a legal response to state involvement with pederastic prostitution. Brady, *Masculinity and Male Homosexuality*, 1–3, 89–90.

53. A. K. Stephenson to Mr. Liddell, Home Office solicitor, February 8, 1877, HO 144/20/58480A, NA.

54. James Smith, first petition to the home secretary, April 1877, HO 144 /20/58480, NA.

55. Stephenson to Liddell, February 8, 1877, emphasis in original.

56. Stephenson to Liddell, February 8, 1877.

57. Stephenson to Liddell, February 8, 1877.

58. Smith, first petition to the home secretary.

59. Smith, first petition to the home secretary.

60. Smith, first petition to the home secretary.

61. A. C. Hepburn, memorandum, April 16, 1877, HO 144/20/58480A, NA.

62. "Central Criminal Court April 11," *Times*, April 12, 1877.

63. Jeffery, "Immorality among Boys"; Telegraph Messengers, London, Immorality among Boys, file 1; Telegraph Messengers: Eastern Central District Office and Central Telegraph Office, file 2; Telegraph Messengers, Metropolitan District, Selection of Candidates, file 4; Telegraph Messengers, Additional Inspector, Appointments Branch, Secretary's Office, for enquiring into character and antecedents of candidates, file 7, POST 30/1052, PM.

64. Correspondence re. Badcock, Bruce, Ogilvie et al., 1905–7, Telegraph Messengers Drill: Award of Chevrons, file 4, Post 30/903A, PM.

65. See, for example, Nord, "The Social Explorer as Anthropologist." For a more recent example of the intersections between poverty, youth, and sexuality, see Koven, *Slumming*.

CHAPTER SIX. TAPPED WIRES

1. Previous treatments of the Cleveland Street affair have highlighted its importance as a government conspiracy, a case study in the efficacy of the "gross indecency" provisions of the 1885 Criminal Law Amendment Act for prosecuting any kind of sexual encounter between men, and a window into homoerotic London. See H. Montgomery Hyde, *The Cleveland Street Scandal* (London: W. H. Allen, 1976); Colin Simpson, Lewis Chester, and David Leitch, *The Cleveland Street Affair* (Boston: Little, Brown, 1976); Morris B. Kaplan, *Sodom on the Thames: Sex, Love, and Scandal in Wilde Times* (Ithaca, NY: Cornell University Press, 2005), chapter 3; Jeffrey Weeks, *Sex, Politics, and Society: the Regulation of Sexuality since 1800* (London: Longman, 1981), chapter 5; Theo Aronson, *Prince Eddy and the Homosexual Underworld*, 2nd ed. (London: John Murray, 1996); Trevor Fisher, *Scandal: Sexual Politics in Late Victorian Britain* (Stroud: Sutton, 1995); and H. G. Cocks, *Nameless Offences: Homosexual Desire in the Nineteenth Century* (London: I. B. Tauris, 2003),

144–53; Matt Cook, *London and the Culture of Homosexuality, 1885–1914* (Cambridge: Cambridge University Press 2003), 50–56, 63–64; Sean Brady, *Masculinity and Male Homosexuality in Britain, 1861–1913* (New York: Palgrave MacMillan, 2005), 86, 89, 103.

2. Dublin also had a role, albeit in the chorus. The "Dublin Castle affair" and the associated libel and criminal trials made headlines across Britain throughout the summer of 1884. The secretary of the Dublin Post Office, Gustavus Cornwall, had been accused of sodomy after being investigated by Irish nationalists. Cornwall was revealed as one of a "precious trio" of sexually corrupt Anglo-Irish administrators. See Leon O'Broin, *The Prime Informer: A Suppressed Scandal* (London: Sidgwick and Jackson, 1971), 25–27. William O'Brien, an Irish nationalist MP and editor of the Land League journal, *United Ireland,* published the libel suit–generating accusations and later discussed the experience in his memoir, *Evening Memories* (Dublin: Maunsel, 1920), 18–19. See also H. Montgomery Hyde, *The Other Love: An Historical and Contemporary Survey of Homosexuality in Britain* (London: Heinemann, 1970), 129. According to home rule advocates, Cornwall's sexual corruption mirrored the injustices perpetuated by English executives on colonial Ireland. The scandal not only implicated the GPO in homoerotic networks but also featured powerful elites as the perpetrators of vice. This association would resonate again in the Cleveland Street Scandal, ironically to the GPO's advantage. The fallout from the Dublin Castle affair, and the political impasses it helped create, had subtle but important influences in delineating the villains and heroes of Cleveland Street. See Kaplan, *Sodom on the Thames,* chapter 3.

3. The extensive scholarship on the Cleveland Street scandal tends to replicate this omission, instead highlighting Lord Somerset's coterie, late nineteenth-century gross indecency laws, upper-class masculinities, and the "new journalism" of the 1880s that publicized the affair. See Hyde, *The Cleveland Street Scandal;* Jeffrey Weeks, "Inverts, Perverts and Mary-Annes: Male Prostitution and the Regulation of Homosexuality in the Nineteenth and Early Twentieth Centuries," in *Hidden from History: Reclaiming the Gay and Lesbian Past,* ed. Martin Duberman, Martha Vicinus, and George Chauncey, 195- 211 (New York: New American Library, 1989); Cocks, *Nameless Offenses:* 144–63; Cook, *London and the Culture of Homosexuality,* chapter 2; Brady, *Masculinity and Male Homosexuality,* 86, 89, 103.

4. According to the *Pall Mall Gazette,* Newlove was the "wretched" panderer who offered money to upstanding junior public servants just trying to get ahead. See Kaplan, *Sodom on the Thames,* 168, 188.

5. Henry Labouchère, speech to the House of Commons, February 28, 1890, 341 *Parl. Deb.* (3rd Ser.) (1890), col. 1541.

6. "Did 'My Lord Gomorrah' Smile?" *North London Press,* January 11, 1890.

7. Kaplan, *Sodom on the Thames,* chapter 3, 205. Another notable scandal was the Crawford divorce case in 1886, which implicated the Liberal MP Charles Dilke.

8. See Matt Houlbrook, "Soldier Heroes and Rent Boys: Homosex, Masculinities, and Britishness in the Brigade of Guards, circa 1900–1960," *Journal of British Studies* 42 (2003): 351–88. Houlbrook explores the relationship between national

identity building, military spectacles, masculine representations, and the construction of homosexuality.

9. Duncan Campbell-Smith, *Masters of the Post: The Authorized History of the Royal Mail* (London: Allen Lane, 2011), 183–92.

10. Secretary's Office, Confidential Enquiry Branch Proposed Revision, 1907, Historical Summary, POST 30/1492, PM. See also Post Office Establishment Books, 1877–89, PM.

11. The infrastructure required to deal with parcel delivery was as extensive as that required for the telegraph. New delivery systems, new staff, and new storage spaces were hastily put into service. In London, the GPO acquired Coldbath Fields Prison to handle the massive influx of parcels. The prison, which had closed in 1877, was fought over by the GPO and urban park advocates such as the Metropolitan Garden Association, who thought converting the eight-acre site into a public park would provide health and moral benefits to the working-class dwellers of Clerkenwell. The GPO won out, with help from the local parish council, who argued that "1500 respectable Post Office Servants" moving into the area would help raise the rates, and thus the tone, of the neighborhood. Those respectable employees were reportedly less than thrilled about working at a site named for a prison, so in 1888 the GPO formally changed the site's name back to its sixteenth-century moniker, Mount Pleasant, the name it bears today.

12. The bombings stopped in late January 1885, possibly in part because of Gladstone's embrace of home rule, and certainly because of infighting between various factions of Irish American Fenians. See Kenneth R. M. Short, *The Dynamite War: Irish-American Bombers in Victorian Britain* (Atlantic Highlands, NJ: Humanities Press, 1979), chapter 8, epilogue; Bernard Porter, *The Origins of the Vigilant State* (London: Weidenfeld and Nicolson, 1987), chapters 3–4. British authorities uncovered and foiled the last Fenian bomb plot, meant to occur during Queen Victoria's Jubilee in 1887.

13. Frederick E. Baines, *Forty Years at the Post Office: A Personal Narrative,* 2 vols. (London: Richard Bentley and Son, 1895), 1:168.

14. Porter, *The Origins of the Vigilant State,* chapter 4.

15. Henry Fawcett, Post Office Detention and Opening of Suspicious Letters, April 4, 1881, 260 Parl. Deb. (3rd Ser.) (1881) col. 565.

16. Evidence of postal censorship and procedures governing the removal of seditious, obscene, or otherwise offensive material from circulation can be found in the file series POST 23/9, PM. See also Howard Robinson, *The British Post Office: A History* (Princeton: Princeton University Press, 1948), 352.

17. Thomas Crook, "Secrecy and Liberal Modernity in Victorian and Edwardian Britain," in *The Peculiarities of Liberal Modernity in Imperial Britain,* ed. Simon Gunn and James Vernon (Berkeley: University of California Press, 2011), 79–82; Robinson, *The British Post Office,* 337–52.

18. Porter, *The Origins of the Vigilant State,* 32–33.

19. The Special Branch of the Metropolitan Police did not make its existence known until 1887. Porter, *The Origins of the Vigilant State,* 79.

20. Robinson, *The British Post Office,* 408.

21. Baines, *Forty Years at the Post Office,* 1:153.

22. Baines, *Forty Years at the Post Office,* 1:39.

23. "How a Telegram Is Sent," *Little Folks,* September 1, 1882, 162.

24. Report of Postmen Committee, 1891, POST 30/1052, PM.

25. A subordinate notes of Blackwood: "The cause of temperance, or, rather, total abstinence from intoxicants, he lost no chance in furthering." Baines, *Forty Years at the Post Office,* 1:178.

26. The Telegraph Messenger Institute was modeled on the church-based urban boys' clubs that had been springing up in Britain's cities since the mid-1880s. The Telegraph Messenger Institute may be the only secular, state-run example of such an organization in this early period. See Michael J. Childs, *Labour's Apprentices: Working-Class Lads in Late Victorian and Edwardian England* (Montreal: McGill-Queen's University Press, 1992), chapter 7. For an elaboration of boy culture, class, and nationalism, see Seth Koven, "From Rough Lads to Hooligans: Boy Life, National Culture and Social Reform," in Andrew Parker, Mary Russo, Doris Sommer, and Patricia Yaeger, *Nationalisms and Sexualities* (London: Routledge, 1992).

27. Memorandum from Thomas Jeffery to Arthur Blackwood, December 17, 1880, Post Circulation, Boy Force, file 3, POST 30/468, PM.

28. Thomas Jeffery to Arthur Blackwood, August 4, 1886, Telegraph Messengers: Employment and Conditions of Service, file 8, POST 30/1052, PM.

29. See Alan Clinton, *Post Office Workers: A Trade Union and Social History* (London: Allen & Unwin, 1984), 128–40; Martin L. Daunton, *Royal Mail: The Post Office since 1840* (London: Athlone, 1985), 261–63.

30. Baines, *Forty Years at the Post Office,* 1:242.

31. *Account of the Celebration of the Jubilee of the Uniform Inland Penny Postage* (London: Richard Clay and Sons, 1891), 53.

32. Baines, *Forty Years at the Post Office,* 2:76.

33. "A Telegraph Boy's Story," *Boy's Own Paper,* May 21, 1892, 539.

34. Ascott R. Hope, "My Last Scrape," *Young England,* November 1, 1886, 509.

35. Weeks, "Inverts, Perverts, and Mary-Annes," 204.

36. Excerpts from unpublished letters quoted in Timothy D'Arch Smith, *Love in Ernest: Some Notes on the Lives and Writings of English "Uranian" Poets from 1889 to 1930* (London: Routledge and Kegan Paul), 1970, 29.

37. The "labyrinth" of London's sexual and social underworlds has been well documented. See Judith Walkowitz, *City of Dreadful Delight: Narratives of Sexual Danger in Late Victorian London* (Chicago: University of Chicago Press, 1992), chapters 1, 3, 7; Deborah Nord, "The Social Explorer as Anthropologist: Victorian Travelers among the Urban Poor," in *Visions of the Modern City: Essays in History, Art, and Literature,* ed. William Sharpe and Leonard Wallock (Baltimore: Johns Hopkins University Press, 1987), 122–34; D. L. Pike, *Metropolis on the Styx: The Underworlds of Modern Urban Culture, 1800–2001* (New York: Cornell University Press, 2007).

38. This incident is alluded to in a summary report, The History of the Position of Boy Messengers and Their Recruitment, 1870–1915, POST 57/27, PM; Notes of Constable Luke Hanks, July 4, 1889, DPP 1/95/3, file 3, NA.

39. Notes of Constable Luke Hanks, July 4, 1889.

40. Hyde, *The Cleveland Street Scandal,* 20; Simpson, Chester, and Leitch, *The Cleveland Street Affair,* 86.

41. Statement of Charles Swinscow, July 4, 1889, DPP 1/95/3, file 3, NA.

42. Baines, *Forty Years in the Post Office,* 2:74–75.

43. Statement of Charles Swinscow, July 4, 1889, DPP 1/95/3, file 3, NA.

44. Police statement of George Wright, July 4, 1889, DPP 1/95/3, file 3, NA.

45. Police statement of Charles Thickbroom, July 4, 1889, DPP 1/95/3, file 3, NA.

46. GPO officials deemed most London telegraph boys to be of the wrong class for clerkships and telegraphy.

47. Statements of Swinscow and Wright, July 4, 1889.

48. Copy of warrant for Henry Newlove and Charles Hammond, July 6, 1889, DPP 1/95/, file 3, NA.

49. Correspondence between postmaster general and the Treasury, November 18–16, 1889, POST 1/219, PM.

50. Notes of Constable Luke Hanks, July 7, 1889, DPP 1/95/3, file 3, NA.

51. Report of Inspector Frederick Abberline, July 18, 1889, DPP 1/95/3, file 3, NA.

52. Notes of Constable Sladden [assistant to Abberline], n.d. 1889, DPP 1/95/3, file 3, NA.

53. Statements of Swinscow, Wright, and Thickbroom, July 4, 1889.

54. It is also possible he was tipped off by the journalist W. T. Stead, who had commented on Veck's and Newlove's hearings in his paper two weeks previously and had excellent connections with Scotland Yard. Simpson, Chester, and Leitch, *The Cleveland Street Affair,* 84, 167–70.

55. Ernest Parke, "Charges of Abominable Crimes against Peers and Officers," *North London Press,* September 28, 1889, quoted in *Reynolds's Weekly,* "Last Week's Latest News," October 6, 1889.

56. Telegraph boys' status as aspiring working-class youth both conflicted with and resonated with working-class sexual underworlds. For broader contexts see G. S. Jones, *Outcast London: A Study in the Relationships between Classes in Victorian Society* (Oxford: Clarendon, 1971); Leslie Hall, *Sex, Gender and Social Change in Britain Since 1880* (Basingstoke: Macmillan, 2000); Seth Koven, *Slumming: Sexual and Social Politics in Victorian London* (Princeton: Princeton University Press, 2004); Frank Mort, *Dangerous Sexualities: Medico-moral Politics in England since 1830,* 2nd ed. (London: Routledge, 2000), parts 2–3; and Anna Davin, *Growing up Poor: Home, School and Street in London 1870–1914* (London: Rivers Oram, 1996).

57. W. T. Stead, *Occasional Notes, Pall Mall Gazette,* September 12, 1889.

58. W. T. Stead, "A Little Child Shall Lead Them," *Pall Mall Gazette,* November 30, 1889.

59. This was not the first time Stead had suppressed knowledge of youthful homosexual practices. His *Maiden Tribute of Modern Babylon* series of articles was likely inspired by a report on male prostitution. His use of the Minotaur as a metaphor for lustful elites could be an allusion to the bisexual appetite of the original

mythic beast. However, male prostitution was not explicitly mentioned. See Walkowitz, *City of Dreadful Delight*, 98, 118, 278.

60. See Walkowitz, *City of Dreadful Delight*, chapter 2; Jerry White, *London in the Nineteenth Century: "A Human Awful Wonder of God"* (London: Vintage, 2008), chapter 10. On the homoerotic aspects of the West End, see Cook, *London and the Culture of Homosexuality*, 13–18.

61. The account in the *Pall Mall Gazette* significantly altered the setting—and timing. In "The Scandal of Cleveland Street: Threatened Prosecution for Libel and Consequent Exposure," published in response to Parke's accusations in the *North London Press*, it claimed, "The facts of the case are simple. In a house of ill-fame in Cleveland-Street, off Tottenham-court-road, last September, the police seized two persons [Veck and Newlove]." *Pall Mall Gazette*, November 18, 1889.

62. Augustus Stephenson to Richard Webster, attorney general, September 15, 1889, DDP 1/95/1, Correspondence, NA, emphasis in original.

63. Labouchère, speech to House of Commons, February 28, 341 Parl. Deb. (3rd Ser.) (1890), col. 1548.

64. Labouchère, speech to House of Commons, February 28, 341 Parl. Deb. (3rd Ser.) (1890), col. 1536.

65. See Hyde, *The Cleveland Street Scandal*, chapter 4.

66. "Lord Euston's Case," *Reynolds's Weekly*, January 19, 1890.

67. The likelihood, however, that a male brothel would advertise its whereabouts to the uninitiated, whatever the lure, is doubtful.

68. Euston was a fan of horse racing and had previously been married to the actress Kate Cook, whose bigamous marriage had attracted its own notoriety. Her love life, like Euston's sporting bachelor persona, was of a stridently heterosexual nature.

69. Hyde, *The Cleveland Street Scandal*, 158; Simpson, Chester, and Leitch, *The Cleveland Street Affair*, 167.

70. "Between Ourselves," *London Victualler*, December 10, 1889.

71. "Euston's Name Cleared," *Daily Telegraph*, January 16, 1890.

72. Quoted in Simpson, Chester, and Leitch, *The Cleveland Street Affair*, 164.

73. Charles Whibley, review of *The Picture of Dorian Gray*, *Scots Observer*, July 5 1890, quoted in Hyde, *The Cleveland Street Scandal*, 240.

74. UK 1901 Census, RG13 Islington, www.1901censusonline.com.

75. Simpson, Chester, and Leitch, *The Cleveland Street Affair*, 225.

76. Kaplan, *Sodom on the Thames*, 186.

CHAPTER SEVEN. MARTIAL MERCURIES

1. R. C. Tombs to Secretary S. A. Blackwood, February 2, 1891, Boy Messengers Drill, POST 33/273, PM. This description of the telegraph boys' styling of their caps suggests a similarity to what the historian Andrew Davies identifies as youth gang fashion in Manchester and Birmingham in the 1890s (this look was nicknamed

"peaky blinders" in Birmingham). Andrew Davies, *The Gangs of Manchester: The Story of the Scuttlers, Britain's First Youth Cult* (Milo Books, 2009), chapter 1; Andrew Davies, "The Real Peaky Blinders," HistoryExtra blog, August 22, 2019 www.historyextra.com/period/victorian/real-peaky-blinders-podcast-historian-andrew-davies-gangs-who.

2. For a discussion of postal workers' relationships to the wider labor movement, see Alan Clinton, *Post Office Workers: A Trade Union and Social History* (London: George Allen and Unwin, 1984), chapters 4, 6, 8.

3. H. Clegg, A. Fox, and A. F. Thompson, *A History of the British Trade Unions,* vol. 1 (Oxford: Oxford University Press, 1964), 216.

4. Clinton, *Post Office Workers,* 134–40; Martin Daunton, *Royal Mail: The Post Office since 1840* (London: Athlone, 1984), 259.

5. Clinton, *Post Office Workers,* 135; Daunton, *Royal Mail,* 259–63; Duncan Campbell-Bannerman, *Masters of the Post: the Authorized History of the Royal Mail* (London: Allen Lane, 2011), 201–2.

6. W. A. Chambers, "Postmen's Grievances," *North London Press,* September 28, 1889, cited in Clinton, *Post Office Workers,* 135.

7. Herbert Joyce to undersecretary of state, October 15, 1889, DPP 1/95/1, NA.

8. The South Kensington extravaganza was more subdued and static in design than the one staged at the museum. It had one model post office, complete with telegraph instruments, but the displays consisted mainly of documents, artifacts, and machinery. Its guest list, however, was irreproachable: the Prince of Wales made an appearance at 10:30 on the opening night, arriving shortly after the conclusion of over two hours of speeches. He reportedly amused himself by sending telegrams to France and looking over telegraphed proofs of the following day's news dispatches. *Account of the Celebration of the Jubilee of Uniform Inland Penny Postage* (London: Richard Clay and Sons, 1891), 159.

9. "Fourth Edition: The Penny Postage Jubilee at Guildhall Last Night/Meeting of Postmen on Clerkenwell Green," *Pall Mall Gazette,* May 17, 1890.

10. "Latest Labour Movement: Postmen's Grievances," *Reynolds's Weekly,* May 18, 1890.

11. "The Postmen's Strike: Scenes at the Chief Offices, Several Hundred Dismissals, Attitudes of Officials and Men," *Daily News,* July 11, 1890: "The Crisis in the Post Office," *Aberdeen Weekly Journal,* July 11, 1890; "The London Postmen," *Evening Post,* July 11, 1890; "The Postmen," *Times,* July 11, 1890; Henry Swift, *A History of Postal Agitation, from Fifty Years Ago till the Present Day* (London: C. Arthur Pearson, 1900), 218–21.

12. "The Postmen's Strike," *Daily News.*

13. "The Postmen's Strike," *Daily News.*

14. Postmen's Strike 1890: Strikers Dismissed and Reinstated, POST 33/2844A, PM; "The Postmen's Strike," *Daily News.*

15. "The Postmen's Strike," *Daily News;* "The Crisis in the Post Office," *Aberdeen Weekly Journal.*

16. "The London Postmen," *Reynolds's Weekly,* July 13, 1890.

17. "The Postmen's Strike," *Daily News;* "The Postmen," *Times.*

18. Postmen, Their Duties and Pay, 1891, POST 30/598, PM.

19. Clinton, *Post Office Workers,* 145.

20. Joyce to undersecretary of state, 15 October 1889.

21. Postmen, Their Duties and Pay, 5, appendix, 29.

22. Testimony of Freeling J. Lawrence, head of Appointment Branch, Postmen, Their Duties and Pay, appendix, 28–30.

23. Exchange between Henry Badcock, London telegraph controller, and Mr. Gardiner, inspector of postmen, Eastern Central District, testimony of Gardiner, Postmen, Their Duties and Pay, appendix, 35, 34.

24. Night Boy Messengers: Service Not Pensionable, 1913 (historical summary), POST 30/2630B; Night Duty—Effect on Youths: Reports of Medical Officers, 1875, POST 30/276D; Night Duty: Minimum Age of Employment, 1890, POST 30/574B, PM.

25. Gardiner, Postmen, Their Duties and Pay, appendix, 34.

26. Postmen, Their Duties and Pay, 5.

27. Postmen, Their Duties and Pay, Recruiting Classes, summary of testimony, 238.

28. Mr Hill, Testimony of Freeling Lawrence, Postmen's Report appendix, 32, 33.

29. Herbert Joyce, Testimony of Mr. Gardiner, Postmen's Report appendix, 35.

30. Haia Shpayer-Makov, "The Appeal of Country Workers: The Case of the Metropolitan Police," *Historical Research* 64 (1991): 186–203, doi: 10.1111 /j.1468–2281.1991.tb01793.x.

31. Postmen, Their Duties and Pay, 6.

32. Henry Cecil Raikes, postmaster general, to Treasury, May 13, 1891, in Postmen, Their Duties and Pay, ix.

33. As drilling started at the Central Telegraph Office, it is likely that it was implemented in direct response to the revelations of the Cleveland Street scandal.

34. James Fergusson, postmaster general, to Robert Tombs, November 28, 1891, Boy Messengers Drill, POST 33/273, PM.

35. R. Tombs to Stevenson Arthur Blackwood, December 19, 1891, Boy Messengers Drill, POST 33/273, PM.

36. R. C. Tombs to S. A. Blackwood, January 26, 1892, Boy Messengers Drill, POST 33/273, PM.

37. S. A. Blackwood, Post Office Circular 902, February 23, 1892, Boy Messengers Drill, POST 33/273, PM.

38. Blackwood, Post Office circular 902; Code of Permanent Rules as to Dress, etc., for Telegraph Messengers, 1891, POST 61/7, PM.

39. Report of the Controller, London Postal Section, on the Appearance of Boy Messengers, November 27, 1891, POST 61/7; Boy Messengers Drill, POST 33 /273, PM.

40. S. A. Blackwood, "Telegraph Messengers Drill," *Daily Telegraph,* August 19, 1892.

41. S. A. Blackwood to War Office, August 19. 1892, Boy Messengers Drill, POST 33/273, PM.

42. London's drill scheme was organized by postal district. Southwestern District boys drilled at the Wellington and Chelsea Barracks. Those in the Southeast District drilled at the recreation grounds on Union Road near Clapham; Eastern District Boys drilled in militia barracks skirting Victoria Park and West Ham Park. In North London, the GPO borrowed the 21st Finsbury Middlesex Rifles headquarters on Penton Street; Western District boys drilled at Kensington Barracks; Western Central District boys drilled at Somerset House; and the Eastern Central District messengers continued drilling at Charterhouse.

43. Copy of Memorandum Handed by P.M.G. [Postmaster General Arnold Morley] to the Secretary of State for War in Connexion with Mr. Arnold Forster's Motion, April 1896, Enlistment of Ex Soldiers and Sailors, file XX, POST 30/1802, PM.

44. Copy of Memorandum handed by P.M.G. to the Secretary of State for War.

45. Employment of Army Reserve Men as Postmen: Digest of Reports from Surveyors and Selected Postmasters, February 1893, POST 30/1802, PM.

46. Secretary Blackwood's minute to the Postmaster General Arnold Morley, Army Scheme as Affecting Telegraph Messengers, July 11, 1893, Enlistment of Ex Soldiers and Sailors, file X, POST 30/1802, PM.

47. Cremer had gained international recognition for his diplomatic interventions on the Continent. He would go on to win the first Nobel Peace Prize in 1903. The trades represented by the deputation included the Amalgamated Carpenters, Engineers, Tailors, and Saddlemakers.

48. Howard Evans, B. Lucraft, and William Morrison, Report of the Proceedings at a Deputation to the Postmaster General from the International Arbitration League, November 18, 1892, POST 33/273, PM.

49. Morrison, Report of the Proceedings.

50. Evans, Report of the Proceedings.

51. W. Maddison, Report of the Proceedings.

52. Charles Freake, Report of the Proceedings."

53. Maddison, Report of the Proceedings.

54. Report on Committee of Employment, Employment of Ex Soldiers and Sailors, file XIX, POST 30/1802, PM.

55. Employment of Ex Soldiers and Sailors, file XI, POST 30/1802, PM.

56. The Northern District GPO acquired drill facilities at the First London Volunteer Engineers grounds at Barnsbury Park in Islington, as well as the Third Middlesex Volunteers Drill Hall on Priory Road in Hornsey; Northwest District Boys also drilled at St Johns Wood Barracks. In the Southeast District, the GPO borrowed the Mantle Road Board School in Brockley and the Holly Hedge House in Blackheath. The Southwest district used the drill hall on St Georges Road in Wimbledon and the grounds of the Fourth Volunteer Battalion, East Surrey Regiment, at 27 St Johns Hill, Clapham Junction. The GPO also borrowed drill grounds in the southeast suburbs of Norwood and Dulwich.

57. Telegraph Messengers Drill, Ireland, 1895, Boy Messenger's Drill: Introduction and Abolition, Part 1, POST 33/273, PM.

58. Seth Koven, "From Rough Lads to Hooligans: Boy Life, National Culture and Social Reform," in *Nationalisms and Sexualities,* ed. Andrew Parker, Mary Russo, Doris Sommer, and Patricia Yaeger (New York: Routledge, 1992): 365–91; John Springhall, *Youth, Empire and Society: British Youth Movements, 1883–1940* (London: Croom Helm, 1977), chapters 3, 4; Michael Childs, *Labour's Apprentices: Working-Class Lads in Late Victorian and Edwardian England* (Montreal: McGill University Press, 1992), chapter 7; John Gillis, *Youth and History: Tradition and Change in European Age Relations, 1770–Present* (London: Academic Press, 1981), chapter 3.

59. Letters from M. E. Brown and H. W. Saunders to G. W. Webb, January 3, 1893, Indoor Boys Messenger Uniform, POST 30/548A, PM.

60. See, for example, "Telegraph Boys on Parade," *Daily News* June 15, 1895.

61. "Drilling H.M.'s Telegraph Lads: Military Exercises That Are Compulsory," *Chums,* December 19, 1894, 262.

62. "Drilling H.M.'s Telegraph Lads."

63. Boy Messenger's Drill, folder II, POST 33/273, PM. Telegraph boys also lined the north side of the mall during Edward VII's coronation.

64. Express Delivery Service: Employment of Boy Messengers to Wait in Theatre Ticket Queues, Convey People across London, etc. Not Allowed, 1904, POST 30/1129B, PM.

65. Daunton, *Royal Mail,* 205–6; Employment of Ex Soldiers and Sailors, file XX, POST 30/1802, PM; memorandum from Spencer Walpole, secretary, to Henry Fitzalan-Howard, postmaster general, December 6, 1897, Soldier Scheme, POST 30/1052, PM.

66. Secretary's response to memorandum by R. Bruce, asst. controller, EC District, February 27, 1906, Telegraph Messengers Drill: Award of Chevrons, POST 30/903A, PM.

67. John Gambril Nicholson, excerpt from unpublished letter, quoted in Timothy D'Arch Smith, *Love in Ernest: Some Notes on the Lives and Writings of English "Uranian" Poets from 1889 to 1930* (London: Routledge and Kegan Paul, 1970), 29.

68. Standing Committee on Boy Labour in the Post Office, Fourth Annual Report, 1914, 6.

69. Arthur Blackwood remained involved in the Telegraph Messenger Institute throughout his tenure as secretary.

70. John Springhall, *Coming of Age: Adolescence in Britain, 1860–1960* (Dublin: Gill and Macmillan, 1986); Springhall, *Youth, Empire and Society;* Gillis, *Youth and History;* Childs, *Labour's Apprentices;* Harry Hendrick, *Images of Youth: Age, Class, and the Male Youth Problem, 1880–1920* (Oxford: Clarendon Press, 1990); Koven, "From Rough Lads to Hooligans."

71. Dr. Macnamara, 19 March 1903, 119 Parl. Deb. (4th Ser.) (1903) col. 1293.

72. Mr. Ogilvie, drill inspector, to George Murray, secretary, March 27, 1903, Telegraph Messenger's Drill: Issue of Revised Syllabus, POST 33/273, PM.

73. Dr. Macnamara, March 19, 1903, 119 Parl. Deb. (4th Ser.) (1903) col. 1294.

74. Springhall, *Youth, Empire and Society,* chapter 3; Koven, "From Rough Lads to Hooligans," 380.

75. Hendrick, *Images of Youth,* 5.

76. Reginald Bray, *Boy Labour and Apprenticeship* (London: Constable, 1911), v–vi.

77. Historians such as Harry Hendrick and Michael Childs may have ignored the relationship between expanding female labor and contracting boys' employment because they understand the boy labor crisis as a problem of perception and not a result of rising unemployment or any sudden structural economic change. They both acknowledge that the decline of apprenticeship gradually altered—but did not decimate—youth labor prospects in the late Victorian and Edwardian eras. See Childs, *Labour's Apprentices,* xvii; Hendrick, *Images of Youth,* 9, Chapter 2, 3.

78. According to the youth reformer Reginald Bray, "Urban life, with its temptations, prematurities, sedentary occupations, and passive stimuli" worked on youths "just when an active, objective life is most needed." He explained his seemingly nonsensical labeling of urban delivery services jobs as "sedentary occupations" by referring to the extended downtime between tasks, when unsupervised boys had "considerable opportunities for pilfering and drinking." Bray, *Boy Labour and Apprenticeship,* 146.

79. Daunton, *Royal Mail,* 206.

80. Report by Mr. Cyril Jackson on Boy Labour, 1909, appendix, vol. XX, in *Report of the Royal Commission on the Poor Laws and Relief of Distress,* 1909, Cd. 4632.

81. Report by Mr. Cyril Jackson.

82. Bray, *Boy Labour and Apprenticeship,* 132.

83. Herbert Samuel to Sir Mathew Nathan, secretary, March 21, 1910, Boy Messengers, Unsatisfactory Prospects, file IX, POST 30/1762, PM. Samuel was friendly with George Bernard Shaw, Beatrice and Sidney Webb, and other Fabian luminaries such as J. A. Hobson, Charles Trevelyan, and Ramsay MacDonald.

84. Boy Messengers, Educational Classes, file I, POST 63/27, PM.

85. Letter from Herbert Samuel, postmaster general, to Edward Redford, secretary of the post office for Scotland, January 29, 1912, file 1, POST 30/3311, PM.

86. Henry Rippon-Seymour studied at Sweden's Royal Central Gymnastics Institute in Stockholm. He had authored and reviewed publications on physical exercises, and before accepting the post of instructor of physical exercises at the Edinburgh Post Office had been a physical instructor for the Provincial Committee for the Training of Teachers, the Dundee Physical Training College, and the Edinburgh City Police. He also held a concurrent post as the chief instructor of gymnastics at George Watson's College, an elite Edinburgh public school.

87. Henry Rippon-Seymour to Edinburgh GPO secretary, January 22, 1912, POST 30/3311, PM.

88. Henry Rippon-Seymour, Suggested Scheme for the Systematic Physical Training of Telegraph Messengers, January 22, 1912, POST 30/3311, PM.

89. Rippon-Seymour, Suggested Scheme.

90. Postmaster general's response to memorandum "Boy Messengers, Suggestion that Physical Training Should Be Compulsory," February 6, 1912, POST 30/3311, PM.

91. The GPO findings were summarized by the London Board of Education official James Veysey. On the whole he agreed with Rippon-Seymour's championing of physique but thought there was "little need for taking such a gloomy and serious view of the physical condition of the Boy Messenger," because on average the London messenger was "physically superior to that of 10 or 15 years ago." For Veysey the school inspector, this was not a result of GPO initiatives but of London board school and London County Council initiatives. See Physical Training of Boy Messengers in the Post Office, POST 30/3311, PM.

92. Springhall, *Youth, Empire, and Society;* Childs, *Labour's Apprentices,* chapter 7.

93. "Edith Grenfell, Penzance, Cornwall, during WW1 Female Messenger," in "Telegram Messenger Boys: Our Forgotten Heroes of Yesteryear," ca. 2010, compiled by Roger Green and Keith Cheshire, Reference Library, PM.

94. "Edith Grenfell, Penzance, Cornwall."

95. Girl Probationers, Employment in Place of Boy Messengers, historical memorandum, 1915, POST 30/3806A, PM.

96. Girl Probationers.

97. Administrators reasoned that these girl messengers would eventually be absorbed by the burgeoning telephone department. London officials also reported favorably on Reuters's practice of hiring female messengers, although Samuel balked at the idea of allowing girls to deliver messages in the city, a common practice at Reuters.

98. Daunton, *Royal Mail,* chapters 6–7.

99. Henry James, *In the Cage* (London: Martin Secker, 1924 [1898]).

100. Patrick Joyce, *The State of Freedom: A Social History of the British State since 1800* (Cambridge: Cambridge University Press, 2013), 129.

101. London Postal Service circular 25, February 12, 1916, London Postal Service: Boy Messengers, Orders and Notices Book, POST 14/346, PM.

102. Notice, September 3, 1915, Boy Messengers, Orders and Notices Book, POST 14/346, PM.

103. Girl Probationers.

104. R. Bruce, London Postal Service circular 138, September 16, 1915, London Postal Service: Boy Messengers, Orders and Notices Book, POST 14/346, PM.

105. Vera Brittain, *Testament of Youth: An Autobiographical Story of the Years* (London: Penguin, 1994 [1933]), 438.

CHAPTER EIGHT. VOICES ON THE WIRES

1. "Thrilling Story by Titanic's Surviving Wireless Man," *New York Times,* April 19, 1912.

2. J. W. C., "The Telephone System of the British Post Office," *St-Martins-le-Grand,* vol. 9, 1899, 50.

3. This chapter complements recent scholarship by Helen Glew on women telephone operators. We used different sources to reach some overlapping conclusions, but our emphases diverge. Helen Glew, " 'Maiden Whom We Never See: Cultural

Representations of the 'Lady Telegraphist' in Britain ca. 1880–1930 and Institutional Responses," *Information and Culture* 55 (2020): 30–50, doi: 10.7560/IC55103.

4. Most accounts of the GPO telephone network focus on its complex and contested history and ultimate unprofitability. See Arthur Hazlewood, "The Origin of the State Telephone Service in Britain," *Oxford Economic Papers* 5, no. 1 (1953): 13–25; Howard Robinson, *The British Post Office: A History* (Princeton: Princeton University Press, 1948), chapter 28; C. R. Perry, *The Victorian Post Office: The Growth of a Bureaucracy* (Woodbridge, Suffolk: Boydell, 1992), chapters 6, 7; Duncan Campbell-Bannerman, *Masters of the Post: The Authorized History of the Royal Mail* (London: Allen Lane, 2011), 192–95. More recently, historians have explored the telephone's influence on business culture. See Graeme J. Milne, "Business Districts, Office Culture, and the First Generation of Telephone Use in Britain," *Journal for the History of Engineering and Technology* 80 (2010): 199–213, doi: 10.1179/175812110X127141333537 59; Graeme J. Milne, "British Business and the Telephone, 1878–1911," *Business History* 49 (2007): 163–85, doi: 10.1080/00076790601170280; Christopher Beauchamp, "The Telephone Patents: Intellectual Property, Business, and the Law in the United States and Great Britain, 1876–1900," *Enterprise and Society* 4 (2008): 591–601.

5. Jeremy Leon Stein, "Ideology and the Telephone: The Social Reception of a Technology, London 1876–1920," PhD diss., University College London, September 1996, 68.

6. Perry, *The Victorian Post Office,* 149.

7. Telephones, InterDepartmental Telephonic Communication, Connection of Government Offices by Switch Room at Treasury, Establishment of System, 1881, POST 30/1153 B, BTA.

8. Perry, *The Victorian Post Office,* 182–85.

9. Stein, "Ideology and the Telephone," 74.

10. W. Napier, "Ineffective Calls," *National Telephone Journal,* September 1906, 114–15; Margaret Sweeny, "The Service from an Operators' Point of View," *National Telephone Journal,* May 1908, 32.

11. Arnold Morley, "Report from the Select Committee on the Telephone Service," *Times,* February 5, 1895.

12. Stein, "Ideology and the Telephone," 144.

13. See Stein, "Ideology and the Telephone," 101–34. He outlines a mutually reinforcing cycle of City investment and concentration of telephone services in the business sector.

14. Circular advertisement for Bell's Telephones, 1877, EHA 5608, BTA.

15. Affluent women also used the telephone, particularly as venues catering to women shoppers began installing telephones. See Stein, "Ideology and the Telephone," chapter 3 nn.130–31.

16. This argument has appeared in popular histories of the telephone. See D Occomore, *Number, Please! A History of the Early London Telephone Exchanges from 1880 to 1912* (Romford, Essex: Ian Henry, 1995), 38.

17. Florence J. Minter, "The Selection of Operators," *National Telephone Journal,* December 1906.

18. Minter, "The Selection of Operators."

19. Minter, "The Selection of Operators."

20. Telephone Operators: Status and Pay, 1897–1914, file IX, Semi-official Correspondence with Treasury, POST 30/1117, part 2, BTA.

21. Austen Chamberlain to GPO secretary, June 6, 1901, Telephone Operators: Status and Pay, 1897–1914, file IX, Semi-official Correspondence with Treasury, POST 30/117, part 2, BTA.

22. Memorandum to GPO secretary, "Telephone Operators, Wages," June 13, 1901, Telephone Operators: Status and Pay, 1897–1914, file IX: Semi-official Correspondence with Treasury, POST 30/117, part 2, BTA.

23. George Murray, GPO secretary, to Austen Chamberlain, June 20, 1901, Telephone Operators: Status and Pay, 1897–1914, file IX: Semi-official Correspondence with Treasury POST 30/117, part 2, BTA.

24. Murray to Chamberlain, June 20, 1901.

25. GPO circular to surveyors, July 17, 1901, Telephone Operators: Status and Pay, 1897–1914, file X, Status and Pay and Selection, POST 30/117, part 2, BTA.

26. GPO circular to surveyors, September 5, 1903, Telephone Operators: Status and Pay, 1897–1914, file XVIII, Condition of Admission to Higher Scale, POST 30/117, part 2, BTA.

27. "The Wages Question in the Post Office: Proceedings of the Committee of Enquiry; The Case for the Postal Telegraph Service in the Provinces," reprinted from *Telegraph Chronicle*, 1903, Odds & Ends, 1881–1905, 148/PT/2/1/1, UWMRC.

28. Perry, *The Victorian Post Office*, 138.

29. See H. Clegg, A. Fox, and A. F. Thompson, *A History of the British Trade Unions*, vol. 1 (Oxford: Oxford University Press, 1964); E.J. Hobsbawm, "General Labour Unions in Britain, 1889–1914," in *Labouring Men: Studies in the History of Labour* (London: Weidenfeld and Nicholson, 1964); Paul Thompson, *Socialists, Liberals, and Labour: The Struggle for London* (London: Routledge and Kegan Paul, 1967). For a discussion of postal workers' relationships to the wider labor movement, see Alan Clinton, *Post Office Workers: A Trade Union and Social History* (London: George Allen and Unwin, 1984), chapters 4, 6, 8. Women's participation in the larger movement has been well documented, but as telephone operators and telegraphists tended to be categorized as "salaried ladies," their particular contributions to the new unionism have been underresearched. See Sheila Lewenhak, *Women and Trade Unions: An Outline History of Women in the British Trade Union Movement* (London: Benn, 1977); Norbert C. Soldon, *Women in British Trade Unions, 1874–1976* (Dublin: Gill and Macmillan, 1978); David Rubinstein, *Before the Suffragettes: Women's Emancipation in the 1890s* (Brighton: Harvester, 1986); Sonya Rose, *Limited Livelihoods: Gender and Class in Nineteenth-Century England* (Berkeley: University of California Press, 1992).

30. The Wages Question in the Post Office"; Clinton, *Post Office Workers*, 239.

31. Clinton, *Post Office Workers*, 239.

32. "Annual Conference," *Telegraph Chronicle and Civil Service Recorder*, April 15, 1910, 56; Records of the Postal Telegraph Clerks' Association, MSS 148

/PT/2/4/17, UWMRC. See also Report from the Select Committee on Post Office Servants, Parliamentary Papers (1912): 9:306.

33. Telephonists, Late Duties of Female Telephonists, file III, 1910; file V, 1912; file VI, 1913; file IX–XI, 1914, POST 30/3002A, BTA.

34. Draft circular, April 21, 1914, Telephone Instructions, London and Provinces: Employment of Female Telephonists at Night, file X, POST 30/3002A, BTA.

35. Telephone Instructions, London and Provinces.

36. Brian McCuskey, "The Kitchen Police: Servant Surveillance and Middle-Class Transgression," *Victorian Literature and Culture* 28, no. 2 (2000): 362, www.jstor.org/stable/25058524.

37. "The Wicked Telephone Girl," *Every Week,* December 27, 1895, 54.

38. "That Dreadful Telephone Girl," *Every Week,* January 10, 1896, 63.

39. "All through the Telephone," *New London Journal,* August 17, 1907, 369.

40. J. W. C., "The Telephone System of the British Post Office."

41. Memoranda, 18 February 1909–3 May 1909, Interdepartmental Telephonic Communication: Treasury Exchange, file 3, POST 30/1153 B, BTA.

42. Hansard Watt, "To Any Telephone Girl," *Pall Mall Magazine,* February 1911, 236.

43. "An Assisted Order," *London Journal,* July 28, 1900, 86.

44. "From the City," *Judy,* July 6, 1904, 947; "The Telephone Girl," *Judy,* July 14, 1906, 327.

45. "Girls at Telephone Exchange Will Disappear before New Invention of Automatic Service," *Dundee Evening Telegraph,* November 23, 1911, 5.

46. "The System of Telephone Calls," *Aberdeen Journal,* June 13, 1900, 7.

47. "Telephone Invention: The Exchange Girl Superseded," *London Daily News,* October 23, 1902, 9.

48. "'Number, Please?': Human Machines," *Manchester Courier,* June 13, 1913, 1.

49. W. H. Gunston, "The Relation of the Staff to the Public," *National Telephone Journal,* October 1906, 138.

50. "'Number, Please?'"

51. "The Telephone Exchange," *Chambers's Journal,* March 16, 1889, 176.

52. "The Telephone Exchange."

53. "'Number, Please?'"

54. "The Telephone Exchange."

55. William Chauncy Cartwright to Sydney Buxton, postmaster general, November 12, 1907, Foreign Office: Miss Adams, Telephone Operator, FO 366/1143, NA.

56. "Telephone Etiquette," *National Telephone Journal,* May 1908, 34.

57. Michael Heller, "British Company Magazines, 1878–1939: The Origins and Functions of House Journals in Large-Scale Organisations," *Media History* 15 (2009): 146, 149, 150, doi: 10.1080/13688800902781850. See also See also J. H. Weiner, *Papers for the Millions: The New Journalism in Britain, 1850s to 1914* (New York: Greenwood, 1988); James Curran, "Media and the Making of British Society, c. 1700–2000," *Media History* 8 (2002): 135–54; R. J. Morris, "Clubs, Societies, and

Associations," in *The Cambridge Social History of Britain, 1750–1950*, vol. 3, ed. F. M. L. Thompson (Cambridge: Cambridge University Press, 1990).

58. *St-Martins-le-Grand* was published from 1890 to 1933. It was replaced by the *Post Office Magazine* in 1933, which was in turn replaced by the Post Office Bank's current staff magazine, *Courier,* in 1966. The full print run is available in the reference library of the PM. Limited holdings are also available at the BTA.

59. Heller argues that employee magazines began appealing to lower staff grades in the interwar period, a product of widespread institutionalized industrial welfare. Heller, "British Company Magazines," 153–61.

60. Sally Mitchell, *The New Girl: Girls' Culture in England, 1880–1915* (New York: Columbia University Press, 1995); Kirsten Drotner, *English Children and Their Magazines, 1751–1945* (New Haven: Yale University Press, 1988). See also Penny Tinkler, *Constructing Girlhood: Popular Magazines for Girls Growing up in England, 1920–1950* (London: Taylor and Francis, 1995); Billie Melman, *Women and the Popular Imagination in the Twenties: Flappers and Nymphs* (Basingstoke: Macmillan, 1988), especially chapter 7.

61. Mitchell, *The New Girl,* 4; Melman, *Women and the Popular Imagination,* 7–9, 108–14.

62. "New Feature," *National Telephone Journal,* July 1907.

63. "Telephone Women, I: Ellen Marian Ralph," *National Telephone Journal,* July 1907.

64. Dina Copelman, *London's Women Teachers: Gender, Class and Feminism, 1870–1930.* London: Routledge, 1996. chapters 3, 7; Susan D. Pennybacker, *A Vision for London, 1889–1914: Labour, Everyday Life and the LCC Experiment* (London: Routledge, 1995), chapter 1.

65. "Telephone Women, XCV: Minnie Francis Butler," *National Telephone Journal,* July 1911.

66. "Telephone Women, LV: Fannie Louisa Holmes," *National Telephone Journal,* January 1910.

67. "Telephone Women, LV: Fannie Louisa Holmes."

68. "Telephone Women, XVII: Emily Richards," *National Telephone Journal,* June 1908; "Telephone Women, LVI: Ethel Aitken Epps," *National Telephone Journal,* January 1910.

69. "Telephone Women, LXXXIX: Constance Marion Gregory," *National Telephone Journal,* April 1911.

70. "Telephone Women, XXXIII: Constance A. Forge," *National Telephone Journal,* February 1909.

71. "Telephone Women, XC: Ada Ellis," *National Telephone Journal,* May 1911.

72. "Telephone Women, LV: Fannie Louisa Holmes."

73. "Telephone Women, LXXXIII: Celia Kate Hooper," *National Telephone Journal,* April 1911.

74. "Telephone Women, LVI: Ethel Aitken Epps"; "Telephone Women, XXXIV: Maude Gladman," *National Telephone Journal,* February 1909; "Telephone Women, XXVII: Ada E. Knapman," *National Telephone Journal,* November 1808.

75. "Telephone Women, LV: Fannie Louisa Holmes."

76. A. Duggan, "Helps and Hindrances to Good Operating," *National Telephone Journal,* September 1906.

77. Winnifred Etheredge, "The Operator's Point of View," *National Telephone Journal,* February 1908.

78. Duggan, "Helps and Hindrances."

79. Winnifred Etheredge, "How a Subscriber May Help His Own Service," *National Telephone Journal,* June 1906.

80. Duggan, "Helps and Hindrances."

81. Etheredge, "The Operator's Point of View."

82. Etheredge, "The Operator's Point of View."

83. Etheredge, "How a Subscriber May Help His Own Service."

84. Etheredge, "How a Subscriber May Help His Own Service."

85. According to the business historian Scott Peter, telephone use remained limited to a small cohort of elites well into the 1930s. Scott Peter, "Still a Nice Communications Medium: The Diffusion and Uses of Telephone System in Interwar Britain," *Business History* 53 (2011): 801–20.

86. Duggan, "Helps and Hindrances"; Sweeny, "The Service"; Etheredge, "The Operator's Point of View"; Etheredge, "How a Subscriber May Help His Own Service."

87. See Judith Walkowitz, "Going Public: Shopping, Street Harassment, and Streetwalking in Late Victorian London," *Representations* 62 (1998): 6.

88. Marion Bailey, "Do Subscribers Appreciate a Cheerful Voice?" *National Telephone Journal,* July 1906.

89. Sweeny, "The Service."

90. These locations were chosen for late-night service as they were "found useful by members of Parliament." "Telephone Women, XVII: Emily Richards."

91. Karolina D. Laing, "What It Is to Be a Night Operator: The Difficulties and Responsibilities," *National Telephone Journal,* August 1908.

92. E. M. Buckland, "To an Operator," *National Telephone Journal,* October 1909.

93. Laing, "What It Is."

94. Public call boxes also vexed operators because the majority of their users were unfamiliar with the new technology and impeded an operator's ability to make a swift connection.

95. "Telephonic Instructions and Notes," *Judy,* 9 March 1898, 116.

96. H. Julius Maclure, contract manager, Brighton, "Private House Development from the Contract Point of View," *National Telephone Journal,* May 1906.

97. "Two Belgian Telephone Girls," *Telegraph and Telephone Journal,* November 1914, 46.

98. Agnes N. Avlott, "Wrong Number Trouble," *Telegraph and Telephone Journal,* July 1915, 216, 217.

99. "Telephonists and the Human Element," *Telegraph and Telephone Journal,* August 1915, 242.

1. George Dangerfield, *The Strange Death of Liberal England,* 12th ed. (New York: Capricorn, 1961 [1935]).

2. Dangerfield's insights have been embraced, qualified, and revised by subsequent generations of historians. See Mary Langan and Bill Schwarz, eds., *Crises in the British State, 1880–1930* (London: Hutchinson, 1986), especially Stuart Hall and Bill Schwarz's opening essay, "State and Society." For alternative views, see David Powell, *The Edwardian Crisis: Britain, 1901–1914* (Basingstoke: Palgrave MacMillan, 1996), and Martin Pugh, *State and Society: British Political and Social History, 1870–1992,* 4th ed. (London: Bloomsbury, 2012), chapter 9. Others have noted that although the Victorian consensus dissolved, liberalism endured as a resilient strand in the many fractious discourses of British social and political life. See for example, E. H. H. Green and D. M. Tanner, eds., *The Strange Survival of Liberal England: Political Leaders, Moral Values, and the Reception of Economic Debate* (Cambridge: Cambridge University Press, 2007).

3. Ray Strachey, *The Cause: A Short History of the Women's Movement in Great Britain* (London: G. Bell and Sons, 1928), 311–12.

4. The militant suffrage movement has been the subject of numerous histories. For more recent work, see Laura E. Nym Mayhall, *The Militant Suffrage Movement: Citizenship and Resistance in Britain, 1860–1930* (Oxford: Oxford University Press, 2003); Sandra Holton, *Suffrage Days: Stories from the Women's Suffrage Movement* (London: Routledge, 1996); Maroula Joannou and June Purvis, eds., *The Women's Suffrage Movement: New Feminist Perspectives* (Manchester: Manchester University Press, 1998); June Purvis and Sandra Stanley Holton, eds., *Votes for Women!* (London: Routledge, 2000). On suffrage campaigns and spectacle, see Lisa Tickner, *The Spectacle of Women: Imagery of the Suffrage Campaign, 1907–1914* (Chicago: University of Chicago Press, 1988); Barbara Green, *Spectacular Confessions: Autobiography, Performance Activism, and the Sites of Suffrage, 1905–1938* (London: St Martins, 1997).

5. Erika Rappaport has examined a specific suffragette target: the plate-glass windows of fashionable West End clothing retailers. She locates this tactic squarely in the environment of consumption and burgeoning middle-class women's culture in London. The window smashing was more than just an attack on property: it was both an acknowledgment and a refutation of the treatment of women as objects of display. The spatial, technological, and economic underpinnings of the culture of shopping created the possibility of such revolts. Erika Rappaport, *Shopping for Pleasure: Women in the Making of London's West End* (Princeton: Princeton University Press, 2001), epilogue.

6. See Norman Watson, *Suffragettes and the Post* (self-published, 2010), 16.

7. See Sylvia Pankhurst, *The Suffragette Movement* (London: Virago, 1997 [1931]), 401.

8. Records of Convictions and Dismissals from 1st January 1913 (to 1914), POST 120/159, PM.

9. Letter Boxes: Prevention of Damage to Contents, ca. 1913, POST 30/2563A, PM.

10. Krista Cowman, *Women of the Right Spirit: Paid Organizers of the Women's Social and Political Union (WSPU), 1904–1918* (Manchester: Manchester University Press, 2007), 96, 97.

11. For example, See Sylvia Pankhurst, *The Suffragette: The History of the Women's Militant Suffrage Movement, 1905–1910* (Boston: Women's Journal, 1912), 476; Dangerfield, *Strange Death,* 154, 174.

12. For Dangerfield, influenced by 1930s sexology, this act of gender bending encapsulated the subversive energy at the heart of the "Women's Rebellion," which he characterized as masculine (and very often lesbian as well).

13. See Laurence Senelick, "The Evolution of the Male Impersonator on the Nineteenth Century Popular Stage," *Essays in Theatre* 1 (1982): 29–44; Elaine Aston, "Male Impersonation in the Music Hall: The Case of Vesta Tilley," *New Theatre Quarterly* 4 (1988): 247–57; Martha Vicinus, "The Adolescent Boy: Fin de Siècle Femme Fatale?" *Journal of the History of Sexuality* 5 (1994): 90–114; Martha Vicinus, "Turn of the Century Male Impersonation: Rewriting the Romance Plot," in *Sexualities in Victorian Britain,* ed. Andrew H. Miller and James Eli Adams (Bloomington: Indiana University Press, 1996), 202–7.

14. The scholarship on the Easter Rising is vast. Here I have relied on influential recent studies: Charles Townshend, *Easter 1916: The Irish Rebellion* (Chicago: Ivan R. Dee, 2006); Clair Wills, *Dublin 1916: The Siege of the GPO* (Cambridge, MA: Harvard University Press, 2009); Joost Augusteijn, ed., *The Irish Revolution, 1913–1923* (London: Palgrave, 2002); Fearghal McGarry, *The Rising: Easter 1916* (Oxford: Oxford University Press, 2010).

15. Townshend, *Easter 1916,* 100.

16. See Wills, *Dublin 1916,* 23. A comprehensive online exhibit on the Easter Rising was launched in 2016 to celebrate its centenary: www.rte.ie/centuryireland /index.php/easterrising.

17. Townshend, *Easter 1916,* 100–102; McGarry, *The Rising,* 163–64; Andrew Kincaid, *Postcolonial Dublin: Imperial Legacies and the Built Environment* (Minneapolis: University of Minnesota Press, 2006), 1–4.

18. Kincaid, *Postcolonial Dublin,* 3.

19. Keith Jeffery, *The GPO and the Easter Rising* (Dublin: Irish Academic Press, 2006); Stephen Ferguson, *GPO Staff in 1916: Business as Usual* (Cork: Mercier, 2005).

20. Ferguson, *GPO Staff,* 62, 84–85.

21. Ferguson, *GPO Staff,* chapter 4; Jeffery, *The GPO and the Easter Rising,* 112–21.

22. Ferguson, *GPO Staff,* 63.

23. Ferguson, *GPO Staff,* 164, 165; Jeffery, *The GPO and the Easter Rising,* 137. See also "Two Belgian Telephone Girls," *Telegraph and Telephone Journal,* November 1914, 46.

24. Ferguson, *GPO Staff,* 79.

25. Ferguson, *GPO Staff,* 79, 84.

26. Ferguson, *GPO Staff,* 52.

27. Antoinette Burton, *The Trouble with Empire: Challenges to Modern British Imperialism* (Oxford: Oxford University Press, 2015), 123. See also D. K. Lahiri Choudhury, "India's First Virtual Community and the Telegraph General Strike of 1908," *International Review of Social History* 48, supplement S11 (2003): 45–71.

28. See the CWU's current website, www.cwu.org, accessed October 2, 2019.

29. Conference minutes, June 30, 1920, Telegraph Messengers Drill: Introduction and Abolition, part 2, POST 33/274A, PM; Minute from G. Evelyn P. Murray, secretary, to Frederick G. Kellaway, postmaster general, August 18, 1921, POST 33/274A, PM.

30. Minute from secretary to postmaster general, August 18, 1921.

31. Henry Rippon-Seymour, *Songs from the Somme* (London: Long, 1918).

32. See Thomas Linehan, *British Fascism, 1918–1939: Parties, Ideology, and Culture* (Manchester: Manchester University Press, 2000): 125–26.

33. Linehan, *British Fascism.* See also Martin Pugh, *Hurrah For the Blackshirts! Fascists and Fascism in Britain between the Wars* (London: Pimlico, 2006), chapter 5.

34. Linehan, *British Fascism,* 126; Pugh *Hurrah For the Blackshirts!,* 54, 69. On Barker's life and cultural impact, see James Vernon, "For Some Queer Reason: the Trials and Tribulations of Colonel Barker's Masquerade in Interwar Britain," *Signs* 26 (2000): 37–62; Rose Collis, *Colonel Barker's Monstrous Regiment: A Tale of Female Husbandry* (London: Virago, 2001); Laura Doan, *Fashioning Sapphism: The Origins of a Modern English Lesbian Culture* (New York: Columbia University Press, 2001), chapter 3.

35. Records of Convictions and Dismissals, 1915, POST 120/159, PM.

36. Royal Mail, "Launch of Royal Mail's Investigation Department," Celebrating 500 Years of Royal Mail, http://500years.royalmailgroup.com/gallery/launch-of-royal-mail-s-investigation-department, accessed February 1, 2019.

37. "Charles (Bob) Gibbons 1933 London," ca. 2007, unpublished memoir, "Telegram Messenger Boys: the Forgotten Heroes of Yesteryear," compiled by Roger Green and Keith Cheshire, ca. 2010, Reference Library, PM.

38. "Charles (Bob) Gibbons 1933 London."

BIBLIOGRAPHY

ARCHIVAL SOURCES

Major Collections

The BT (British Telecom) Archives (BTA), London
The Morten Collection, Haringey Archive Service at Bruce Castle, London
The National Archives of the United Kingdom (NA), London
The Postal Museum (PM), London
University of Warwick Modern Records Center (UWMRC), Warwick

Other Document Sources

British Library, London
Manchester Archives and Local Studies, Manchester. Fawcett Collection
Peabody Library, Baltimore MD. Periodical Collections
Victoria and Albert Museum, London, Theatre and Performance Collections
Women's Library, London School of Economics, London, Records of the Association of the Post Office Women Clerks

OFFICIAL SOURCES

Parliamentary Papers (by Date)

HC 202 Vol 41.555. Reports to Postmaster General on Proposal for Transferring to Post Office Control Electric Telegraphs throughout United Kingdom, 1867–68 (Scudamore Report).
C. 304 Vol. 37.703. Report on Reorganization of Telegraph System of the United Kingdom, 1871 (Scudamore Report).
C. 1113 Vol. 23.3. First Report of the Civil Service Inquiry Commission: With Correspondence, 1875 (Playfair Commission).

HC 357 Vol. 13.1. Report from the Select Committee on Post Office (Telegraph Department): Together with the Proceedings of the Committee, Minutes of Evidence, and Appendix, 1876 (Playfair Report).

HC 163 Vol. 44.37. Inter-dept. Committee on Post Office Establishments: Minutes of Evidence, Indices, Summaries, Appendices, 1897 (Tweedmouth Commission).

C. 2170 Vol. 33.465. Committee on Post Office Wages: Report and Appendices of the Committee Appointed to Inquire into Post Office Wages, part I, 1904 (Bradford Committee).

HC 380 Vol.12.1. Index and Digest of Evidence to the Report from the Select Committee on Post Office Servants, 1906 (Hobhouse Committee).

C. 4632 44.921. Royal Commission on the Poor Laws and Relief of Distress, Appendix, vol. XX: Report by Mr. Cyril Jackson on Boy Labour together with a Memorandum from the General Post Office on the Conditions of the Employment of Telegraph Messengers, 1909 (Hamilton Commission).

Parliamentary Debates: 3rd Series; 4th Series.

GENERAL POST OFFICE DOCUMENTS

British Postal Guide, 1870–1916.
Immorality among Boys: Mr. Jeffery's Report and Recommendation, 1877.
Further Substitution of Male for Female Telegraphists, 1878.
Postmen, Their Duties and Pay, 1891.
Post Office Establishment Books, 1870–1916.
Reports of the Postmaster General on the Post Office, 1870–1916.
Standing Committee on Boy Labour in the Post Office, 1911–14.
"Telegram Messenger Boys, Our Forgotten Heroes of Yesteryear. Unpublished memoirs, compiled by Roger Green and Keith Cheshire, ca. 2010.

Newspapers and Periodicals

Aberdeen Weekly Journal
Belgravia
Bow Bells
Boy's Own Paper
The British Juvenile
British Quarterly Review
Capital and Labour
Chambers's Journal
Chicago Daily Tribune
Chums
Civil Service Gazette

Daily Chronicle
Daily News
Daily Telegraph
Dundee Evening Telegraph
The Economist
Edinburgh Review
The Engineer
Englishwomen's Domestic Review
English Women's Journal
Evening Post
Every Week
Fun
Good Words
Illustrated London News
Illustrated Police News
Ipswich Journal
Journal of the Society of the Arts
Judy
The Licensed Victualler
Little Folks
Lloyd's Weekly
London Daily News
London Journal
Longman's Magazine
Manchester Courier
Moonshine
National Telephone Journal
New London Journal
New York Times
North London Press
Pall Mall Gazette
Pall Mall Magazine
The Post
Postman's Gazette
Post Office Gazette
Punch
Quarterly Review
Reynolds's Weekly Newspaper
Saturday Review
The Spectator
The Standard
St-Martins-le-Grand
Sunday Times
Telegraph Chronicle and Civil Service Recorder

Telegraph and Telephone Journal
Telegraphic Journal
Telegraphist
Temple Bar
Time
The Times
United Ireland
Women's Penny Paper
Young England

PRIMARY SOURCES

Account of the Celebration of the Jubilee of the Uniform Inland Penny Postage. London: Richard Clay and Sons, 1891.

Ackerly, J. R. *My Father and Myself.* London: Bodley Head, 1966.

Baines, F. E. *Forty Years at the Post Office: A Personal Narrative,* 2 vols. London: Richard Bentley and Son, 1895.

Banks, Elizabeth. *Campaigns of Curiosity: Journalistic Adventures of an American Girl in London.* Chicago: F. Tennyson Neely, 1894.

Bray, Reginald. *Boy Labour and Apprenticeship.* London: Constable, 1911.

Brittain, Vera. *Testament of Youth: An Autobiographical Story of the Years.* London: Penguin, 1994 (1933).

Chadwick, Edwin. "On the Economy of Telegraphy as Part of a Public System of Postal Communication." *Journal of the Society of Arts* 15, 1867.

Clausen-Thue, W. *The ABC Universal Commercial Electronic Telegraphic Code.* London: Rock Terrace, 1873.

———. *The ABC Telegraphic Code,* 3rd ed. London: Eden Fisher, 1876.

Hill, Rowland. *Post Office Reform: Its Importance and Practicability,* 3rd. ed. London: Charles Knight, 1837.

James, Henry. *In the Cage.* London: Martin Secker, 1924 (1898).

Jevons, W. S. "On the Analogy between the Post Office, Telegraphs, and Other Systems of Conveyance of the United Kingdom as Regards Government Control." In *Methods of Social Reform,* 2nd ed. London: MacMillan, 1904.

Joyce, Herbert. *The History of the Post Office from Its Establishment Down to 1836.* London: Richard Bentley and Son, 1893.

O'Brien, William. *Evening Memories.* Dublin: Maunsel, 1920.

Pankhurst, Sylvia. *The Suffragette: The History of the Women's Militant Suffrage Movement, 1905–1910.* Boston: Women's Journal, 1912.

———. *The Suffragette Movement.* London: Virago, 1997 (1931).

Raikes, Henry St John. *The Life and Letters of Henry Cecil Raikes.* London: Macmillan, 1898.

Rippon-Seymour, Henry. *Songs from the Somme.* London: Long, 1918.

Sims, George, ed. *Living London.* Vol. 3. London: Cassell, 1903.

Strachey, Ray. *The Cause: A Short History of the Women's Movement in Great Britain.* London: G. Bell and Sons, 1928.

Swift, H. G. *A History of Postal Agitation, from Fifty Years Ago till the Present Day.* London: C. Arthur Pearson, 1900.

Thompson, Flora. *Lark Rise to Candleford.* Oxford: Oxford University Press, 1939.

Tombs, R. C. *The King's Post: Being a Volume of Historical Facts relating to the Posts, Mail Coaches, Coach Roads, and Railway Mail Services of and Connected with the Ancient City of Bristol from 1580 to the Present time.* Bristol: W. C. Hemmons, 1905.

Trollope, Anthony. "The Telegraph Girl." In *Anthony Trollope: Later Short Stories,* ed. John Sutherland. Oxford: Oxford University Press, 1995 (1877).

SECONDARY SOURCES

Agar, John. *The Government Machine: A Revolutionary History of the Computer.* Cambridge, MA: MIT Press, 2003.

Alaimo, Kathleen. "The Authority of Experts: The Crisis of Female Adolescence in France and England, 1880–1920." In *Secret Gardens, Satanic Mills: Placing Girls in European History, 1750–1960,* ed. Mary Jo Maynes, Birgitte Søland, and Christina Benninghaus, 149–63. Bloomington: Indiana University Press, 2004.

Allen, Joan, Alan Campbell, Eric Hobsbawm, and John McIlroy, eds. *Histories of Labour: National and International Perspectives.* Pontypool, Wales: Merlin, 2010.

Anderson, Gregory. "The White Blouse Revolution." In *The White Blouse Revolution: Female Office Workers since 1870,* ed. Gregory Anderson, 1–26. Manchester: Manchester University Press, 1988.

Aronson, Theo. *Prince Eddy and the Homosexual Underworld.* 2nd ed. London: John Murray, 1996.

Aston, Elaine. "Male Impersonation in the Music Hall: The Case of Vesta Tilley." *New Theatre Quarterly* 4 (1988): 247–57.

Augusteijn, Joost, ed. *The Irish Revolution, 1913–1923.* London: Palgrave, 2002.

Bailey, Peter. "Parasexuality and Glamour: The Victorian Barmaid as Cultural Prototype." *Gender and History* 2, no. 2 (1990): 148–72, doi: 10.1111/j.1468-0424.1990.tb00091.x.

———. *Popular Culture and Performance in the Victorian City.* Cambridge: Cambridge University Press, 1998.

———. "White Collars, Gray Lives? The Lower Middle Class Revisited." *Journal of British Studies* 38, no. 3 (1999): 273–90, www.jstor.org/stable/176057.

Bayly, C. A. *Empire and Information: Intelligence Gathering and Social Communication in India, 1780–1870.* Cambridge: Cambridge University Press, 1996.

Beauchamp, Christopher. "The Telephone Patents: Intellectual Property, Business, and the Law in the United States and Great Britain, 1876–1900." *Enterprise and Society* 9, no. 4 (2008): 591–601, doi: 10.1093/es/khn084.

Beauchamp, Ken. *History of Telegraphy.* London: Institution of Engineering and Technology, 2001.

Bederman, Gail. *Manliness and Civilization: A Cultural History of Gender and Race in the United States, 1880–1917*. Chicago: University of Chicago Press, 1995.

Beetham, Margaret. "Domestic Servants as Poachers of Print: Reading, Authority and Resistance in Late Victorian Britain." In *The Politics of Domestic Authority in Britain since 1800*, ed. Lucy Delap, Ben Griffin, and Abigail Wills, 185–203. Basingstoke: Palgrave Macmillan, 2009.

Bektas, Yakup. "The Sultan's Messenger: Cultural Constructions of Ottoman Telegraphy, 1847–1880." *Technology and Culture* 41, no. 4 (2000): 669–96, doi: https://doi.org/10.1353/tech.2000.0141.

Boyd, Kelly. *Manliness and the Boys' Story Paper in Britain: A Cultural History, 1855–1940*. New York: Palgrave, 2003.

Brady, Sean. *Masculinity and Male Homosexuality in Britain, 1861–1913*. Basingstoke: Palgrave MacMillan, 2005.

Breward, Christopher. *The Hidden Consumer: Masculinities, Fashion and City Life, 1860–1914*. Manchester: Manchester University Press, 1999.

Briggs, Asa. *Victorian Cities*. Berkeley: University of California Press, 1965.

Burton, Antoinette. *The Trouble with Empire: Challenges to Modern British Imperialism*. Oxford: Oxford University Press, 2015.

Campbell-Bannerman, Duncan. *Masters of the Post: The Authorized History of the Royal Mail*. London: Allen Lane, 2011.

Castells, Manuel. *End of Millennium: The Information Age; Economy, Society, and Culture*. Vol. 3. Chichester: John Wiley and Sons, 2010.

———. *The Informational City: Information Technology, Economic Restructuring, and the Urban-Regional Process*. Oxford: Blackwell, 1989.

Childs, Michael. *Labour's Apprentices: Working-Class Lads in Late Victorian and Edwardian England*. Montreal: McGill University Press, 1992.

Choudhury, D.K. Lahiri. "India's First Virtual Community and the Telegraph General Strike of 1908." *International Review of Social History* 48, Supplement S11 (2003): 45–71.

———. "Sinews of Panic and the Nerves of Empire: The Imagined State's Entanglement with Information Panic, India c. 1880–1912." *Modern Asian Studies* 38 (2004): 965–1002.

———. *Telegraphic Imperialism: Crisis and Panic in the Indian Empire, c. 1830*. Basingstoke: Palgrave Macmillan, 2010.

Clark, Anna. *The Struggle for the Breeches: Gender and the Making of the British Working Class*. Berkeley: University of California Press, 1995.

Clegg, H., A. Fox, and A.F. Thompson. *A History of the British Trade Unions*. Vol. 1. Oxford: Oxford University Press, 1964.

Clinton, Alan. *Post Office Workers: A Trade Union and Social History*. London: George Allen and Unwin, 1984.

Cocks, H.G. "Making the Sodomite Speak: Voices of the Accused in English Sodomy Trials, c. 1800–1898." *Gender and History* 18 (2006): 87–107.

———. *Nameless Offences: Homosexual Desire in the Nineteenth Century*. London: I.B. Tauris, 2003.

Cohen, Deborah. *Family Secrets: Shame and Privacy in Modern Britain*. Oxford: Oxford University Press, 2017.

Cohen, Ed. *Talk on the Wilde Side: Toward a Genealogy of a Discourse on Male Sexualities*. London: Routledge, 1993.

Collini, Stefan. "The Idea of 'Character' in Victorian Political Thought." *Transactions of the Royal Historical Society* 35 (1985): 29–50, doi:10.2307/3679175.

Collis, Rose. *Colonel Barker's Monstrous Regiment: A Tale of Female Husbandry*. London: Virago, 2001.

Cook, Matt. *London and the Culture of Homosexuality, 1885–1914*. Cambridge: Cambridge University Press, 2003.

Copelman, Dina. *London's Women Teachers: Gender, Class and Feminism, 1870–1930*. London: Routledge, 1996.

Cowman, Krista. *Women of the Right Spirit: Paid Organizers of the Women's Social and Political Union (WSPU), 1904–1918*. Manchester: Manchester University Press, 2007.

Cox, Pamela. "Girls in Trouble: Defining Female Delinquency, Britain, 1900–1950." In *Secret Gardens, Satanic Mills: Placing Girls in European History, 1750–1960*, ed. Mary Jo Maynes, Birgitte Søland, and Christina Benninghaus, 192–205. Bloomington: Indiana University Press, 2004.

Crook, Tom. "Secrecy and Liberal Modernity in Victorian and Edwardian Britain." In *The Peculiarities of Liberal Modernity in Imperial Britain,* ed. Simon Gunn and James Vernon, 72–90. Berkeley: University of California Press, 2011.

Curran, James. "Media and the Making of British Society, c. 1700–2000." *Media History* 8 (2002): 135–54.

Dangerfield, George. *The Strange Death of Liberal England*. New York: Capricorn, 1961 (1935).

D'Arch Smith, Timothy. *Love in Ernest: Some Notes on the Lives and Writings of English "Uranian" Poets from 1889 to 1930*. London: Routledge and Kegan Paul, 1970.

Daunton, M. L. *Royal Mail: The Post Office since 1840*. London: Athlone, 1985.

Davies, Andrew. *The Gangs of Manchester: The Story of the Scuttlers, Britain's First Youth Cult*. Milo Books, 2009 (ebook).

Davin, Anna. "City Girls: Young Women, New Employment, and the City, London 1880–1910." In *Secret Gardens, Satanic Mills: Placing Girls in European History, 1750–1960*, ed. Mary Jo Maynes, Birgitte Søland, and Christina Benninghaus, 209–23. Bloomington: Indiana University Press, 2005.

———. *Growing Up Poor: Home, School, and Street in London, 1870–1914*. London: Rivers Oram, 1996.

———. "Women Telegraphists and Typists, 1870–1890." In *Women in Industry and Technology,* ed. Amanda Devonshire and Barbara Wood, 214–15. London: Museum of London, 1986.

Delap, Lucy. *Knowing Their Place: Domestic Service in Twentieth-Century Britain*. Oxford: Oxford University Press, 2011.

Doan, Laura. *Fashioning Sapphism: The Origins of a Modern English Lesbian Culture*. New York: Columbia University Press, 2001.

Dowling, Emma, Rodrigo Nunes, and Ben Trott. "Immaterial and Affective Labor: Explored." *Ephemera: Theory and Politics in Organization* 7, no. 1 (2007): 1–7.

Downey, Gregory. *Telegraph Messenger Boys: Labor, Technology, and Geography, 1850–1950.* New York: Routledge, 2002.

Drotner, Kirsten. *English Children and Their Magazines, 1751–1945.* New Haven: Yale University Press, 1988.

Durham, John. *Telegraphs in Victorian London.* Cambridge: Golden Head Press, 1959.

Dyhouse, Carol. *Girls Growing Up in Late Victorian and Edwardian England.* London: Routledge and Kegan Paul, 1981.

Ewing, E. Thomas. "'A Most Powerful Instrument for a Despot': The Telegraph as a Transnational Instrument of Imperial Control and Political Mobilization in the Middle East." In *The Nation State and Beyond,* ed. Roland Wenzlhuemer and Isabella Löhr, 83–100. Berlin: Springer-Verlag, 2013.

Fari, Simone. *Victorian Telegraphy before Nationalization.* Basingstoke: Palgrave Macmillan, 2015.

Ferguson, Stephen. *GPO Staff in 1916: Business as Usual.* Cork: Mercier, 2005.

Feurer, Rosemary. "The Meaning of 'Sisterhood': The British Women's Movement and Protective Labor Legislation, 1870–1900." *Victorian Studies* 31, no. 2 (1988): 233–60, www.jstor.org/stable/3827971.

Fisher, Trevor. *Scandal: Sexual Politics in Late Victorian Britain.* Stroud: Sutton, 1995.

Foucault, Michel. "Governmentality." Translated by Rosi Braidotti. In *The Foucault Effect: Studies in Governmentality,* ed. Graham Burchell, Colin Gordon, and Peter Miller, 87–104. Chicago: University of Chicago Press, 1991.

Galvan, Jill. *The Sympathetic Medium: Feminine Channeling, the Occult, and Communications Technologies, 1859–1919.* Ithaca, NY: Cornell University Press, 2010.

Gilbert, Pamela. *Mapping the Victorian Social Body.* Albany: SUNY Press, 2004.

Gillis, John. *Youth and History: Tradition and Change in European Age Relations, 1770–Present.* London: Academic Press, 1981.

Glew, Helen. *Gender, Rhetoric, and Regulation: Women's Work in the Civil Service and London County Council, 1900–1955.* Manchester: University of Manchester Press, 2016.

———. "'Maiden Whom We Never See: Cultural Representations of the 'Lady Telegraphist' in Britain ca. 1880–1930 and Institutional Responses," *Information and Culture* 55 (2020): 30–50, doi: 10.7560/IC55103.

Goodland, Lauren. *Victorian Literature and the Victorian State.* Baltimore: Johns Hopkins University Press, 2003.

Graham, Stephen, and Simon Marvin. *Splintering Urbanism: Networked Infrastructures, Technological Mobilities, and the Urban Condition.* London: Routledge, 2001.

Green, Barbara. *Spectacular Confessions: Autobiography, Performance Activism, and the Sites of Suffrage, 1905–1938.* London: St Martins, 1997.

Green, E. H. H., and D. M. Tanner, eds. *The Strange Survival of Liberal England: Political Leaders, Moral Values, and the Reception of Economic Debate.* Cambridge: Cambridge University Press, 2007.

Gunn, Simon. *The Public Culture of the Victorian Middle Class: Ritual and Authority in the English Industrial City, 1840–1914.* Manchester: Manchester University Press, 2000.

Hadley, Elaine. *Living Liberalism: Practical Citizenship in Mid-Victorian Britain.* Chicago: University of Chicago Press, 2010.

Hammerton, A. James. "Pooterism or Partnership? Marriage and Masculine Identity in the Lower Middle Class, 1870–1920." *Journal of British Studies* 38 (1999): 291–321, www.jstor.org/stable/176058.

Haralson, Eric. *Henry James and Queer Modernity.* Cambridge: Cambridge University Press, 2003.

Hardt, Michael. "Affective Labor." *Boundary* 2, no. 2 (1999): 89–100, www.jstor.org/stable/303793.

Hardt, Michael, and Antonio Negri. *Empire.* Cambridge, MA: Harvard University Press, 2009.

Hartman, Heidi. "Capitalism, Patriarchy, and Job Segregation by Sex." *Signs* 1, no. 3 (1976): 137–69.

Hazlewood, Arthur. "The Origin of the State Telephone Service in Britain." *Oxford Economic Papers* 5, no. 1 (1953): 13–25, www.jstor.org/stable/2661863.

Headrick, Daniel. "A Double-Edged Sword: Communications and Imperial Control in British India." *Historical Social Research* 35, no. 1 (2010): 51–65, www.jstor.org/stable/20762428.

———. *The Invisible Weapon: Telecommunications and International Politics, 1851–1945.* Oxford: Oxford University Press, 1991.

———. *The Tools of Empire: Technology and European Imperialism in the Nineteenth Century.* Oxford: Oxford University Press, 1981.

Headrick, Daniel, and Pascal Griset. "Submarine Telegraph Cables: Business and Politics, 1838–1939." *Business History Review* 75 (2001): 543–78.

Heller, Michael. "British Company Magazines, 1878–1939: The Origins and Functions of House Journals in Large-Scale Organizations." *Media History* 15, no. 2 (2009): 143–66, doi: 10.1080/13688800902781850.

Hendrick, Harry. *Images of Youth: Age, Class, and the Male Youth Problem, 1880–1920.* Oxford: Clarendon, 1990.

Herbert, Amanda. "Gender and the Spa: Space, Sociability, and the Self at British Health Spas, 1670–1714." *Journal of Social History* 43, no. 2 (2009): 361–83, doi:10.1353/jsh.0.0260.

Hicks, Mar. *Programmed Inequality: How Britain Discarded Women Technologists and Lost Its Edge in Computing.* Cambridge, MA: MIT Press, 2017.

Hilton, Matthew. "'Tabs', 'Fags,' and the 'Boy Labour Problem' in Late Victorian and Edwardian Britain." *Journal of Social History* 28, no. 3 (1995): 587–607.

Hindmarch-Watson, Katie. "Lois Schwich, the Female Errand Boy: Narratives of Female Cross-Dressing in Late-Victorian London." *GLQ* 14, no. 1 (2008): 69–98, www.muse.jhu.edu/article/224861.

Hobsbawm, E. J. "General Labour Unions in Britain, 1889–1914." In *Labouring Men: Studies in the History of Labour.* London: Weidenfeld and Nicholson, 1964.

Holton, Sandra Stanley. *Feminism and Democracy: Women's Suffrage and Reform Politics in Britain, 1900–1918.* Cambridge: Cambridge University Press, 1986.

———. *Suffrage Days: Stories from the Women's Suffrage Movement.* London: Routledge, 1996.

Houlbrook, Matt. "Soldier Heroes and Rent Boys: Homosex, Masculinities, and Britishness in the Brigade of Guards, 1900–1960." *Journal of British Studies* 42 (2003): 351–88, doi:10.1086/374294.

Hugill, Peter J. *Global Communications Since 1844: Geopolitics and Technology.* Baltimore: Johns Hopkins University Press, 1999.

Humphries, Stephen. *Hooligans or Rebels? An Oral History of Working-Class Childhood and Youth, 1889–1930.* Oxford: Oxford University Press, 1981.

Hunt, Bruce J. "Doing Science in a Global Empire: Cable Telegraphy and Electrical Physics in Victorian Britain." In *Victorian Science in Context,* ed. Bernard Lightman, 311–33. Chicago: University of Chicago Press, 1997.

Hunt, Tristram. *Building Jerusalem: The Rise and Fall of the Victorian City.* London: Weidenfeld and Nicolson, 2004.

Hyde, H. Montgomery. *The Cleveland Street Scandal.* London: W. H. Allen, 1976.

———. *The Other Love: An Historical and Contemporary Survey of Homosexuality in Britain.* London: Heinemann, 1970.

Jackson, Louise. *Child Sexual Abuse in Victorian London.* London: Routledge, 2000.

Jeffery, Keith. *The GPO and the Easter Rising.* Dublin: Irish Academic Press, 2006.

Joannou, Maroula, and June Purvis, eds., *The Women's Suffrage Movement: New Feminist Perspectives.* Manchester: Manchester University Press, 1998.

John, Angela V., ed. *Unequal Opportunities: Women's Employment in England, 1800–1918.* Oxford: Blackwell, 1986.

Johnson, Paul. *Saving and Spending: The Working-Class Economy in Britain, 1870–1939.* Oxford: Clarendon, 1985.

Jordanova, Ludmilla. *Sexual Visions: Images of Gender in Science and Medicine between the Eighteenth and Twentieth Centuries.* Madison: University of Wisconsin Press, 1989.

Joyce, Patrick. "The End of Social History?" *Social History* 20 (1995): 73–91, www.jstor.org/stable/4286248.

———. *The Rule of Freedom: Liberalism and the Modern City.* New York: Verso, 2003.

———. *The State of Freedom: A Social History of the British State since 1800.* Cambridge: Cambridge University Press, 2013.

Kaplan, Morris. *Sodom on the Thames: Sex, Love, and Scandal in Wilde Times.* Ithaca, NY: Cornell University Press, 2005.

Kaur, Amarjit. "A History of Forestry in Sarawak." *Modern Asian Studies* 32 (1998): 117–47, www.jstor.org/stable/312971.

Killen, Andreas. *Berlin Electropolis: Shock, Nerves, and German Modernity.* Berkeley: University of California Press, 2006.

Kincaid, Andrew. *Postcolonial Dublin: Imperial Legacies and the Built Environment.* Minneapolis: University of Minnesota Press, 2006.

Koven, Seth. "Borderlands: Women, Voluntary Action, and Child Welfare in Britain, 1840–1914." In *Mothers of a New World: Maternalist Politics and the Origins of the Welfare State,* ed. Seth Koven and Sonya Michel, 94–135. London: Routledge, 1993.

———. "From Rough Lads to Hooligans: Boy Life, National Culture, and Social Reform." In *Nationalisms and Sexualities,* ed. Andrew Parker, Mary Russo, Doris Sommer, and Patricia Yaeger, 365–91. New York: Routledge, 1992.

———. *Slumming: Sexual and Social Politics in Victorian London.* Princeton: Princeton University Press, 2004.

Langan, Mary, and Bill Schwarz, eds. *Crises in the British State, 1880–1930.* London: Hutchinson, 1986.

Latour, Bruno. *Science in Action: How to Follow Scientists and Engineers through Society.* Cambridge, MA: Harvard University Press, 1987.

———. "Technology Is Society Made Durable." In *A Sociology of Monsters: Essays on Power, Technology and Domination,* ed. John Law, 103–31. London: Routledge, 1991.

———. *We Have Never Been Modern.* Translated by Catherine Porter. New York: Harvester Wheatsheaf, 1993.

Law, John. *Organizing Modernity: Social Ordering and Social Theory.* Oxford: Blackwell, 1994.

Lee, C. H. "The Service Sector, Regional Specialization, and Economic Growth in the Victorian Economy." *Journal of Historical Geography* 10, no. 2 (1984): 139–55, doi: 10.1016/0305-7488(84)90115-4.

Levine, Philippa. *Victorian Feminism, 1850–1900.* Tallahassee: Florida State University Press, 1987.

Lewenhak, Sheila. *Women and Trade Unions: An Outline History of Women in the British Trade Union Movement.* London: Benn, 1977.

Lewis, Jane, and Celia Davies. "Protective Legislation in Britain, 1870–1990: Equality, Difference and Their Implications for Women." *Policy and Politics* 19, no. 1 (1991): 13–26, doi: 10.1332/030557391782454340.

Linehan, Thomas. *British Fascism, 1918–1939: Parties, Ideology and Culture.* Manchester: Manchester University Press, 2000.

Markovitz, Stefanie. *The Crimean War in the British Imagination.* Cambridge: Cambridge University Press, 2009.

Marsden, Ben, and Crosbie Smith. *Engineering Empires: A Cultural History of Technology in Nineteenth-Century Britain.* Basingstoke: Palgrave Macmillan, 2005.

Mayhall, Laura E. Nym. *The Militant Suffrage Movement: Citizenship and Resistance in Britain, 1860–1930.* Oxford: Oxford University Press, 2003.

McCuskey, Brian. "The Kitchen Police: Servant Surveillance and Middle-Class Transgression." *Victorian Literature and Culture* 28, no. 2 (2000): 359–75, www .jstor.org/stable/25058524.

McDowell, Linda. *Working Bodies: Interactive Service Employment and Workplace Identities*. Chichester: Wiley-Blackwell, 2011.

McGarry, Fearghal. *The Rising: Easter 1916*. Oxford: Oxford University Press, 2010.

McIlroy, John. "Waving or Drowning? British Labor History in Troubled Waters." *Labor History* 53, no. 1 (2012): 91–119, doi: 10.1080/0023656X.2012.650435.

Melman, Billie. *Women and the Popular Imagination in the Twenties: Flappers and Nymphs*. Basingstoke: Macmillan, 1988.

Menke, Richard. *Telegraphic Realism: Victorian Fiction and Other Information Systems*. Stanford: Stanford University Press, 2008.

Milne, Graeme J. "British Business and the Telephone, 1878–1911." *Business History* 49, no. 2 (2007): 163–85, doi: 10.1080/00076790601170280.

———. "Business Districts, Office Culture, and the First Generation of Telephone Use in Britain." *Journal for the History of Engineering and Technology* 80, no. 2 (2010): 199–213, doi: 10.1179/175812110X12714133353759.

Mitchell, Sally R. *The New Girl: Girls' Culture in England, 1880–1915*. New York: Columbia University Press, 1996.

Morris, R. J. "Clubs, Societies, and Associations." In *The Cambridge Social History of Britain*, vol. 3, *1750–1950*, ed. F. M. L. Thompson. Cambridge: Cambridge University Press, 1990.

Mort, Frank. *Dangerous Sexualities: Medico-moral Politics in England since 1830*. London: Routledge, 1987.

Morus, Iwan Rhys. *Bodies/Machines*. Oxford: Berg, 2002.

———. "The Nervous System of Britain: Space, Time and the Electric Telegraph in the Victorian Age." *British Journal for the History of Science*, 33, no. 4 (2000): 455–75, www.jstor.org/stable/4028030.

———. *Shocking Bodies: Life, Death and Electricity in Victorian England*. Stroud: History Press, 2011.

Moscucci, Ornella. *The Science of Woman: Gynaecology and Gender in England, 1800–1929*. New York: Cambridge University Press, 1990.

Mullin, Kate. *Working Girls: Fiction, Sexuality, and Modernity*. Oxford: Oxford University Press, 2016.

Nead, Lynda. *Victorian Babylon: People, Streets, and Images in Nineteenth-Century London*. New Haven: Yale University Press, 2000.

Nord, Deborah. "The Social Explorer as Anthropologist: Victorian Travelers among the Urban Poor." In *Visions of the Modern City: Essays in History, Art, and Literature*, ed. William Sharpe and Leonard Wallock. Baltimore: Johns Hopkins University Press, 1987: 122–34.

———. *Walking the Victorian Streets: Women, Representation, and the City*. Ithaca, NY: Cornell University Press, 1995.

O'Broin, Leon. *The Prime Informer: A Suppressed Scandal*. London: Sidgwick and Jackson, 1971.

Occomore, D. *Number, Please! A History of the Early London Telephone Exchanges from 1880 to 1912*. Romford, Essex: Ian Henry, 1995.

Olcott, Teresa. "Dead Centre: The Women's Trade Union Movement in London, 1874–1914." *London Journal* 2 (1976): 33–50.

Oppenheim, Janet. *"Shattered Nerves": Doctors, Patients, and Depression in Victorian England*. Oxford: Oxford University Press, 1991.

Osborne, Thomas. "Security and Vitality: Drains, Liberalism, and Power in the Nineteenth Century." In *Foucault and Political Reason: Liberalism, Neoliberalism and Rationalities of Government,* ed. Andrew Barry, Thomas Osborne, and Nikolas Rose, 99–117. Chicago: University of Chicago Press, 1996.

Otter, Chris. "Making Liberalism Durable: Vision and Civility in the Late Victorian City." *Social History* 27, no. 1 (2002): 1–15, www.jstor.org/stable /4286834.

———. "Making Liberal Objects: British Techno-social Relations, 1800–1900." *Cultural Studies* 21, no. 5 (2007): 570–90, doi: 10.1080/09502380701278962.

———. *The Victorian Eye: A Political History of Light and Vision in Britain, 1800–1910*. Chicago: University of Chicago Press, 2008.

Pennybacker, Susan D. *A Vision for London, 1889–1914: Labour, Everyday Life and the LCC Experiment*. London: Routledge, 1995.

Perry, C. R. *The Victorian Post Office: The Growth of a Bureaucracy*. Woodbridge, Suffolk: Boydell Press, 1992.

Peter, Scott. "Still a Nice Communications Medium: The Diffusion and Uses of the Telephone System in Interwar Britain." *Business History* 53, no. 6 (2011): 801–20, doi: 10.1080/00076791.2011.578131.

Peters, John Durham. *The Marvelous Clouds: Toward a Philosophy of Elemental Media*. Chicago: University of Chicago Press, 2015.

———. *Speaking into the Air: A History of the Idea of Communication*. Chicago: University of Chicago Press, 1999.

Petrow, Stefan. *Policing Morals: The Metropolitan Police and the Home Office, 1870–1914*. Oxford: Clarendon, 1994.

Pike, David. *Metropolis on the Styx: The Underworlds of Modern Urban Culture, 1801–2001*. Ithaca, NY: Cornell University Press, 2007.

Poovey, Mary. *Uneven Developments: The Ideological Work of Gender in Mid-Victorian England*. Chicago: University of Chicago Press, 1988.

———. "Writing about Finance in Victorian England: Disclosure and Secrecy in the Culture of Investment." *Victorian Studies* 45, no. 1 (2002): 17–41, www.muse .jhu.edu/article/43751.

Porter, Bernard. *The Origins of the Vigilant State*. London: Weidenfeld and Nicolson, 1987.

Potter, Simon J. "Webs, Networks, and Systems: Globalization and the Mass Media in the Nineteenth- and Twentieth-Century British Empire." *Journal of British Studies,* 46, no. 3 (2007): 621–46, doi: 10.1086/515446.

Powell, David. *The Edwardian Crisis: Britain, 1901–1914*. Basingstoke: Palgrave, 1996.

Price, Leah, and Pamela Thurschwell, eds. *Literary Secretaries/Secretarial Culture.* Aldershot: Ashgate, 2005.

Pugh, Martin. *Hurrah For the Blackshirts! Fascists and Fascism in Britain between the Wars.* London: Pimlico, 2006.

———. *State and Society: British Political and Social History, 1870–1992.* 4th ed. London: Bloomsbury, 2012.

Purvis, June, and Sandra Stanley Holton, eds. *Votes for Women!* London: Routledge, 2000.

Rabinbach, Anson. *The Human Motor: Energy, Fatigue, and the Origins of Modernity.* Berkeley: University of California Press, 1992.

Rappaport, Erika. *Shopping for Pleasure: Women in the Making of London's West End.* Princeton: Princeton University Press, 2001.

Robinson, Howard. *Britain's Post Office: A History of Development from the Beginnings to the Present Day.* Oxford: Oxford University Press, 1953.

———. *Carrying British Mail Overseas.* London: George Allen and Unwin, 1964.

———. *The British Post Office: A History.* Princeton: Princeton University Press, 1948.

Rose, Sonya. *Limited Livelihoods: Gender and Class in Nineteenth-Century England.* Berkeley: University of California Press, 1992.

Ross, Ellen. *Love and Toil: Motherhood in Outcast London.* Oxford: Oxford University Press, 1993.

Rotunno, Laura. *"Blackfriars, the Post Office Magazine:* A Nineteenth-Century Network of the 'Happy Ignorant,'" *Victorian Periodicals Review* 44, no. 2 (2011): 141–64, doi: 10.1353/vpr.2011.0019.

Rubenstein, David. *Before the Suffragettes: Women's Emancipation in the 1890s.* Brighton: Harvester, 1986.

Savage, Mike. "Class and Labour History." In *Class and Other Identities: Gender, Religion and Ethnicity in the Writing of European Labour History,* ed. Lex Heerma van Voss and Marcel van der Linden, 55–72. Oxford: Berghan, 2002.

Savoy, Eric. "'In the Cage' and the Queer Effects of Gay History." *Novel: A Forum on Fiction* 28, no. 3 (1995): 284–307.

Sconce, Jeffrey. *Haunted Media: Electric Presence from Telegraphy to Television.* Durham, NC: Duke University Press, 2000.

Sedgwick, Eve Kosofsky. *Epistemology of the Closet.* Berkeley: University of California Press, 1990.

———. "Queer Performativity: Henry James's *The Art of the Novel.*" *GLQ* 1 (1993): 1–16, doi:10.1215/10642684–1-1-1.

Senelick, Laurence. "The Evolution of the Male Impersonator on the Nineteenth-Century Popular Stage." *Essays in Theatre* 1, no. 1 (1982): 29–44.

Shelangoskie, Susan. "Anthony Trollope and the Social Discourse of Telegraphy after Nationalization." *Journal of Victorian Culture* 14 (2009): 72–93, doi:10.3366/E1355550209000605.

Short, Kenneth R. M. *The Dynamite War: Irish-American Bombers in Victorian Britain.* Atlantic Highlands, NJ: Humanities Press, 1979.

Showalter, Elaine. *Sexual Anarchy: Gender and Culture in the Fin de Siècle.* London: Bloomsbury, 1991.

Shpayer-Makov, H. "The Appeal of Country Workers: The Case of the Metropolitan Police." *Historical Research* 64, no. 154 (1991): 186–203, doi:10.1111/j.1468-2281.1991.tb01793.x.

Simpson, Colin, Lewis Chester, and David Leitch. *The Cleveland Street Affair.* Boston: Little, Brown, 1976.

Soldon, Norbert C. *Women in British Trade Unions, 1874–1976.* Dublin: Gill and Macmillan, 1978.

Springhall, John. *Coming of Age: Adolescence in Britain, 1860–1960.* Dublin: Gill and Macmillan, 1986.

———. *Youth, Empire and Society: British Youth Movements, 1883–1940.* London: Croom Helm, 1977.

Standage, T. *The Victorian Internet: The Remarkable Story of the Telegraph and the Nineteenth Century's Online Pioneers.* New York: Walker, 1998.

Stedman Jones, Gareth. *Outcast London: A Study in the Relationship between Classes in Victorian Society.* London: Penguin, 1984.

Stein, Jeremy Leon. "Ideology and the Telephone: The Social Reception of a Technology, London 1876–1920." PhD diss., University College London, September 1996.

Stevens, Hugh. "Queer Henry in the Cage." In *The Cambridge Companion to Henry James,* ed. Jonathan Freedman, 120–38. Cambridge: Cambridge University Press, 1998.

Sutherland, Gillian. *In Search of the New Woman: Middle Class Women and Work in Britain, 1870–1914.* Cambridge: Cambridge University Press, 2015.

Taylor, Barbara, and Anne Phillips. "Sex and Skill: Notes towards a Feminist Economics." *Feminist Review* 6, no. 1 (1980): 1–15, doi:10.1057/fr.1980.20.

Thomas, Kate. *Postal Pleasures: Sex, Scandal, and Victorian Letters.* Oxford: Oxford University Press, 2012.

———. "A Queer Job for a Girl: Women Postal Workers, Civic Duty and Sexuality, 1870–80." In *A Queer Place: Sexuality and Belonging in British and European Contexts,* ed. Kate Chedgzoy, Emma Francis, and Murray Pratt, 50–70. London: Ashgate, 2002.

Thompson, Paul. *Socialists, Liberals, and Labour: The Struggle for London.* London: Routledge and Kegan Paul, 1967.

Thrift, Nigel. "New Urban Eras and Old Technological Fears: Reconfiguring the Goodwill of Electronic Things." *Urban Studies* 33, no. 8 (1996): 1463–93, doi:10.1080/0042098966754.

Tickner, Lisa. *The Spectacle of Women: Imagery of the Suffrage Campaign, 1907–1914.* Chicago: University of Chicago Press, 1988.

Tillotson, Shirley. "'We May All Soon Be 'First-Class Men': Gender and Skill in Canada's Early Twentieth Century Urban Telegraph Industry." *Labour/Le Travail* 27 (1991): 97–125, www.jstor.org/stable/25130246.

Tinkler, Penny. *Constructing Girlhood: Popular Magazines for Girls Growing Up in England, 1920–1950.* London: Taylor and Francis, 1995.

Tosh, John. *A Man's Place: Masculinity and the Middle-Class Home in Victorian England*. New Haven: Yale University Press, 1999.

Townshend, Charles. *Easter 1916: The Irish Rebellion*. Chicago: Ivan R. Dee, 2006.

Tully, John. "A Victorian Ecological Disaster: Imperialism, the Telegraph, and Gutta-Percha." *Journal of World History* 20, no. 4 (2009): 559–79, www.jstor.org/stable/40542850.

Turner, Stephen. "Whatever Happened to Knowledge?" *Social Studies of Science,* 42, no. 3 (2012): 477–78, doi:10.1177/0306312712436555.

Upchurch, Charles. *Before Wilde: Sex between Men in Britain's Age of Reform*. Berkeley: University of California Press, 2009.

Vernon, James. *Distant Strangers: How Britain Became Modern*. Berkeley: University of California Press, 2014.

———. "For Some Queer Reason: The Trials and Tribulations of Colonel Barker's Masquerade in Interwar Britain." *Signs* 26, no. 1 (2000): 37–62, www.jstor.org/stable/3175380.

Vicinus, Martha. "The Adolescent Boy: Fin de Siècle Femme Fatale?" *Journal of the History of Sexuality* 5, no. 1 (1994): 90–114, www.jstor.org/stable/3704081.

———. "Turn of the Century Male Impersonation: Rewriting the Romance Plot." In *Sexualities in Victorian Britain,* ed. Andrew H. Miller and James Eli Adams, 202–7. Bloomington: Indiana University Press, 1996.

Vincent, David. *The Culture of Secrecy: Britain, 1832–1998*. Oxford: Oxford University Press, 1998.

———. "Government and the Management of Information, 1844–2009." In *The Peculiarities of Liberal Modernity in Imperial Britain,* ed. Simon Gunn and James Vernon, 165–81. Berkeley: University of California Press, 2011.

———. *I Hope I Don't Intrude: Privacy and Its Dilemmas in Nineteenth-Century Britain*. Oxford: Oxford University Press, 2015.

———. *Privacy: A Short History*. Cambridge: Polity, 2016.

Walkowitz, Judith. *City of Dreadful Delight: Narratives of Sexual Danger in Late Victorian London*. Chicago: University of Chicago Press, 1992.

———. "Going Public: Shopping, Street Harassment, and Streetwalking in Late Victorian London." *Representations* 62 (1998): 1–30, www.jstor.org/stable/2902937.

———. "Science and the Séance: Transgressions of Gender and Genre in Late Victorian London." *Representations* 22, no. 2 (1988): 3–29, doi:10.2307/2928407.

Watson, Norman. *Suffragettes and the Post*. Self-published, 2010.

Weeks, Jeffrey. *Between the Acts: Lives of Homosexual Men, 1885–1967*. London: Routledge, 1990.

———. "Inverts, Perverts, and Mary-Annes: Male Prostitution and the Regulation of Homosexuality in the Nineteenth and Early Twentieth Centuries." In *Hidden from History: Reclaiming the Gay and Lesbian Past,* ed. Martin Duberman, Martha Vicinus, and George Chauncey, 195–211. New York: New American Library, 1989.

———. *Sex, Politics and Society*. London: Longman, 1981.

Weeks, Kathi. "Life within and against Work: Affective Labor, Feminist Critique, and Post-Fordist Politics." *Ephemera: Theory and Politics in Organization* 7, no. 1 (2007): 233–49.

Weiner, J.H., ed. *Papers for the Millions: The New Journalism in Britain, 1850s to 1914.* New York: Greenwood, 1988.

Wenzlhuemer, Roland, *Connecting the Nineteenth-Century World: The Telegraph and Globalization.* Cambridge: Cambridge University Press, 2013.

———. "The Development of Telegraphy, 1870–1900: A European Perspective on a World History Challenge." *History Compass* 5, no. 5 (2006): 1720–42, doi:10.1111/j.1478-0542.2007.00461.x.

White, Jerry. *London in the Nineteenth Century: "A Human Awful Wonder of God."* London: Vintage, 2008.

Wills, Clair. *Dublin 1916: The Siege of the GPO.* Cambridge, MA: Harvard University Press, 2009.

Zimmeck, Meta. "Jobs for Girls: The Expansion of Clerical Work for Women, 1870–1930." In *Unequal Opportunities: Women's Employment in England 1800–1918,* ed. Angela John, 153–78. Oxford: Oxford University Press, 1986.

ONLINE SOURCES

Ancestry.co.uk

Communications Workers' Union main website, www.cwu.org.

Davies, Andrew. "The Real Peaky Blinders." HistoryExtra podcast, August 22, 2019, www.historyextra.com/period/victorian/real-peaky-blinders-podcast-historian-andrew-davies-gangs-who/.

Easter Rising Online Exhibit by Century Ireland, produced by Boston College and hosted by RTE (Raidió Teilifís Éireann) Ireland, www.rte.ie/centuryireland/index.php/easterrising, accessed May 5 2020.

McVey, Victor. *Telegraphic Codes and Message Practice,* www.jmcvey.net/cable/index.htm.

Old Bailey Online, www.oldbaileyonline.org.

Royal Mail. "Launch of Royal Mail's Investigation Department," Celebrating 500 Years of Royal Mail, http://500years.royalmailgroup.com/gallery/launch-of-royal-mail-s-investigation-department/, accessed May 5, 2020.

INDEX

Fischer, Henry (CTO controller), 59, 65, 66, 140
Freake, Charles (politician), 143
freedom, 3, 40, 86, 105, 112–113, 124, 126, 135, 143, 181, 184, 185
Freud, Sigmund, 184

gambling, 18, 28, 40, 53, 59, 60, 62. *See also* racing
gender, 3, 9, 13, 14, 17, 48, 75, 78–79, 88, 105, 108, 202n30, 203n34, 204n40, 215n11, 238n12; and discretion, 44, 50, 159; and division of labor, 4, 6, 14, 39, 43, 50–51, 57, 63–67, 85, 97, 153–154, 166–167, 183, 186; and division of space, 10, 59, 60, 157; and labor organizing, 66, 85, 87; and technology, 53, 62, 203n34; and telecommunications consumers, 30, 177; and wages, 54, 58
General Post Office (GPO): administration, 5, 8, 12, 13, 20, 22, 23, 26, 31–32, 34–36, 38, 41–43, 46–47, 50, 52–53, 55, 57, 62, 64–69, 72, 84, 86, 88, 90–91, 95–87, 100, 103, 111, 115–118, 123, 133–142, 146–147, 150, 153, 154, 157, 163, 165–167, 181, 183, 192, 197n5; architecture of, 22, 189; Clearing House Branch, 53; Coldbath Fields Prison (Mount Pleasant), 141, 222n11; Confidential Enquiry Branch, 110, 111, 114, 115, 116, 118, 121, 123, 124, 135, 138, 144, 185; electricians, 38, 39, 76; Field Telegraph Corps, 115; finances of, 20–21, 26, 43, 55, 65, 232n4; gendered division of labor, 5, 37, 39, 43, 50, 53–57, 64–67, 71–85, 87, 88, 97, 153–154, 157, 166–167, 183; headquarters, 16, 22, 26, 31, 71, 89, 91, 115, 120, 136, 188, 191, 193; hierarchies, 23, 36, 41, 44, 58, 63, 67, 137; hiring policies, 57, 65, 71, 87, 91–94, 101, 107, 131, 138, 140–141, 144, 149, 153–154; infrastructure (*see* London, infrastructure; telecommunications, infrastructure); internal police force, 108, 111, 114, 116, 194 (*see also* Confidential Enquiry Branch); Investigations Branch, 185, 193; lavatories, 19, 23, 94, 110, 120–122, 126; militarization, 12, 13, 89, 95, 118, 120,

130–131, 133–134, 142, 144–146, 148, 151, 192, 194, 222n8, 228n56; Missing Letter Branch, 36, 98–100, 108, 114, 117, 139, 207n1; nationalization, 2, 13, 16, 17, 19–21, 26–30, 32, 42–43, 51, 59, 89, 91, 94, 69, 84, 89, 91, 94, 138, 160, 173, 205n11; night shifts, 51, 64–66, 71–74, 84, 85, 97, 100–104, 106, 108, 139, 153, 166–167, 178; parcel post, 26, 34, 39, 114, 114, 137, 222n11; pensions, 34, 38, 55, 164; Post Office Rifles regiment, 89, 115, 119, 141; Post Office Rifles Volunteers Regiment Band, 89, 168; in the press, 37, 66, 110, 121, 125 (*see also* telegraphy, press depictions of); progressivism of, 43, 114, 128, 148, 150, 152, 185; racial, ethnic hiring exclusions, 57, 212n16; reputation of, 43, 107, 113; responses to labor organizing (*see* labor, organizing); Returned Letter Branch, 53; rural specificities, 20, 26, 57, 85, 147, 153–154 (*see also* London, metropolitan specificities); sick leave, 73, 81, 82, 84, 108; spatial order of, 53, 56, 71, 99, 100, 107, 118, 183, 222n11; *St-Martins-le-Grand* (periodical), 159, 168, 172, 235n58; Sunday shifts, 71, 72, 75, 84–85, 89, 137, 180; surveillance practices of (*see* censorship; espionage); wages, 32, 34–36, 43, 54, 55–58, 65–66, 68, 71–72, 74, 84, 91–92, 101, 104, 107–108, 117–118, 135, 137, 158, 161, 164–166, 175, 183, 185, 212n20. *See also* postal workers; telegraph boys; telegraphists; telephone operators
Gibbons, Bob (telegraph boy), 194
Gladstone, William, 20, 33, 131, 142, 222n12
Glasgow, 29, 31, 78, 114
Gloucester, 193
Good Words (periodical), 42
governmentality, 198n6
Graham, Sir James (politician), 27, 36
Great War. *See* World War I
Greenwich, 180, 183
Gregory, Constance Marion (telephone operator), 174
Grenfell, Edith (telegraph girl), 153, 154
Guardsmen, 96–97
gutta-percha, 205n21

heteronormativity, 97, 129
heterosexuality, 11, 54, 56, 78, 162, 225n68
Holmes, Fanny Louisa (telephone operator), 174, 175
Home Office, 98, 99, 104, 105, 107, 108, 131, 135; Hepburn, A.C., 107
homoeroticism, 90, 97, 100, 103, 104, 112, 119, 120–21, 124, 131, 147, 193, 211n79, 220n1, 221n2, 225n60
homosexuality, 11, 52, 69, 91, 99, 100, 101, 102, 103, 105, 107, 129, 130, 218n35, 222n8, 224n59; Maryannes, 112, 129, 130; prosecution of, 104, 127. *See also* sexuality; sodomy
House of Commons, 96, 112, 128, 131
House of Parliament, 25, 27, 37, 236n90

Illustrated London News, 49, 60, 61
immorality, 99–101, 103, 105, 108, 114, 139, 149, 209n49
In the Cage (1898), 1, 52
Indian Uprising (1857), 38
industrial labor, 6–9, 19, 21, 85, 149, 161, 166, 201n22, 202n30, 235n59
information 1, 12, 46, 111, 113, 199n15, 200nn16,17, 201n23; flows, 4, 5, 12, 14, 31, 34, 46, 63, 90, 96, 115, 137, 183, 192, 195 158, 183, 191, 195, 200n16
International Arbitration League, 143, 192
intimacy, 2, 7, 9, 11, 15, 44, 46, 47, 68, 79, 90, 138, 157, 204n43
invisibility, 1, 3, 7, 14, 96, 97
Ireland, 18, 23, 36, 42, 78, 108, 144, 183, 189, 191, 207n1, 221n2. *See also* Irish
Irish: anti-imperialism, 111; nationalism, 12, 115, 116, 131, 188–191, 221n2. *See also* Ireland; Fenians

James, Henry (writer), 1, 52, 154
jealousy, 1, 79, 168
Jeffery, Thomas (GPO administrator), 36, 98–108, 117, 124, 139
Jevons, William Stanley (economist), 19, 20
journalism, 1, 10, 17, 18–20, 22, 23, 29–31, 42, 43, 49–50, 54, 86, 95, 125, 131, 203n40; depictions of homosexuality, 104, 110–113, 121, 126, 224n54; depictions of telegraphy, 5, 10, 16–18, 22–23,

33, 41, 54–55, 64–66, 71, 85, 89, 168–171; depictions of telegraph boys, 93–94, 112, 117, 120, 121, 129–130, 136–137, 146; political, 85, 110–112, 125–126, 129, 130, 135; Press Association, 37; press cables, 18, 20, 30, 37, 40, 51, 59, 60, 62, 64, 65, 74
Joyce Committee, 137–140, 142
Joyce, Herbert (GPO administrator), 135, 137–139, 144
Joyce, Patrick, 35, 38, 198n6
Judy (periodical), 169, 179

Kenney, Jessie (WSPU), 186–187

labor, 2–14, 17, 31–36, 40–47, 50–57, 64–80, 90, 92, 97, 107, 114, 155, 157, 163–175, 183, 197n5, 200n17, 202n30, ; "pink collar," 9, 43 (*see also* gender; women's work); organizing, 36–37, 51, 53, 55, 59, 66, 113, 118, 135–138, 144, 233n29; strikebreaking, 31, 42; strikes, 12, 14, 31–32, 37, 39, 41–42, 54, 68, 86–87, 135–139, 191, 207n1. *See also* "boy labour crisis"; postal workers; telecommunications workers; telegraphists; telephone operators
Labouchère, Henry (MP), 111, 128
Laing, Karolina (telephone operator), 178, 179
Lang, Andrew, 45
Leeds, 59
Leeman, George (MP), 27–28
legal system, 45, 95, 98, 99, 108–109, 111–112, 121, 127–128, 130, 132, 135, 219n51, 220n52, 221n3, evidence, 102, 104–107, 124, 129, 219n51; legality of opening mail, 27, 116, 156; libel, 98–99, 111, 128, 221n2, 225n61. *See also* espionage; sodomy
lesbianism, 238n12
Liberal Party, 27, 65, 68, 111, 131, 153, 183, 221n7
liberalism, 3, 4, 13, 14, 17, 27, 44, 69, 116, 150, 183–184, 198n6, 198n7, 237n2
Licensed Victualler, the (periodical), 93, 129
Limerick, 42
Liverpool, 5, 31, 59, 64, 71, 114, 162

of the workplace, 4, 46, 77–79, 155, 162, 177. *See also* homosexuality; telegraph boys

Smith, James, 104–107, 220n52

smoking, 93, 217n13

social engineering, 144

social hierarchy, 9, 17, 23, 34, 45, 67

socialism, 148

social geography, 2, 4, 13, 24, 149

social inequality, 2, 91, 200n15

social utility, 17, 43

social uplift, 17, 69, 152, 201n22

sociology, 148, 201n27, 202n30

sodomy, 90, 98, 103, 104, 105, 107, 108, 120, 209n51, 221n2. *See also* homosexuality; sexuality

Somerset House, 95, 228n42

Somerset, Lord Arthur, 110, 112, 113, 123, 127, 128, 221n3

Songs of the Somme, 193

sound reading, 81–83

South Kensington Museum of Science and Art (now Victoria and Albert Museum), 86

Spectator (periodical), 41

spiritualism, 48, 200n16, 202n31, 210n62, 211n63

staff magazines, 172, 235n59

standardization, 9, 39, 98, 157, 178

state intervention, 12, 17, 19, 134

Stead, W.T. (journalist), 126, 224n54, 224n59. See also *Pall Mall Gazette*

Stephenson, Augustus (lawyer), 104–105, 107, 126, 127

Stockholm, Sweden, 230n86

Stoker, Bram, 48

Strachey, Ray (WSPU), 184

strangers, 11, 42, 50, 56, 91

Strowger, Almon (inventor), 170

suburbs, 5, 25, 137, 142, 144, 155, 228n56

Sunday Times (newspaper), 89, 93, 94

surveillance, 4, 12, 14, 28, 36, 108, 112, 115, 207n1

Swift, Henry, 36

telecommunications, 1, 5–6, 44, 47, 164, 166, 175, 199nn12,15, 200n16; as manual or intellectual labor, 8, 35, 38–39, 50, 52, 71, 76, 80, 88, 164–165, 171, 181; consumers, 7, 10, 13, 15, 29, 52; human aspect, 180–181; infrastructure, 2, 51, 211n63 (*see also* pneumatic tubes; wires); innovations in technology 8, 36, 65, 70, 88; international, 40, 62, 64–65; private telecommunications companies, 18, 19, 58, 192, 193; professional associations, 37, 52 (*see also* PTCA); rural/urban differences, 5, 6, 20, 26, 39, 49, 56, 58–60; wages, 183, 184

telecommunications workers, 1–4, 8–10, 12, 14, 43, 165, 183, 201n25, 202n31, 211n63; as conduits of information, 2, 164, 171; gendered labor divisions, 10, 55, 159, 164–165, 169, 183; interference in operations, 168; participation in Easter Rising, 190–191. *See also* Easter Rising (1916)

telegrams, 1, 2, 18, 21, 39–41, 86, 207n41; cost to consumer, 17–19, 20, 26, 29–30, 47, 71, 114, 116, 157; delivery rules, 95–96, 153, 155; perceptions of, 28, 116–117, 153, 157, 186; privacy of, 31, 33, 36–37, 41, 48–52, 94, 115, 131

Telegraph and Telephone Journal (periodical), 180

telegraph boys, 1, 2, 4, 6, 8, 11–14, 23, 29, 35, 63, 93–95, 153, 117, 121, 129, 148, 164, 183, 186, 194, 217n13, 231n91; as apprentices, 93, 140, 146, 230n77; corporal system, 94, 101, 139, 141, 146, 147; as civil servants, 94, 112; class, 101, 103, 119, 130, 131, 150, 224nn46,56; delivery rules, 95–97, 218n23; discipline of, 93, 98, 102, 107, 109, 140–145, 147, 217n4; educational campaigns, 147, 149, 150–151, 192; families of, 143, 150; fines against, 108, 195; fitness, 13, 134, 143–145, 148, 151–152, 192–193, 231n91; and homosexuality, 12, 99, 110, 144, 193–194; informal tasks, 54, 146; labor organizing, 136, 144; as legal witnesses, 104 (*see also* legal evidence); leisure time, 97, 98, 144, 145, 148; militarization of, 89, 115, 118, 130, 131, 133–134, 139–143, 145, 148, 151, 155, 192, 222n8, 227n33, 228n42; qualifications, 92, 131, 149, 192; prospects after

Founded in 1893,
UNIVERSITY OF CALIFORNIA PRESS
publishes bold, progressive books and journals
on topics in the arts, humanities, social sciences,
and natural sciences—with a focus on social
justice issues—that inspire thought and action
among readers worldwide.

The UC PRESS FOUNDATION
raises funds to uphold the press's vital role
as an independent, nonprofit publisher, and
receives philanthropic support from a wide
range of individuals and institutions—and from
committed readers like you. To learn more, visit
ucpress.edu/supportus.